1000 HANDY
HOUSEHOLD HINTS

1000 HANDY HOUSEHOLD HINTS

Lizzie Evans

Contents

First published in Great Britain in 1982 by
Octopus Books Limited
59 Grosvenor Street
London W1

ISBN 0 86273 029 5

Made and printed in Great Britain by
Richard Clay (The Chaucer Press) Limited
Bungay, Suffolk

Illustrations by Advertising Arts

"A Stitch in Time Saves Nine"

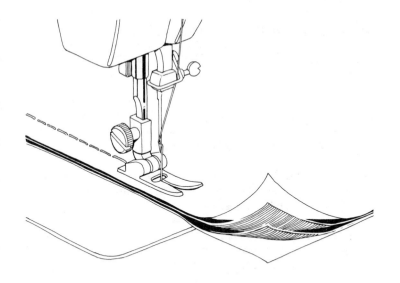

Tips on handiwork, household maintenance and plants

Knitting
and sewing tips

NOTES FOR KNITTERS

Secure stitches: If you are slipping some stitches off your knitting needle, hold them secure by threading a pipe cleaner through them. The ends can be bent under so the stitches do not slip off.

Clothes peg clamp: Keep a large spring clothes peg with your knitting. When you stop temporarily, clamp the needles together with it. This will keep stitches from slipping off and your work becoming unravelled.

New for old: Re-use knitting wool from discarded sweaters by winding it tightly round a piece of wood or stiff cardboard, then dipping it in lukewarm water. Leave it to dry naturally and it will lose all its kinks.

Quick measure: Mark one of your knitting needles with coloured nail varnish into inches or centimetres, it saves hunting for the tape measure.

Back into shape: Plastic knitting needles that have gone out of shape can be straightened if you either hold them in the steam of a boiling kettle or plunge them in near-boiling water, then when you take them out of the steam or water you will be able to straighten them between your fingers. Put them into cold water immediately afterwards to set the shape.

Wool in order: Keep your knitting wool pristine by putting it in a plastic freezer bag with a loose elastic band around the top. If you're using several colours at once, use a plastic bag with small holes in it and thread the different wools through them. They will stay untangled that way. Single balls of wool can also be put in a small cardboard box. Make a hole in the lid for the wool to go through, then seal the box with sticky tape.

Light on dark: Use light needles when you knit or crochet dark yarn, dark needles with light. It is much easier to count the stitches that way and doesn't strain your eyes.

Instant information: When you buy wool, wind a small piece round one of the printed wrappers and put it on one side. Then if you need to buy some more you have instant information to hand, to take to the shop with you.

Look – no join: To make an inconspicuous join in knitting wool, thread a darning needle up from the new skein and darn the wool in and out of several inches of the old yarn. Remove needle, pull straight, then twist between the palms of your hands for a smooth look.

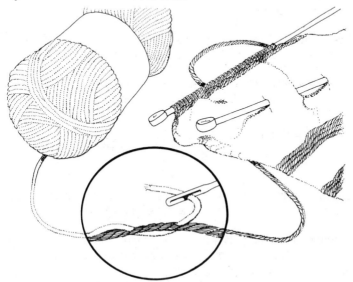

Untangled yarns: If you are knitting with two strands of yarn at once, thread the ends together through an empty cotton reel before you start. It keeps them smooth and untangled.

Lining up seams: When stitching together two large pieces of knitting or crochet, mark the seams first at intervals with coloured wool tags, so that you can line them up like seam notches to check that both sides are even.

Hook replaces needle: Use a crochet hook instead of a needle to 'sew' up side seams in textured or knobbly knitted garments.

Cuffs in place: Sew a couple of rows of spool elastic thread through the cuffs of heavy knit sweaters with a running stitch, then if you push up the sleeves, they will stay put.

MONEY SAVERS

Bird patterns: Don't throw away bird or flower patterned fabric, cut the shapes out and use them to decorate plain curtains or covers.

Useful ends: Don't throw away nearly used reels of cotton. Use the thread for tacking seams or hems.

New sheets from old: Sheets that are worn in the centre can be cut in half and then turned sides to middle, joined and re-used.

Blouse and petticoat: When making a blouse for a school child, give it an extra long tail and it will act as a petticoat, too, under her skirt.

Shirts into pillowcases: Don't throw away old white shirts, the backs from two of them will make a pillowcase.

Patchwork pieces: Hunt round charity shops and jumble sales for clothes you can adapt for yourself or the children and for patchwork pieces.

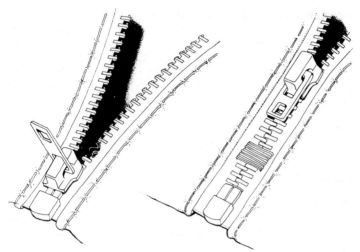

Mend a zip: If the zip fastener has broken at the base it can be salvaged: pull the slide down below the broken teeth, cut them out, then pull the slide up above the gap matching it on both sides. Stitch the zip together again just above the break.

Cushion stuffing: Use cut pieces of old knitwear, or cut up tights as a stuffing for cushions or soft toys.

Ironing board cover: The legs of pyjama trousers make good covers for an ironing board.

Button bank: Always save buttons and zips from discarded clothes.

Tape let down: Use iron-tape for the hemlines of children's dresses or boys' trousers. As the child grows, they are easier to let down that way. The tape will pull off easily after the garment has been laundered several times.

Extend a belt: A too-short belt can be lengthened easily if you undo it, remove the buckle, add a short length of narrow elastic to the buckle end, then replace it.

11

Woollen ties: Odd lengths of coloured wool can be crocheted into decorative chains to tie up Christmas or birthday presents.

Restore a tape: A limp linen tape measure can often be given a new lease of life if you iron it between two sheets of waxed paper.

Extend a hem: Make a horizontal tuck in the hem turn-up on children's dresses, or trousers, using the longest machine stitch: it will not show and can be let down later on as the child grows.

Extend a blanket: Blanket too short for the bed? Then sew a wide strip of discarded blanket of similar material to the bottom end, where it will be tucked in and unnoticeable.

New lining: Worn linings on otherwise good coats, jackets and skirts can be replaced. Carefully unpick the old lining, press out flat, then use as a pattern for a replacement one.

Flannel supply: Worn bath towels can be cut up and hemmed to provide a steady supply of flannels and face cloths.

Pretty napkins: Make a set of table napkins out of a worn tablecloth, edge them with decorative machine stitching.

Toddlers' pants: Discarded nappies can be turned into useful towelling pants for toddlers. Use two nappies per pair of pants.

Curtain hint: Switch your curtains around to opposite ends of the window every time you take them down for washing or cleaning, so that they keep their colour more evenly.

Add a band: If the hemline of a child's dress is too short for her, but the rest of it fits well, add a band of contrasting colour round the hem, team it up with a matching bow, buttons or belt.

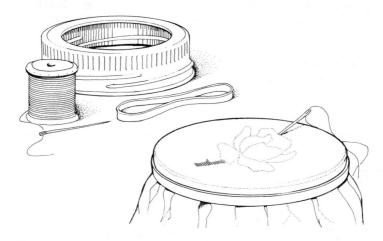

Embroidery frame: A metal fruit jar ring and an elastic band make a perfect miniature embroidery frame for small work.

Budget handkerchiefs: An old cotton shirt can be cut into squares and hemmed to make cheap handkerchiefs.

Needle sharpener: Blunt sewing machine needles can be sharpened if you 'stitch' them through a piece of sandpaper.

MACHINE SEWING

Fluff remover: Use a pastry brush to remove fluff from working parts of your sewing machine.

Curved seams: Use a shallow zig-zag stitch if you are machining curved trouser seams, it will take strain and wear and tear better than a straight one.

Stop the slip: To stop shiny fabrics from slipping off the table while you machine them, stretch a piece of towelling over the surface.

Slippery seams: When stitching seams on fine slippery fabrics, place a piece of paper underneath to make the job easier. The paper can be torn off afterwards.

Sewing jersey: All jersey fabrics should be sewn with the machine on a shallow zig-zag setting.

Useful bag: Fix a paper bag to the side of your sewing table top with masking tape or drawing pins, then scraps of fabric and cotton can be swept into it, and there is less clearing up to do afterwards.

Stray cottons: Use eyebrow tweezers to pull out stray pieces of cut cotton left in seams.

Sewing plastic: If you are sewing plastic, put it between a sandwich of waxed or greaseproof paper to make machining easier. It tends to stick otherwise. After the job has been done, the paper will tear away easily, leaving the stitching intact.

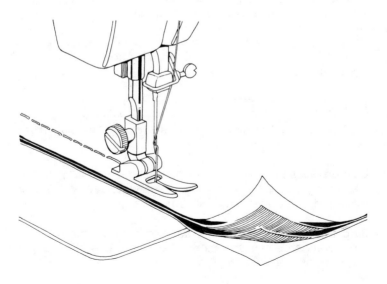

Tangled towelling: Looped fabrics like terry towelling will often get entangled between the needle and foot of the sewing machine. Avoid this by placing a sheet of tissue on top of the material before you start. It is easily torn away afterwards.

Machine seams for knitted garments: Use your sewing machine to seam hand-knitted or machine-knitted garments; use the loosest tension and a narrow zig-zag setting if your machine has one.

Eye in focus: Put a piece of white paper under the foot of your sewing machine when you are threading the needle, it makes the eye show up more clearly.

Surplus oil: Always stitch a few lines on a piece of blotting paper after you have oiled your sewing machine. This will blot up any surplus oil that might otherwise mark your fabrics.

Easy smocking: Mock smocking can be made easily on a zig-zag sewing machine: simply make four rows of gathers about $\frac{1}{2}$ centimetre ($\frac{1}{4}$ inch) apart, using a shirring foot with ordinary cotton, then embroider v's in a contrasting colour on it using the zig-zag stitch.

Breaking thread: If the top thread tends to break on your sewing machine, the tension is usually too tight. But it could be that you are using too fine a needle. If the bottom thread keeps breaking, it could be tight tension, which needs to be adjusted on the bobbin case, or you may have overwound the bobbin.

Powder for plastic: If you are top-stitching plastic material, smooth some talcum powder or French chalk over the area before you start, it will make it easier to work.

Be prepared: To save time when sewing a garment with a lot of seams, thread up two spools of cotton so you have a replacement ready when the first runs out.

Professional effect: Before sewing a decorative shell edging, or crocheting an edge on fine materials, take the thread out of your sewing machine, set it on the largest stitch length and run it along the edge. This will give you a row of minute, evenly spaced holes to guide you in getting a regular, professional effect with your stitching.

DRESSMAKING

Hem marker 1: A sink plunger marked on its wooden handle, makes a good hem marker for long skirts. It stands up by itself on the floor leaving your hands free to pin the skirt hem.

Hem marker 2: To mark a hemline, stretch a piece of string between two chairs, or a chair and table, at the desired height. Rub the string thoroughly with a piece of chalk, then put on the garment and turn slowly making sure the fabric brushes against the string all round. The chalk will mark the hem at the required spot.

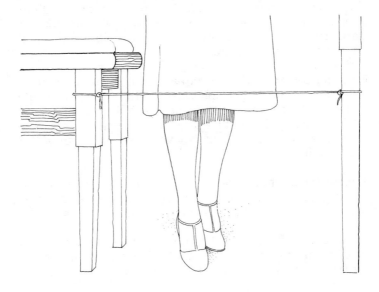

Nap in the right direction: If you're working with fabric which has a nap, like corduroy, mark the reverse side with an arrow to save sewing mistakes; use masking tape for the job, or stitch an arrow in contrasting cotton, chalk will tend to rub out. When the nap runs downwards, the colour appears lighter; if upwards the fabric looks darker.

Double thread: If you're working with double thread, knot each thread separately to prevent it pulling through. The cotton is much less likely to snarl up or twist.

Matching patterns: Match up stripes and tartans by turning the seam allowance under on one side and ironing it. Lay it alongside the seamline on the other piece, right sides upwards, matching it as you go and cover in place with transparent sticky tape. Stitch in the usual way, then remove the tape before pressing the seam.

Sewing scrap-book: Make a file or scrap-book of off-cuts of fabric and extra buttons from clothes that you make, for instant replacements if a button or a patch is required.

Hitting the spot: If you're putting snap fasteners on a garment, sew the projecting part on first, rub it with tailor's chalk, then press it against the side where the other half of the fastener is to go. It will mark the spot for you.

Heavy seams: Having difficulty in working with heavy material? Run a bar of soap along the wrong side of the seam before you start stitching. The needle will go through the fabric more easily and, when you come to press it, the seam will stay flatter.

Narrow belts: Iron-on hemming tape makes a good backing for narrow fabric belts.

Elastic threading: Attach a small safety pin to each end of the elastic when you are threading it through a waistline casing, that way you can monitor its progress as you pull it through.

17

Difference in arm measurements: When making a dress with a perfect fit, be sure to measure both arms for length and width. Many people find there is a difference between one arm and the other.

Shoulder straps: Sewing a dress with skinny shoulder straps? Then make another set of straps to sew over your bra straps, so they will be less noticeable.

Towel roll: Ironing the 'roll' into a tailored collar? Wrap a damp towel round a rolling pin and lay the collar over it to get the required curve. A padded rolling pin also makes a good sleeve board.

Removing pattern creases: Always iron paper patterns lightly before you use them to remove creases which might make them inaccurate.

Couture look: Give a couture look to a dress by making crochet covers for the buttons in sewing silk that matches the colour exactly. Use a double crochet stitch and either stuff with cotton wool until it is the right shape or stretch over a mould.

Scalloped finish: If you want a scalloped finish on a seam or hem, use rick-rack braid, letting only every other point show as you stitch, tucking the others into the seam allowance or up behind the hemline.

Heavy gathering: Use button thread on the bobbin if you are gathering heavy fabric by sewing machine. Loosen the tension first, do two rows on the longest stitch size available, then pull both sets of threads at once.

Sewing on patches: If you're sewing decorative patches or badges on to fabric, always glue them in place first with a dab of fabric glue, it makes them easier to work with. Failing that, spray the backs with spray starch, which will stick them in place while you sew, but will come out in the first wash.

Fabric loops: Always cut the fabric on the cross when making hand-made fabric loops, it will curve better and is much easier to sew.

Paper patterns: To make paper patterns last longer, spray them before you use them with a proprietary fabric protector.

Hemline hold-up: If you are hemming a fine fabric, use hairgrips to hold up the hemline while you are working on it, rather than pins, which would leave a mark.

Hold for pattern pieces: Use a clothes peg to hold pattern pieces together while you are working with them.

BUTTONS AND BUTTONHOLES

Correct tension: To avoid buttons being sewn on too tightly, separate the button from the fabric underneath with a matchstick while you stick it in place, or place a pin on top of the button between the holes so that the stitching goes over the pin at right angles to it.

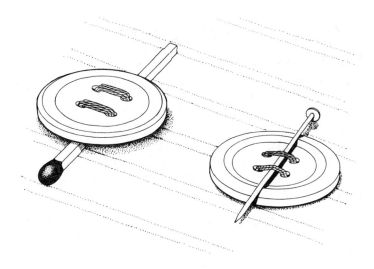

Fraying buttonholes: To stop buttonholes fraying while you stitch them, paint the cut edges with colourless nail varnish, allow to dry, then carry on stitching. Alternatively, mark the buttonhole in the first place with nail varnish and cut a slit through the centre when it is dry.

Long-life buttons: Dab the stitched centre of a button, front and back, with clear nail varnish before you wear a garment for the first time. The buttons will stay put much longer.

Buttons on shirts: The buttons on a tight fitting shirt will stay in place better if you sew them on with shirring elastic instead of thread. The same goes for the buttons on a button-through dress.

Button stitching: Buttons with four holes in them will stay put almost indefinitely if you stitch them, two by two, with separate lengths of thread. Then, if one side goes, the other should hold the button in place.

Button loops: Shoe lace makes good, inexpensive button loops.

DARNING, SEWING, AND EMBROIDERY

Use for off-cuts: Save long off-cuts of fabric from loosely woven material. When they are unravelled, they can be used as matching yarn for top-stitching, etc.

Tapestry repairs: When doing tapestry or needlepoint, tack some spare lengths of wool to the back of the work when you finish. They will come in handy later if you need to do any repairs to the work.

Templates: Cut patchwork templates from stiffened iron-on interlining instead of card, and use in place of heavy backing.

Threading a needle: Difficult needle threading is made easier if you spray hair lacquer on to the end of the cotton to stiffen it.

Fringe benefit: When making a fringe on the edge of a piece of fabric, mark the depth you require, then cut the fabric at intervals up to that point, being very careful not to snip across the vertical threads. The cross-threads stroke out much more easily if they are in short lengths.

Fine needle for beads: If you find you don't have a needle fine enough to take the beads you are threading, put a little melted candle-wax on the thread instead and twist it into a point before it hardens. Or, if the thread is really fine, paint some nail varnish on it and allow that to dry before using.

Curtain linings: When attaching curtain linings to the back of the curtain fabric, stop the stitches from going through to the outside of the curtain by putting a strip of cardboard between the two as you stitch.

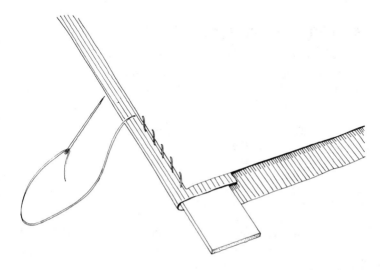

Hemming plastic: When working with plastic fabrics, turn up seam allowances and hemlines ready for stitching with sticky tape instead of pins.

Drawstrings: Always stitch drawstrings in place at centre back, so that they won't pull out accidentally.

Darning thread: Always use thinner rather than thicker thread for darning holes in fabric; heavy yarns tend to tear what is already a fragile, worn area.

Prevent snarling: To stop a length of sewing thread from snarling, always knot, or secure the end, which was nearest to the spool.

Large darns: Darn large items like sheets on the sewing machine; place a piece of paper underneath the hole and sew back and forwards over it, taking in the torn fabric edges until you have filled up the gap. When the fabric is washed, the paper will dissolve and the darn will remain intact.

WORTH NOTING

Pincushion: Stitch your pincushion on to a circle of elastic, so that you can wear it round your wrist as you work. Or stick pins and needles into a bar of soap, it lubricates them at the same time.

Quick check tape: A piece of worn tape measure stuck on to a sewing box, or the side of a sewing machine, is useful for quick check-ups on hem lengths, etc.

Jars for scraps: Small screw-top jars are useful for holding scraps of ribbon and lace.

Cut above plastic: Always cut out material on a plastic table cloth. The scissors move more easily over its slippery surface.

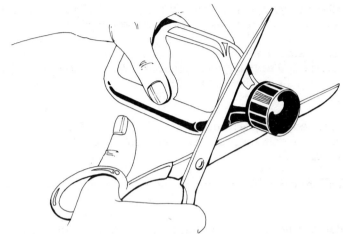

Scissor sharpeners: Sharpen scissors by making scissor movements round the neck of a sturdy glass medicine bottle or wine bottle. Or, cut through some glasspaper several times.

Red-hot needle: Use a red-hot metal knitting needle to poke holes into home-made leather or plastic belts, straps, etc.

Useful tail-comb: The tail from a tail-comb makes a useful instrument for poking out awkward corners or turning narrow tubes of fabric inside out.

Cushion settlers: If you are using small pieces of plastic foam as a cushion filling, add one or two larger pieces, this will stop the rest from settling down at one end only.

Finding an end: Push a drawing pin into the top of a reel of thread and wind the loose end around that. It is much easier to find.

Small things in store: Save matchboxes, then sticky-tape them together into a doll-size chest of drawers, to hold items like small pins, hooks, eyes, fasteners when you are sewing.

Cutlery tray: A plastic cutlery tray makes a good storage place for cotton reels and other sewing items.

Seam dampener: Use empty roll-on deodorant bottles (provided the ball is detachable), well rinsed out and refilled with water, to run along and dampen side seams before ironing.

Ever-ready needle: Push a piece of foam plastic into the centre of a cotton spool; use it to house a needle, ready for use next time.

Pins that grip: Before using pins on slippery fabric, poke them into soap: they will grip better that way.

Safety pin holder: Use a pipe cleaner to house safety pins – thread them on to it, then bend into a loop and twist the ends together. Large buttons can also be threaded on this way.

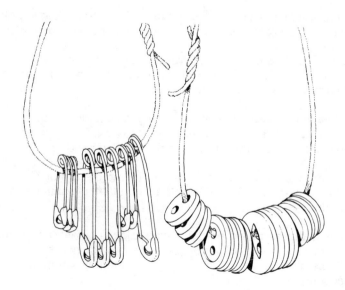

Instant mending: Keep an extra emergency sewing kit in the bedroom, so that buttons that are shed, hems that come down, whilst you are dressing, can be mended instantly, on the spot.

Darning mushroom: An electric light bulb makes a good darning mushroom for stockings and socks. The mushroom-shaped bulbs are heavier weight and therefore the best sort to use.

Money protector: Sew a small zip into the inside pocket of a child's jacket or blazer so that money and other items can be kept safely there.

Cover up: Making a dress to wear while entertaining or working around the house? Then make up an apron in matching fabric, so it is less noticeable when you wear it.

Long needle holder: Save a disused clinical thermometer case to house extra long sewing needles.

Slipping straps: To stop shoulder straps from slipping, run a couple of rows of machine stitching along them at shoulder-top level, using elastic thread in a matching colour.

Scissor store: Screw a cuphook to the side corner of your work table; it is useful for holding scissors which would otherwise tend to disappear under materials when not in use.

Pins to a magnet: Keep a small magnet in your sewing basket, it's ideal for quickly picking up spilled pins.

Filling for small items: Drained, dried coffee grounds make an ideal filling for very small items like pin cushions or tiny home-made toys.

Do it yourself

NAILING AND DRILLING

Thin into thick: When nailing, always nail through the thinner piece of wood into the thicker. Where possible, use nails three times longer than the thinner piece of wood.

Stagger the line: Avoid nailing in a straight line along the grain – staggering the line will reduce the chances of the wood splitting.

Dust catcher: When drilling into a ceiling, keep the dust out of your eyes by pushing the drill bit through the bottom of a yogurt pot – this will then act as a cup to catch the dust in.

Drilling hint: When drilling wood, rest the piece you are drilling on a piece of scrap, this will stop the wood from splintering as the drill breaks through.

Stepladder plus: Nail a strip of wood right around the top of the platform on your stepladder to stop nails and tools from falling off while you're working. Another strip nailed vertically will stop you knocking your can of paint over – put a rubber band around both the can and the strip of wood. Leather loops nailed to the side will come in handy for holding pliers, hammer, etc.

Avoid mess: If you want to avoid mess when drilling a hole in a wall, tape the open end of a paper bag to the wall just below the point where you intend drilling. If the tape is likely to damage the wall surface, use adhesive (blue) putty instead.

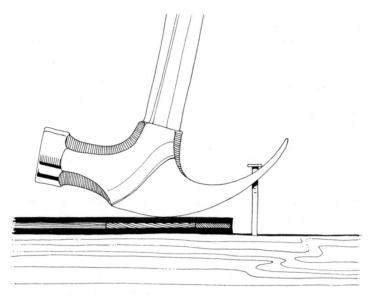

Saving the surface: When using the claw of a hammer to remove nails from a piece of wood, slip a thin piece of scrap wood under the hammer head – this will save the surface from damage.

Tight screws: If you find it difficult to get screws as tight as you would like, drill a hole through the handle of your screwdriver, then slip a large nail through and use this for extra leverage.

Finding a wall stud: When drilling into a hollow (stud) wall use a compass to check for the wall studs. Move it slowly over the surface of the wall, the needle will move when you pass it over the nails in the studs.

Finding a joist: When fixing anything into a ceiling you will need to find a convenient joist and fix into that. Joists run at right angles to the floorboards in the room above – find out roughly where the joist is by tapping (there will be no echo, the sound will be dull), then do a final test with a bradawl or small drill (there will be no cavity behind).

Prevent cracking: When nailing into a plastered wall, stick a piece of sticky tape to the wall first – this helps to prevent the plaster from cracking and leaves a clean hole.

Keeping screws in place: If you find that a metal screw tends to work its way loose, put a dab of nail varnish under the head before tightening it.

Prevent wood splitting: Blunting a nail point by giving it a couple of taps with a hammer will help to prevent wood from splitting.

Wax on screws: Screws are easier to insert and remove if you dip them in a little wax polish. If oil fails to shift a rusty screw, try a few drops of vinegar. Leave for a few minutes before trying again.

Thumb safety: Avoid hitting your thumbs when hammering small nails – push them through a piece of thin card and use the card to hold the nail in place. Tear the card away once the nail has taken hold.

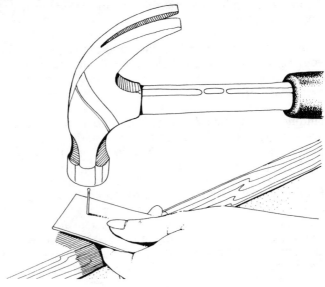

Screw lore: Screws should be turned clockwise when being inserted, anti-clockwise when being removed. Remember 'Left is loose and right is tight'.

Tighten a screw: A loose screw can often be cured in the following way. Remove the screw, break off a piece of match and wedge it in the hole, then replace the screw.

Loosen a screw: To shift a tight screw, heat the tip of the screwdriver before attempting to loosen it.

Fizz away rust: A rusted bolt can be freed by wiping with a cloth soaked in any fizzy drink. If this doesn't work, try ammonia.

QUICK AND EASY SOLUTIONS

Keeping hooks in place: To keep self-adhesive wall hooks firmly in place, coat the sticky surface with nail varnish before putting up.

Avoiding damp: When creating a flower bed next to the outside wall of the house, make sure that you never leave earth piled up against the wall – this can form a 'bridge' over the damp proof course that will allow damp to rise up the walls of the house.

Mending cracks: If you're not a dab hand with a plastering trowel, get rid of small cracks by mixing up plaster to the consistency of thick paint and, using a brush – not a trowel – cover the cracks.

Emergency plunger: In an emergency you can make a plunger for unblocking sinks by wrapping a sponge in a plastic bag and tying it tightly to the end of a stick (the handle of a wooden spoon would do nicely).

Reduce pipe strain: When removing the U-trap from a sink, use a piece of wood wedged in the U to reduce the strain on the pipes.

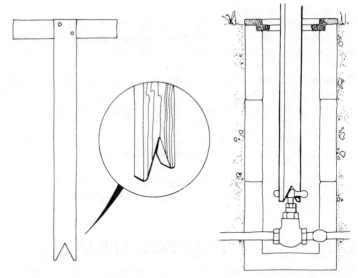

Turning a stopcock: In an emergency the water board's stopcock can be turned with the aid of a long piece of wood with a V shaped notch cut out of the end. Stopcocks, like ordinary taps, are turned off in a clockwise direction.

Filling large holes: When filling large holes in plaster, build the filler up layer by layer, allowing each to dry before applying the next. If you try to do it all at once the filler won't take properly.

Glue spreaders: Lolly sticks make useful glue spreaders and mixers – keep a few in your 'glue drawer'.

Clear drains: Instead of dumping coffee grounds in the bin, pour them down the sink, they help to keep drains free from grease and do not clog it as tea leaves do. External drains can be kept clear by pouring washing soda dissolved in boiling water down them occasionally.

Bonded ends: Nylon cord or rope can be prevented from fraying by melting the cut end over a low flame, causing the threads to bond together.

Successful plaster: When mixing plaster, you will avoid lumps if you add plaster to water instead of water to plaster. You can slow up the hardening of plaster by adding a little vinegar.

Prevent dry rot: Airbricks are vital to prevent dry rot (they allow air to circulate under the floor) never block them.

Mending linoleum: Linoleum that has come away from the floor at the edges can be refixed easily. Simply work some linoleum cement under the offending edge with a knife, weight it down with books and leave for 24 hours. The seam where two pieces of linoleum are joined should be sealed. This can be done simply by running a piece of sticky tape along the seam and covering this with shellac.

Rush repair: If the edges of rush matting squares come unravelled they can be stuck back into place with ordinary clear adhesive.

Toothpaste 'glue': Posters can be fixed temporarily to a painted wall with toothpaste. This is easy to remove when the time comes – it will just scrape off. It can also be used on wallpaper with care.

Paper store: A cuphook makes a handy place for storing important pieces of paper, just spear them on the hook.

Non-stick snow: When shovelling snow, a light coating of wax on the blade will prevent the snow from sticking.

Corn pads: You can stop picture frames from making marks on the wall by sticking corn plasters to the bottom corners.

TILE TIPS

Laying tiles: Before laying or cutting plastic, cork or linoleum tiles, warm them lightly in a cool oven. That way they will cut more easily and adapt themselves to the contours of the floor.

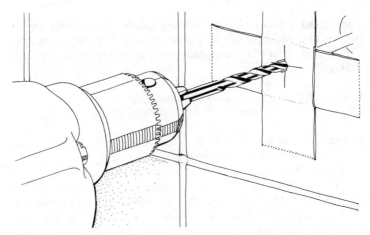

Drilling ceramics: Ceramic tiles can be difficult to drill into as the hard shiny surfaces cause the bit to skate about. To prevent this and ensure accuracy and safety when drilling, stick masking tape over the place to be drilled.

Getting rid of a tile: To remove a damaged tile, scrape away the grouting (the stuff around the edge of the tile), then drill a hole in the centre of the tile and carefully chip away, using a hammer and cold chisel. Be sure to wear protective goggles to protect your eyes. When the tile has been chipped away, simply scrape out the old adhesive.

Avoid cracking: If you have to cut polystyrene tiles, you can do so without cracking them by heating the knife first in boiling water.

FURNITURE AND WOOD

Petrol for dry rot: If you have a piece of furniture that has dry rot, you can kill it off by painting the affected area with petrol – be sure to do this outside and away from naked flames.

Vinegar and glue: Glued furniture joints can be freed by brushing with vinegar.

Saw accuracy: For absolute accuracy when sawing wood, don't just make a pencil mark. With a sharp knife and a steel rule score the line in the wood. Then make a second line a fraction to the waste side of the first, holding the knife at an angle. The result will be a tiny groove that will guide the saw and prevent it from wandering.

Chip away old paint: Old paint can be cleared from the head of a stubborn screw by striking it sharply with a hammer. If this fails, use an old screwdriver as a chisel to chip the paint away.

Getting rid of a wobble: If you have a table or chair with a short leg making it wobble, put some plastic wood on a piece of wax paper and put the leg down on it. When the plastic wood has dried, remove the wax paper and trim and sand to match.

Window sill groove: Most window sills have a shallow groove running lengthwise underneath them on the outside. This stops rain running from the front to the back of the sill and soaking the wall directly underneath. If your window sill doesn't have one, just glue a thin strip of wood to the underneath instead.

Candle grease: A plane will glide over wood more easily if rubbed with a candle.

Finding rough patches: When fine sanding a piece of wood, a stocking pulled over your hand and rubbed lightly over the wood will help you locate any slightly rough patches.

Good sanding: When sanding you will do a better job, and the paper will last longer, if you damp the backing and use the paper wrapped around a block of wood.

New knots: Don't paint straight over knots in new wood – the resin often causes a brown stain to appear through the paint. First give them a coat of knotting (from a DIY shop) to seal them.

ELECTRICAL

Plug wiring: Keep a note of the correct way of wiring a plug in a place where you can always find it when you need it (on the inside of a tool box or the handle of a screwdriver, for example). The new colour coding for the wires is as shown below left.

This replaces the previous colour coding which you will have on older appliances (below right)

NEW COLOUR CODE	**OLD COLOUR CODE**
GREEN/YELLOW = EARTH (E)	GREEN = EARTH (E)
BROWN = LIVE (L)	RED = LIVE (L)
BLUE = NEUTRAL (N)	BLACK = NEUTRAL (N)

If the plug has a two core flex, leave the earth terminal blank.

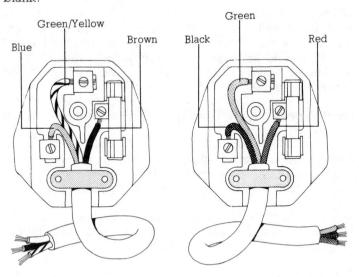

Sorting out wires: Plastic tags from bread packs can come in handy for sorting out a tangle of wires. Clip one on to each flex and label it using a permanent marker; that way you'll be able to keep track of which flex is which.

Blown fuse: To save time and effort when a fuse blows, label all fuses and keep an emergency tool kit (a torch, a card of fuse wire, a screwdriver and a pair of pliers) next to the fuse box.

Scissors for stripper: When stripping wire, if you don't have a proper stripper, use a pair of sharp nail scissors – cut into the wire then rotate the scissors until the insulation comes free.

Dust bulbs: Light bulbs will last longer, and give off more light, if you dust them regularly (switch off first). Bulbs tend to overheat if there is a build-up of dust.

Broken bulb: If a bulb breaks while you are removing it, leaving a jagged stump to be removed, embed it in the end of a bar of soap and use this to provide leverage. Discard the soap after use.

Fuse tester: For a quick and easy fuse tester, remove the end of a metal-cased torch. Place one end of the fuse on the end of the battery and the other on the torch case. If the bulb lights (with the torch switched on) then the fuse has not blown.

Household maintenance

THE OUTSIDE

Unblock a drain: If you have no drain rods and must unblock an outside drain, you can sometimes save the expense of calling a plumber by using an ordinary garden hose with water flowing through it. Work from the dry side of the blockage and be sure to wash the hose thoroughly afterwards.

Clear gutters: In autumn, gutters tend to get clogged with leaves, causing overflows and blockages. To prevent the leaves from settling in the gutter, fix a strip of chicken wire along the top.

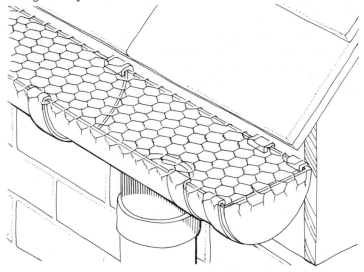

Damp detection: Mould or algae on an outside wall can be removed by scraping away, then washing the affected area with bleach diluted one to one with water. Leave to dry then repeat the bleach treatment the next day. If the mould reappears look for the source of the damp.

Window repair: Polythene sheeting can be used for an emergency repair to a broken window. To hold it in place without tearing, use thin battens over the top of the sheeting, with the nails passing through the battens and the polythene edge into the window frame.

PLUMBING

Burst pipes: Bandages and epoxy-resin adhesive can be used to repair burst pipes in an emergency. Mix up the adhesive according to the manufacturer's instructions and spread on the pipe and the bandage, then simply wrap the bandage tightly around the burst section of pipe. This should last long enough for you to get a plumber.

Thawing pipes: Don't use a blow torch to thaw frozen pipes – unless you're very careful you'll damage the pipe or even set fire to the house. Instead use a hair dryer, a hot water bottle, or cloths wrung out in hot water.

Avoid blockages: Never throw fatty or greasy food into the sink, this causes blockages.

Clearing a drain: If all else fails, try clearing a blocked drain like this. First pour down two kettles of boiling water, then a small amount of paraffin. Leave for twenty minutes and then pour down another two kettles of water.

Mending a washbasin: As a temporary measure, a cracked washbasin can be repaired by sticking strips of linen tape to the outside and covering these with gloss paint. Heavy duty waterproofing tape, of the kind sold in hardware stores for temporary repairs to pipes, will also work well.

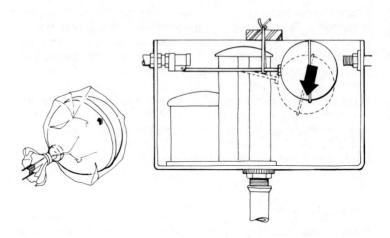

Punctured ball-floats: A plastic bag can be used to make an emergency repair to a punctured ball-float in the lavatory cistern – wrap the bag around the ball and seal with an elastic band. Cistern overflows can often be cured by bending the float arm downwards slightly. If the cistern itself is leaking you can cut the water off, while maintaining a supply elsewhere in the house, by placing a piece of wood across the tank and tying the arm float to this.

Cold tank insulation: When insulating a loft, remember that the cold water tank will now need insulating as well to prevent it from freezing. Never place insulation underneath the tank as this will cut it off from warmth from the rest of the house.

Repair a plumbing joint: A leak in a plumbing joint may be caused by worn threads. Undo the joint and wind a piece of cotton tightly around one of the threads. The joint should then screw back to give a tight fit.

Stop that dripping noise: The noise from a dripping tap can be prevented by tying a piece of string between the tap and the plughole. The water will now run down the string without dripping.

Prevent freezing: In winter even the smallest amount of water in unlagged pipes can freeze and cause a blockage. To prevent this, keep basin and bath plugs in place, especially at night.

HANDY THINGS TO KNOW

Fill that gap: Small gaps between door and window frames and the surrounding wall can be sealed with a flexible filler. For larger gaps, partially fill with old newspaper, then cover with filler.

A door that sticks: If a door sticks, find the offending area using carbon paper. Place some with the carbon side facing the inside of the door, on the frame and close the door. Repeat this, working your way around the door. The black marks will show where the door is rubbing. Sand the offending areas down, or just lubricate by rubbing with a candle.

Stiff lock: To free a lock that has jammed, smear the key with a little petroleum jelly and jiggle it about in the lock. A lock that is simply stiff can be lubricated by rubbing the key with a pencil, then working the graphite into the lock in the same way.

Preventing scratches: Regular use of a plastic washing up bowl prevents cutlery from chipping and scratching your sink.

Ending a squeak: A squeaky floorboard can sometimes be cured by lubricating the edges with talcum powder.

Smooth moving door: Soap can be used to silence a creaking door (just rub a little into the hinges) and make tight fitting drawers run smoothly (rub along the top and bottom edges.

Painting and decorating

HINTS FOR PAINTERS

Stair painting: When painting stairs, paint every other tread and allow these to dry before painting the others – that way you'll still be able to use them.

Ceiling paint: When painting a ceiling, remember that a water stain will keep coming through emulsion paint – use a matt oil-based paint instead.

Mildew problem: Mildew can be removed before painting by application of a little household bleach. Never paint over mildew or it will come back through the paint.

Mask with petroleum jelly: Small fittings on doors and windows that are too much trouble to mask or remove can be protected from paint by rubbing them with a little petroleum jelly before painting.

Ideal dust cloth: Don't throw away any old or discoloured shower curtains – they will make ideal dust cloths when painting.

Spray thinly: Spray paints give better results if applied in many thin coats rather than a few thick ones.

Keep leftovers: When you've finished a painting job, always make sure you have a small amount of paint left over for any little bits of patching up that are needed in the future – paint manufacturers may well alter a colour and you could find it hard to match later.

Sample patch: Some wallpapers will bleed colour through emulsion paints. Before repainting check by painting a sample patch in an unseen place.

Decorator's clothes: Old pyjamas make useful clothes to paint and decorate in.

A tight fit: The best way to keep paint from drying out is to put the lid on as tightly as possible and then cover it with kitchen foil.

Keep off the glass: Freshly dried paint can be removed from glass by washing with a solution of water and vinegar (3 parts warm water to 1 part vinegar). Or, when painting window frames, keep the glass free of paint by placing dampened strips of newspaper around the edges of each pane. The paper will stay in place until after you've finished painting. You can also remove paint by scraping with a single-edged razor blade (see page 329 for safety).

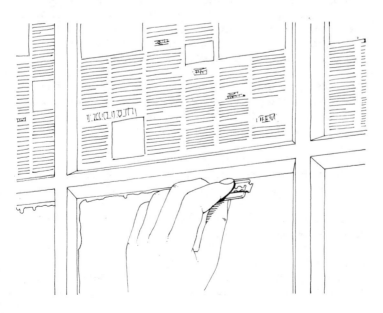

Colour matching: Before you start painting, dab a sample of the colour on to a sheet of white paper – this will give you a useful guide to take with you when it comes to matching curtains, carpets, etc.

Follow the sun: If paint is allowed to get hot while drying, the finish will be spoiled. When decorating a house exterior, follow the sun round, painting a section of wall as it falls into shadow. That way you'll know that the paint has a chance to dry properly.

Painting radiators: Don't use metallic paint on radiators, it will tend to absorb heat rather than letting it out into the room.

Avoid dark colours: Don't use dark colours out of doors if it can be avoided – they absorb heat and therefore tend to blister and fall off more quickly than light colours.

Distemper test: When removing distemper, check whether an area is completely clear by testing with a wet sponge. If the water from the sponge is absorbed from the surface straight away, there is still a residue of distemper left that will cause your paint to peel and flake.

Care with emulsion: Never use emulsion paint on areas that are subject to wide variations in temperature (radiators, window frames, etc.). Emulsion paint is fairly inflexible when it dries and will tend to crack and fall off.

Drainpipes: When painting drainpipes, hold a piece of cardboard between the pipe and the brickwork behind, so that you do not mark the wall.

Natural cords: Do not paint the sash cords themselves, as this will tend to make them perish.

Rub before painting: Before applying a coat of gloss paint or before painting over a gloss surface, always rub down with medium-grade glasspaper.

Non-stop: Try not to interrupt your work, if you are painting a wall or ceiling. If you stop for more than twenty minutes, a join line will show afterwards.

Painting order: If painting a whole room, start with the ceiling, then do the woodwork, followed by the walls and lastly the skirting board.

WAYS TO HANDLE PAINT

Drip tray: To prevent the inevitable drips of paint that run down the side of the can dripping on to the floor, fix a paper plate to the bottom of the can. You can do this by putting a few drops of paint on to the middle of the plate.

Working at heights: When painting, especially when working at heights, decant a quantity of paint into a small tin, you'll find it easier to handle than a large one.

Brush wipe: A thin piece of wire or string stretched across the top of a tin makes a useful brush wipe.

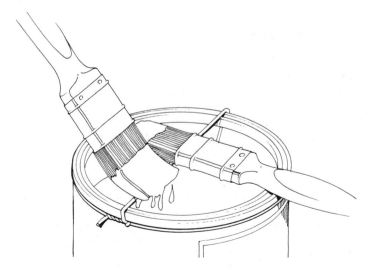

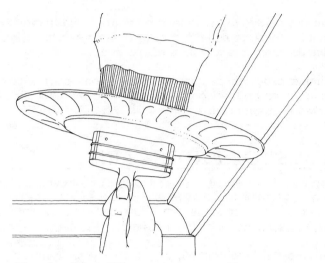

Catching the drips: When painting a ceiling, prevent paint from running down your wrist by pushing the brush handle through a paper plate.

Sweet smell: A teaspoon of vanilla essence in a can of paint will help to prevent unpleasant odours.

Keeping the flies away: A small amount of insect repellant in a can of paint will keep away flies while the paint dries.

Paint stirrer: A wire coat hanger bent in two makes a useful paint stirrer.

Try a little butter: When cleaning your hands after painting, you may well find that white spirit makes your skin chap. Try a little oil or butter instead – rub on thoroughly, then wash off with hot soapy water.

Paint level: When you've finished painting and before you put the tins away, make a mark with the paint on the side of the tin showing the level of the paint inside. Later on when you come to look for paint, you'll be able to see at a glance how much there is and of what colour.

Re-use spirit: When using white spirit to clean gloss paint from brushes, do not throw away the dirty spirit after you have finished. If the liquid is left for a few days the paint residue will sink to the bottom leaving clean white spirit which can be carefully poured off and re-used.

Protect lights: Light fixtures can be protected from drips when painting a ceiling by wrapping them in plastic bags, sealed at the top with a rubber band.

Use jam jars: If you're painting a piece of furniture, jam jar lids placed under each leg catch drips and stop paint going on the floor as you paint the end of the legs.

Small store of paint: Store very small amounts of leftover paint in cleaned nail varnish jars. The small amounts and the brush built into the handle of the jar make an ideal combination for repairing those little scratches.

Better grip: A piece of thick foam rubber wrapped around the handle of your paint brush gives you a better grip and makes a long paint job less tiring.

Paint strainer: Lumpy paint can be strained through old tights or stockings.

Stop a skin forming: A thin layer of white spirit poured on to the top of gloss paint before closing the lid and putting it away will help to stop a skin from forming.

HINTS FOR HANGING WALLPAPER

Correct view: Never make a final decision about a wallpaper or paint in artificial light and always view a colour against a neutral background.

Choosing a shade: If you are decorating to a single colour, remember that when large amounts of a colour are used it tends to concentrate itself, so choose a shade slightly paler than the one you think you want.

Getting rid of blisters: If you find that despite your best efforts you still have a few blisters in your wallpaper after it's dried, try this tip. Fill a syringe with paste and inject it into the blister. Allow time for the paper to absorb the paste then gently flatten the blister. Finally go over the area with a roller.

Alum water: When stripping wallpaper, dissolve 10 ml (2 teaspoons) of alum (obtainable from chemists) in 500 ml (1 pint) of warm water. Then, using a roller or brush, wet the wall thoroughly. Leave to dry and you'll find that the paper comes off easily.

Filling holes: Cracks in plaster can be filled with old newspaper before skimming with plaster. Nail holes can be hidden by filling with toothpaste. If necessary add food colour to match the wall. Nail holes in wallpapered walls can be filled with the aid of a box of crayons. Match the wallpaper, then soften the tip of the crayon over a match and use this to plug the hole.

Neat finish: After papering leave the surplus paper around light switches, etc., to dry thoroughly before trimming – this makes it easier to get a neat finish.

Prevent spots: Grease spots on existing paper, especially in the kitchen, will tend to come through any new paper placed on top. To prevent this, coat the offending spot with a clear varnish, or even nail varnish remover, before papering.

Tear a patch: When patching wallpaper never *cut* the patch. Tear out an irregular patch, making the tear *away* from the pattern (see also page 277 for treating stains).

Stain remover: A piece of stale bread can be used to remove light stains and marks from wallpaper.

Whisking paste: Use a whisk to save time when mixing wallpaper paste.

Wallpaper paste: Always use the recommended paste for the type of wallpaper you are using. Throw out any paste left over, as it will not keep.

The right paper: Resist buying wallpapers that are not suitable for the walls you are going to hang them on. Kitchens need washable papers, that are also steam and heat resistant, as do bathrooms. Paper over the stairwell walls should also be washable.

Lining paper: Walls which are painted or distempered need a lining paper first. Hang it horizontally to avoid bulky lines where there is one join on top of another.

Brush rest: When papering, save yourself making a sticky mess by stretching a piece of string across the top of your paste bucket. Use this to rest your brush on while hanging the paper.

Repairing scratches: Small scratches in wallpaper can be fixed by taking a scrap of paper with the same design, wetting it and, using a small paint brush, taking some of the colour from the scrap to repair the scratch.

Faded paper: When repairing a tear in wallpaper that's been up for some time you may find that it has faded so the new piece stands out. Soaking the new piece in lemon juice will fade it slightly to match. Otherwise, leave it in strong sunlight and sprinkle a little salt on it.

Finding screw holes: When repapering, you can save yourself hours of searching for screw holes by popping a match stick into each one, leaving about $3\,mm$ ($\frac{1}{8}$ inch) protruding. When you smooth down the paper the end of the match will poke through, indicating where the holes are.

Delicate papers: When hanging very light or delicate papers, paste the wall instead of the paper – you'll find them much easier to hang.

Wallpaper near cookers: Don't hang vinyl wallpaper near a cooker – the surface will be damaged by splashes from hot food.

Symbols: These international symbols are now beginning to appear in wallpaper pattern books and on product labels:

~~	spongeable	▌▐	paste-the-wall
≈	washable	► ○	free match
≋	super-washable	► ◄	straight match
▬	scrubbable	► ◄	offset match
☼	sufficient light fastness	50 cm 30	design repeat distance offset
☼	good light fastness	▐ ⟩	duplex
◥	strippable	⟨≈⟩	co-ordinated fabric available
◥	peelable	↑	direction of hanging
⊻	ready pasted	↓↑	reverse alternate lengths

How many rolls of wallpaper do you need?: Standard wallpapers come in rolls approximately 10.05 m (11 yards) long and 530 mm (21 inches) wide. The chart gives the number of rolls required according to the height of the walls and the distance round the room. Allow extra for matching patterns.

NUMBER OF ROLLS REQUIRED

Distance around the room (doors and windows included)

WALLS Height from skirting	9 m (30')	10 m (34')	12 m (38')	13 m (42')	14 m (46')	15 m (50')	16 m (54')	17 m (58')	18 m (62')	19 m (66')	21 m (70')	22 m (74')	23 m (78')	24 m (82')	26 m (86')	27 m (90')	28 m (94')	30 m (98')
2.15–2.30 m (7'–7'6")	4	5	5	6	6	7	7	8	8	9	9	10	10	11	12	12	13	13
2.30–2.45 m (7'6"–8')	5	5	6	6	7	7	8	8	9	9	10	10	11	11	12	13	13	14
2.45–2.60 m (8'–8'6")	5	5	6	7	7	8	9	9	10	10	11	12	12	13	14	14	15	15
2.60–2.75 m (8'6"–9')	5	5	6	7	7	8	9	9	10	10	11	12	12	13	14	14	15	15
2.75–2.90 m (9'–9'6")	6	6	7	7	8	9	9	10	10	11	12	12	13	14	14	15	15	16
2.90–3.05 m (9'6"–10')	6	6	7	8	8	9	10	10	11	12	12	13	14	14	15	16	16	17
3.05–3.20 m (10'–10'6")	6	7	8	8	9	10	10	11	12	13	13	14	15	16	16	17	18	19

Decorating record: When you've finished decorating, make a note, such as the one below, of how many rolls you needed and how long it took, along with any particular difficulties. Keep this somewhere safe and you'll find it a boon when you come to redecorate.

ROOM

Paint, walls	Type ....
	Manufacturer ....
	Colour ....
	Quantity ....
	Washable ....
Paint, woodwork	Type ....
	Manufacturer ....
	Colour ....
	Undercoat ....
Wallpaper	Type ....
	Manufacturer ....
	Pattern ....
	Adhesive ....
	Number of rolls ....
	Washable ....

Any particular problems? ....

TOOLS AND EQUIPMENT

Prevent rust: Mothballs, charcoal or chalk kept in a tool box will help to absorb moisture and so prevent rusting. Another way to prevent metal tools from rusting, is to give them a rub down with car wax before putting them away. Oil works just as well but tends to be removed more easily. You can also remove rust from tools by rubbing them with a typewriter eraser.

Non-slip: A hammer head will not slip if it is kept clean and is slightly roughened with emery paper.

Nail store: Ice cube trays, which are too cracked for use in the refrigerator, come in handy for storing small nails, screws and other oddments. Screws, nuts, bolts and washers, needed for a repair job, can also be kept easily to hand by sticking them in a line on a strip of sticky tape.

Prevent metal scratching: When using pliers to handle metal with a delicate finish, slip the fingertips from two old gloves (leather if possible) over the ends of the jaws to prevent scratching.

Pliers as a vice: You can use pliers as a small vice to hold things in place when you are glueing them together, for example, if you wrap a strong piece of wire around the handles to secure them.

Chalk stops slipping: A screwdriver blade can be prevented from slipping by being rubbed with chalk before it is used.

PAINT BRUSH CARE

Foil wrap: If you need to take a break from painting (either overnight, or just for a few hours) wrap the bristles of your brush in kitchen foil. This keeps them soft without you having to go to the trouble of washing and drying the brush.

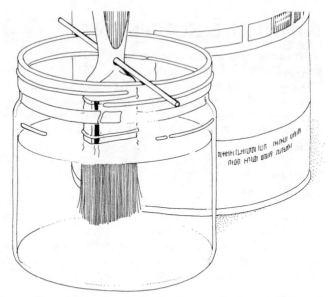

Brush soaking: Use the hole in the end of a paintbrush (make one if there isn't one already) to suspend the brush when soaking it in cleaning fluid. Thread a stick through and rest this on top of a container holding the fluid. The jar must be deeper than the brush. This will keep the bristles off the bottom of the jar and stop them from being damaged.

Soak in oil: Paint brushes last longer and are easier to clean, if, before being used for the first time, they are soaked overnight in linseed oil.

Soft brushes: Before putting clean brushes away, rinse them in a fabric softener, this helps to keep them soft and pliable.

Soak away stiffness: Vinegar can be used to soften paint brushes which have gone stiff (especially those used for gloss paint). Heat the vinegar to just below boiling and immerse the brushes in it for a few minutes. Then take the brushes out and the vinegar will evaporate. To make sure the brushes are clean, rinse before using again.

Best buys: Always buy the best possible brushes. Cheap ones are a poor investment, as they tend to shed bristles.

Simply white: Keep one set of brushes for white paint only. Once a brush has been used for colour, however well you clean it, some colour will remain and will show up on white paintwork.

Protecting brushes: After cleaning paintbrushes, wrap them in newspaper when they are almost dry to keep the bristles soft and to protect them from moths. Always store brushes flat.

Paint rollers: When using paint rollers, foam rubber or mohair sleeves are best for gloss paint and distemper. Felt and lambswool are the best for other types of paint.

Plant
and garden tips

IN THE GARDEN

Storing tools: When putting garden tools away for the winter, coat the metal parts with oil then bury them in a bucket of sand. This will keep rust at bay.

Hose handle: A short length of old garden hose can be split down the middle and slipped over the handle of a metal bucket to protect your hands.

Handy tool holders: Use a length of old hose to make handy tool holders for the garden shed or workroom. Cut off a piece 50 mm (2 in) long, then slit it along its length with a sharp knife. Nail it to a wall or piece of board and use like a spring clip.

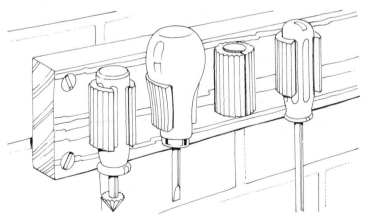

Bring on the plants: When replacing windows, save the old glazed frames. Propped against a wall, they make ideal cold frames for the garden to bring plants on ahead of the season.

Foil the elements: Protect young trees from the elements in winter by wrapping the length of their trunks in kitchen foil.

CUT FLOWERS

Trimmed and fresh: To keep flowers fresh as long as possible, change the water and cut off a small piece of the stems every day. If the stems are hard and woody (rose stems, for example), they should be crushed at the ends to encourage the absorption of water.

Charcoal in the water: If you can't change the water every day, put a piece of charcoal or a copper coin in the water with the flowers.

The long and the short of it: Flowers with short stems can be made to stand properly in a tall vase if the bottom of the vase is filled with screwed-up newspaper.

Lower leaves: Do not allow the lower leaves of flowers to trail in the water: remove them. If you leave them in the water they will rot and the flowers won't last as long as they should.

Mint green: When arranging flowers, consider using sprigs of fresh herbs, such as mint, thyme or rosemary for greenery – that way an extra fragrance will be provided, as well as extra colour.

Odds and evens: If you are arranging a small number of flowers it is easier with an odd number than an even.

Longer-lasting tulips: To make tulips last longer, make a series of small holes down the whole length of their stems.

Clear water: To keep a flower vase free from slime and to avoid the stale smell that can be caused by flower water, add just a few drops of bleach to the water. This will not harm the flowers.

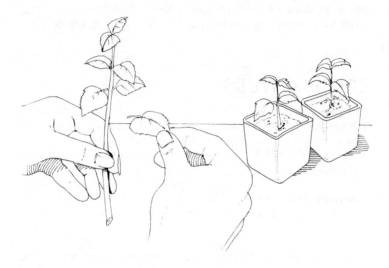

INDOOR PLANTS

Taking cuttings: Many plants can be grown quite easily from cuttings. They make ideal gifts or you can arrange to trade cuttings with your friends. The easiest method is by stem cutting. Select a plant with a soft stem. Pick a young shoot that is about 50 mm (2 in) long, choosing one with several leaf nodes (places from which leaves sprout). Make the cut with a sharp knife just below one of the nodes. Gently pull off the leaves from this node. Plant in a cutting mixture.

Shiny leaves: Polish heavy-leaved indoor plants, such as rubber plants, with cotton wool soaked in olive oil or milk.

Good mulch: Old tea-leaves, emptied on to the soil around houseplants, make a good mulch.

Ready together: When growing mustard and cress together, start the cress off three or four days before the mustard – if you do this they'll be both ready at the same time.

Plant drainer: Save broken crockery and use it at the bottom of plant pots to provide proper drainage.

Holiday care: Before going on holiday, put your plants in the bath with a little water and cover the top of the bath with polythene, leaving a few gaps to let the air in. Draw the curtains if the sun is likely to reach them through the window. The polythene cover maintains a moist atmosphere for the plants.

Miniature indoor gardens: Use hollow or ornamental bricks as miniature indoor gardens. Stand on a tile or tray before filling the gaps with earth and planting. Choose plants that all require the same treatment.

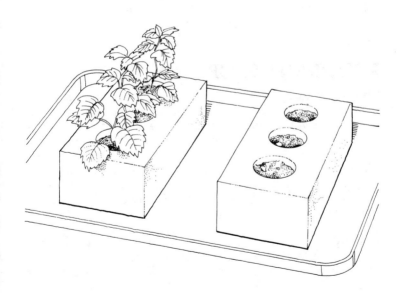

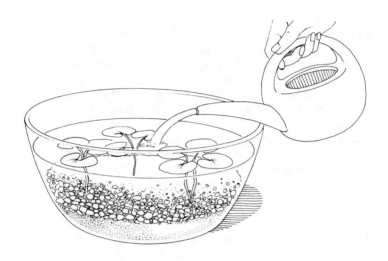

Indoor water gardens: To make an indoor water garden, plant miniature water lilies in 50 mm (2 in) of ordinary soil in a bowl (a transparent bowl is best). Cover the soil with a thin layer of gravel. Increase the depth of water as the plants grow.

POT PLANT PROBLEMS

The following is a selection of hints to help you deal with the most common houseplant problems. It is a good idea to check over your plants in spring and weed out those which have not survived the winter successfully.

Plant not growing: In winter it is quite normal for plants not to grow. If the plant is not growing in spring, the most likely reason is that it has grown too big for its pot. Otherwise it may be underwatered or underfed.

Spindly growth: When a plant grows very tall and spindly with only a few leaves, it means that it has been given too much food and water for the amount of light available. This happens most often in spring, when there is little light about. Cut down on feeding and watering.

Plant growing crooked or twisted: If you look carefully at a plant which has grown twisted, you will see that it has done so in order to get nearer to a source of light. Move the plant so as to give it more light. If the plant is already in plenty of light, turn it regularly, so that the whole plant gets the same amount of light.

Leaves dropping: If the leaves are old, the most likely cause of them dropping is underwatering. If the leaves are fairly young and they turn yellow before dropping, the cause is probably overwatering.

Yellow leaves: If the leaf is yellow but stays on the plant, then the cause is either that the plant is not getting enough light or that the soil or water contains too much lime. If the leaf drops the cause is overwatering.

Leaves loosing their markings: If a plant, which normally has leaves marked with pale cream lines or spots, is losing these markings, it is a sign that the plant is not getting enough light.

Browning of leaf edges: Overwatering, too much direct light or cold draughts, may all cause the edges of the leaves to turn brown.

"It's Not What You Do, It's The Way You Do It"

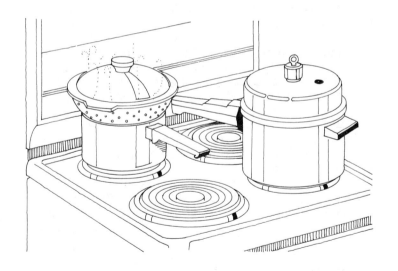

General household hints

General household hints

CLOTHES AND JEWELLERY

Anti-static: A dress that clings to your slip can be separated by running a wire coat hanger between the two as you are dressing. This cuts down the amount of static electricity, which is what makes them stick together.

Glove care: Leather gloves should be pulled off from the tip of each finger and stored flat, not screwed up one inside the other.

Hanging an evening dress: To hang up a long evening dress in the wardrobe without the hem scraping the floor, sew loops on the inside at waist level. Turn inside out and hang like a skirt.

Needles to hand: You can make a useful emergency sewing kit to carry in your purse, by cleaning out an old lipstick container and filling it with pins, needles and a spool of clear nylon thread.

Pack away: When packing a holiday suitcase, always put the heaviest items in first. If possible, put a layer of towelling between bumpy objects, like shoes, and your clothes.

Day-to-day care: Try not to wear any item of clothing more than one day at a time. Clothes last much longer, and look fresher, if they are given a chance to recover before being worn again. Always hang them up when still warm from the body, so that creases drop out.

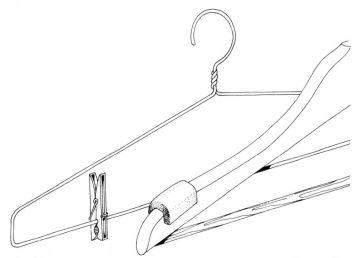

Non-slip: You can stop clothes from slipping off wooden hangers by sticking a piece of foam rubber at each end of the hanger.

Trouser hangers: To make hangers for trousers or skirts, without sewing on loops, fix two clothes pegs on ordinary wire hangers.

Inside-out storage: If possible store black items of clothing inside out to prevent them picking up dust and fluff.

Quick-dry Wellingtons: The inside of wet Wellington boots can be dried quickly with the aid of a hair dryer.

Wet shoes into shape: If leather shoes become thoroughly soaked, stuff them with dry newspaper before leaving to dry – if you don't, they'll dry out of shape.

Extended life: When shoes are new, put stick-on soles over the new soles. Make sure the soles are the right weight. The shoes will now last longer.

Leather costs more: Shoes with leather soles and heels wear out quicker and cost more to repair than plastic soles and heels.

Costume care: After a swim don't just wring a swimsuit out and put it away. Always rinse it in tap water first. The salt in the sea and the chemicals in swimming baths are very bad for material.

No perfume: Never put perfume or deodorant on clothes, both of them will damage the fabric.

Keeping in shape: To help garments to keep their shape, empty all the pockets and do up buttons and zips before putting away. Never put clothes in a wardrobe straight after wearing them – hang them up in the room for a few minutes first.

Roll don't fold: Clothes made of man-made fibres should be rolled rather than folded before putting away.

Real pearls: You can tell real pearls from paste by biting them – real pearls feel gritty. They should be worn as often as possible – contact with the skin helps to maintain their natural colour.

Jewellery cleaner: The impregnated cloths supplied for cleaning spectacle lenses are ideal for cleaning jewellery as well.

Brilliant detergent: Rhinestones can be cleaned by scrubbing gently with hot water containing a detergent, then drying with a soft cloth.

Away with tarnish: A coat of clear nail varnish will stop costume jewellery from tarnishing. Where the finish becomes damaged it can be repaired by rubbing with a stick of the metallic wax sold for brass rubbing in craft shops, then coating with clear nail varnish.

Novel necklace idea: Necklaces are easily damaged if they are jumbled together in a box; they tend to tangle, and getting any one out usually involves abusing the others. One solution is to keep them on a row of small nails or hooks along a dull stretch of wall. Not only will they be kept free from tangles, but you can see at a glance just what you have to choose from. They will also brighten up an otherwise unattractive area.

Linen or cotton: You can tell whether something is linen or cotton by placing a wet finger on the material. If the material is linen the mark will show through straight away.

Metal stains: Don't hang wet or damp garments on wire hangers – the metal can cause staining.

Stop the rub: If socks always wear out at the same point, rub a little paraffin inside your shoes at the offending spot.

Fluff remover: Use a piece of sticky tape wrapped around your finger, sticky side out, to remove dust and fluff from dark material.

Quick zip: A zipper that doesn't run smoothly can be lubricated by rubbing it with a soft pencil – the graphite does the trick.

Smooth metal: If your metal zipper tends to stick, rubbing it with wax will make it glide more smoothly.

Longer jeans: If you have to lengthen an old pair of jeans, remove the white line left at the fold by brushing on permanent blue ink (matched to the colour of the jeans) mixed with a little water.

Dyeing tip: When dyeing fabric in a washing machine, remember that it is much more important for the dye to circulate freely than it is for washing powder. So to be on the safe side, never dye more than half the manufacturer's recommended machine load.

Shoe shine: Baby oil makes very good shoe conditioner – rub some into the leather last thing at night and rub it off in the morning.

Potato buff: Badly scuffed leather shoes should be rubbed with a piece of raw potato before polishing.

Firm patches: Iron-on patches often do not have glue right up to the edges and this can cause them to lift off after a while. The solution is to trim around the edges till you reach the glue.

Hem creases: Use white vinegar to get rid of a stubborn hem crease – damp the material with the vinegar, then press flat with a warm iron.

Steam away creases: If you don't have access to an iron, you can remove the wrinkles from a garment by hanging it up in the bathroom while you have a bath – the steam makes the creases drop out.

Away with shine: Black clothing tends to become shiny with use – this can be got rid of by rubbing with a rag soaked in turpentine. Hang out of doors to remove the smell before wearing.

FURNITURE AND FURNISHING

Carpet pieces protect: Carpet samples make useful door mats. They are also useful for protecting table tops from typewriters, sewing machines, etc.

Even wear: A stair carpet should always be a little longer than the stairs themselves. You will need to move the carpet up or down from time to time and re-fix to ensure even wear.

No more wobble: If the rung or leg of a chair works its way loose, when sticking it back, mix a little sawdust with wood glue – this will keep it tight and stop it from wobbling.

Prevent yellowing: Table linen that is not in constant use should be wrapped in blue tissue paper. This will stop it from yellowing.

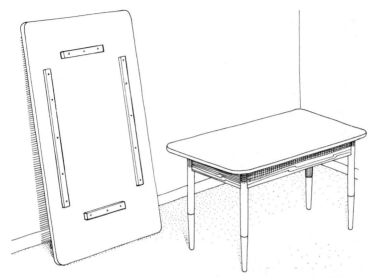

Plywood table top: When entertaining you can extend your dining table by putting a large piece of sturdy plywood over it. With the plywood in place, draw the outline of the table top on the underneath. Remove the plywood and fix strips of wood along the lines you have drawn, so that they fit just outside the original table top area. These will stop the plywood from sliding about when it's in place. Sand any very rough edges. Cover with a table cloth and no-one will be any the wiser.

Flat mats: Cloth table mats can be kept flat when not in use by hanging them on a clip board.

Good for brass – not for nylon: Although it's a good idea to lubricate old-style brass curtain tracks with a little light oil or petroleum spirit, never do this to nylon track or it will jam.

Top with brown paper: Where a bed has a wire spring base, it should always be covered with something, even if only brown paper, to prevent the springs staining the mattress.

Easy movement: An offcut of carpet slipped upside down under a heavy object to be moved will protect the floor and make moving much easier.

New top for old: Revive the look of an old coffee table by covering the top with a piece of material kept in place with a sheet of glass.

Rock – not slide: You will often find that a rocking chair will tend to slide about the floor when used. Keep it in one spot by glueing a strip of velvet (or velvet type) ribbon to the rockers.

No more curls: A rug that curls up at the edges can be kept flat by brushing the back with size. This sealant can be bought in decorating shops.

OUT SHOPPING

Buying a bed: The rule when buying a bed is 'buy in haste, repent at leisure'. Always check the mattress carefully before purchasing. Is it too hard, too soft?

Lists save time: Write shopping lists to correspond with the order in which you visit shops, in order to save time returning for something you forgot the first time around.

Resist temptation: Always take a list when you go shopping and stick to it. Supermarkets are designed to tempt you into buying things you don't really need.

Forward planning: If you have the space for storage, buying things that you will always need in bulk saves time, trouble and money.

Tempting price: Buy clothes in the sales in the shops to save money, but make sure you don't get carried away by tempting prices and start losing your judgement. Check seconds, or goods brought in for the sales, carefully for flaws.

Second-hand TV: If you are buying a second-hand television set, insist on seeing it working. If it is colour, try to find out why they are selling it. Ask if the tube is guaranteed. See the test card to check the colour balance. Second-hand black and white sets are temptingly cheap but be prepared to throw them away if anything major goes wrong; they are not worth repairing.

Shopping in the rain: Keep a sheet of polythene in your shopping bag to protect food in case of rain.

Heavy citrus: When buying citrus fruits, don't just judge the look of the fruit. Weight is the best guide – the heavier is normally the better.

HOUSE CARE

Fitting a duvet cover: When changing duvet covers, keep a couple of pegs handy. Get one of the far corners in place and peg it there, now do the same for the other far corner. Now locate the near corners (don't worry about what's happening to the rest of the duvet). Grasp the two nearest corners and give the whole thing a shake to straighten the middle out before removing the pegs.

Line up: When lining a shelf, cut several liners all at the same time. Put them inside the shelves one on top of the other and when the top one gets dirty, remove it and there will be another one underneath.

Fitted sheets: Save time and money by making your own fitted sheets – just tie a knot in the corners of an ordinary sheet and tuck this under the mattress.

Fingers off: Clear adhesive plastic stuck around switch plates and plugs will keep dirty fingermarks off the wall.

Anti-rust breadbins: Metal breadbins tend to rust at the bottom. To prevent this, glue small pieces of rubber under them to let the air circulate.

. . . and waste bins: A piece of self-adhesive plastic stuck to the inside bottom of a metal waste paper bin will prevent it rusting and staining.

Beat it clean: Never wash the cloth bag of your vacuum cleaner – doing so will allow dust to come through – beat it clean instead.

Dust avoidance: When hanging pictures, place a drawing pin at the top corners of each at the back. This holds the top of the picture slightly away from the wall and prevents the build up of dust.

AROUND THE KITCHEN

A firm board: To stop a pastry board from sliding, lay out a damp cloth underneath it. For a more permanent solution glue strips of rubber to the bottom of the board.

Softening a cork: If you wish to replace the cork in a bottle, but you find that it will not fit, soak it in a little hot water to soften it.

Keep under wraps: Soap lasts longers once it is in use if it is stored in a cupboard in its original wrapping for a while beforehand.

Flexible rubber: When you first fill a new hot water bottle, add a few drops of glycerine to the water. This makes the rubber more flexible and prevents it from perishing.

New knob: When a saucepan lid has lost its knob, replace it with a large piece of cork. Slip a screw through the hole and turn this so that it bites into the cork, holding it firmly in place.

Sharp knives: If kitchen knives are left in a drawer they will blunt each other. Keep them sharp by hanging them on a magnetic knife rack, but always store them handle downwards in case they fall.

Protecting glasses: To prevent glasses from cracking when hot water is poured into them, stand a metal spoon on the bottom before pouring.

Finding blunt areas: When sharpening a knife, look for blunt or worn areas by holding the edge towards the light. Where the knife is blunt it will catch the light and sparkle.

Foam lining: Line the inside of cutlery drawers with foam rubber to cut down on noise, wear and tear.

Magnet gloves: Oven gloves can be kept where they're most needed if you sew a small magnet as near to the outside of them as possible and use this to stick them to the cooker.

Bulletin board: Use the front of your refrigerator as a bulletin board – hold pieces of paper in place with small magnets.

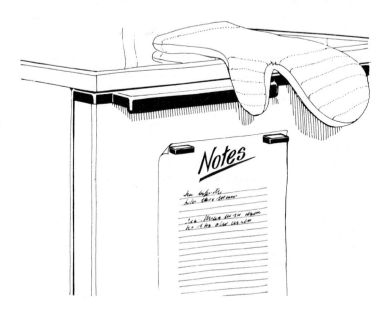

Coming unstuck: You can separate two glasses that are stuck one inside the other, by filling the inside one with cold water and immersing the other in warm to hot water.

Oil a stopper: To free the stopper from a decanter, put a little cooking oil around the stopper and tap gently around the outside until it comes free.

Easy reference: The insides of kitchen cupboards are an ideal place to stick metric conversion charts, favourite recipes – anything you need to have handy.

Lighting up: Damp matches can be made to light by dipping them in nail varnish and then letting this dry before striking.

Firm seals: If you seal a letter with a little raw egg white, it will make it impossible to steam open.

Stubborn lids: For a better grip on a stubborn jar lid, wrap a rubber band around it. If this fails, run a little hot water over the lid.

Better ice cubes: Air in water makes ice cubes slow to freeze. If you use boiled water, which has been allowed to cool, in your trays instead of water fresh from the tap, not only will they freeze quicker but the ice will be crystal clear.

Soup's up: When serving soup to the family, stir an ice cube into the children's bowls. It cools it to suit young mouths, and that way the whole family will be able to start eating at the same time.

No spills: When packing for a picnic, prevent salt and pepper from spilling by taping over the tops of the shakers.

String tidy: To keep string tidy, store it in a funnel. Hang the funnel up with the ball of string inside it and draw the string out through the end of the funnel.

Steel not wheel: Serrated or scalloped-edged knives should only be sharpened on a steel not in a wheel sharpener. Sharpen them only on the non-serrated side of the blade.

Use for egg cartons: Save a few plastic egg cartons for the children to use as throw away paint palettes.

See-through storage: Glass coffee jars, or translucent poly-thene ice cream tubs, are ideal for storing non-perishable foods. The ice cream tubs also make good freezer containers.

Clean milk bottles: Rinse milk bottles in cold water before washing in hot. Hot water will coagulate any remaining milk which, in turn, will stick to the inside of the bottle and be difficult to remove.

Prevent chips: Glue several strips of rubber to the top of your draining board to prevent plates from chipping. A rubber attachment on a tap will do a similar job.

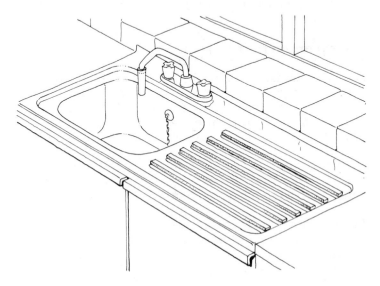

Spaghetti lighter: A piece of raw spaghetti makes a useful taper for lighting pilot lights or anything that's difficult to get to with a match.

No smoke wicks: Candle wicks will not smoke if they are soaked in a little vinegar, then left to dry before using.

Large into small: Instead of damaging candles that are just too big for a holder, dip the ends in a little warm water to soften them into a slimmer shape before inserting.

Sponges in good order: Sponges will become slimy if they are not allowed to dry out thoroughly after use. To revive a slimy sponge, soak it overnight in water containing a little vinegar. Wash the sponge thoroughly before using.

Longer life for rubber gloves: Rubber (not PVC) gloves are easily punctured by long fingernails. Prevent this by putting a piece of cotton wool in the end of each finger.

Stop steel wool rust: Steel wool will not go rusty if it's kept in soapy water. Make sure that it is completely covered with water.

ABOUT THE HOUSE

Placing pictures: If you cut the shape and size of a picture out of paper you will be able to select its correct position without having to make holes in the wall. When you come to mark the nail for the picture use a wet finger – it will dry without leaving anything that will show.

Straighten up: To cure a picture that will not quite hang straight, wrap some adhesive tape around the centre of the wire – this will stop the picture from slipping sideways.

Broken glass: A pad of damp cotton wool is just the thing for picking up tiny fragments of broken glass. Dab the affected area and the pieces of glass will stick to the pad which can then be thrown away.

Wet book: Dry a book that has been dropped in the bath by putting tissues in between each page. Repeat this procedure until the pages are nearly dry, then leave overnight with a sheet of paper between each page and press under a weight. Don't use too heavy a weight or you'll damage the binding.

Test for a damp bed: If you're not sure whether a bed has been properly aired or not, put a hand mirror between the sheets. Leave it for 10 minutes or so, if it has clouded over when you remove it, the bed is damp.

Smooth a chipped surface: Chipped glass and porcelain can be sanded smooth with very fine sandpaper.

Stopcocks and fuse box: Go around the house and mark the various stopcocks showing which way to turn them and what they do. If you do this now you'll be able to find the right one easily in an emergency. Do the same for your fuse box.

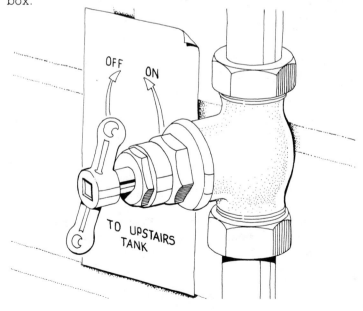

Preserving books: Hot dry air causes the binding of books to crack and the pages to yellow – keep them somewhere cool with a good circulation of air.

Keeping warm: Remember that cellular blankets will only keep you warm if they are sandwiched between you and an ordinary blanket, bedcover or eiderdown.

Threading a rod: Slip a thimble over the end of a rod that has to be threaded through the hem of a curtain and you will prevent it from catching in the fabric.

New candles for old: A broken candle can be repaired by softening both broken ends in a little hot water before ramming the two ends together and holding them there until the wax sets. Hot water will also soften bent candles sufficiently to allow them to be rolled straight on a table top (unless the candle has a delicate finish).

Freeze first: Candles will burn more evenly, and therefore last longer, if they are put in a freezer for a few hours before using.

Slow burner: A candle will burn more slowly, and can be used as a substitute night light, if you sprinkle the top with a little salt.

Safe glue: Flour and water mixed together to make a paste provides a good safe glue for young children.

Musty suitcases: To stop suitcases from smelling musty after they've been out of use for a while, put a few sugar lumps inside them before putting them away.

Coming unstuck: Stamps that have become stuck together will be easier to separate if you put them in the freezer for about half an hour.

Bouncing back: Restore a ping pong ball that has been dented by putting it in hot water with a little salt added.

Tidy cables: Keep electrical cables tidy by winding them into a loop and slipping this inside a cardboard tube.

Select stems: When you are selecting or arranging flowers, hold them at the bottom of their stems and not by the neck, where they are easily bruised.

Salt revival: A dying fire can be revived by throwing a few handfuls of salt on to it.

Seeing in the dark: Put a dab of luminous paint on light switches to make them easy to find in the dark.

GETTING IT ALL TOGETHER

'Wish you were here': Before you go on holiday, decide who you wish to send postcards to and write out names and addresses on sticky labels. This saves taking your address book, wasting valuable holiday time, and makes sure that no one is forgotten. Remember to pack the labels in your suitcase!

Wallet list: Make a note of names and numbers of all credit and identity cards kept in your wallet. If the wallet should get stolen you won't have the dreadful task of trying to recall precisely what was in it. Never keep bank cards together with your cheque book, it makes a forger's life too easy.

Help in a hurry: Save time by keeping near the telephone a list of numbers that are either needed very often, or in a great hurry.

Scribble board: Paint the wall near the telephone in a gloss paint to match the existing wall colour, and use a contrasting coloured crayon to scribble down notes and numbers. These can then be wiped off with a damp cloth.

Pound wise: Keep a one pound note in a pocket of your handbag for use in an emergency.

Spot a case: Spotting your suitcases when they come off the conveyor belt at an airport can be a problem, particularly if they are not very distinctive. Put a strip of brightly coloured sticky tape (the kind used to decorate bicycles) around them to make it easy.

A line in time: To make a neat alteration to a telephone book, write the information on a strip cut from a self-adhesive label. If you do this, and keep to a standard number of lines per person, it will save you eventually having to copy old numbers into a new book.

Prevent ageing: A clipping from a newspaper can be preserved and stopped from yellowing by soaking it for an hour in a saucer in which you have dissolved a milk of magnesia tablet in just a little soda water. Pat off most of the moisture then leave until completely dry.

Getting bags into shape: You can make polythene bags fit particular objects closely by cutting the shape of the object out of thick paper and slipping it inside a polythene bag. Sandwich the bag between two sheets of paper. Now, with a moderate iron, taking care not to go over the opening, the bag will seal itself around the shape you've cut and you can slip out the cut-out and substitute the object in question.

Long life wrapping: Store those bits of Christmas wrapping paper you can't bear to throw away in the long cardboard tube found at the centre of kitchen foil rolls. Iron the wrapping with the iron on low heat to remove creases, roll and insert into the cardboard tube. Now it's ready for next Christmas.

Addresses on file: Instead of using an address book, copy names and addresses on to a card file. That way alterations can be made easily and without mess.

Keeping things upright: A piece of elastic pinned to the front inside of a drawer is ideal for holding small bottles upright, when the drawer is opened or shut.

Silver wrapping: In an emergency, kitchen foil doubles as an attractive silver gift wrap.

On the scent: Use melted candle wax to seal the top of scent bottles, etc., before travelling – that way you can be sure of avoiding an accident.

A good tip: You can protect the tip of your umbrella and the inside of your umbrella stand by lining it with a piece of foam rubber.

NEW WAYS WITH FAMILIAR THINGS

Clear labels: To keep the instructions on prescribed medicine clear, coat the labels with colourless nail varnish straightaway. This will save them from getting smeared or fading.

Useful funnel: Cut off the top from a plastic bottle before throwing it away and you'll have made a useful funnel.

Sealing packets: Use clothes pegs to reseal packets of food temporarily.

Fire lighter: When lighting a fire, use a portable hair dryer as an electric bellows. Hold it some distance away from the fire and use with caution for short periods at a time.

Dry spot: When you have to wash a small part of a garment or remove a stain, dry the affected spot using a hairdryer to avoid leaving an unsightly ring (see also page 228).

Match a lock: Use different shades of nail polish to mark keys and the outside of locks to match. Then you won't have to go through every key on a ring before opening the door.

Pack a pleat: When packing a pleated skirt hold the lower end of the pleats together with paperclips.

Getting a grip: A pair of nutcrackers can be useful for giving a grip on small bottle tops that won't move. Be careful not to use too much force though.

Frost protectors: Dry-cleaning bags placed over plants overnight will help to protect them from frost.

Mini crush: Use a pair of teaspoons, one inside the other, as a mini pestle and mortar when crushing medicine tablets.

Bath salts: Save large coffee jars to use as attractive containers for bath salts. Paint the lids a colour to match the bathroom, using acrylic paint for the purpose.

Wrap around: Self adhesive draught excluder is ideal for wrapping around anything (tennis rackets, for example) where you need a good grip.

Plant container: An old bird cage makes an attractive way of presenting plants. Trailing plants will look particularly good.

Rolling pin: A large wine bottle makes a very good rolling pin. Fill it with iced water and cork it firmly before using.

Display case: Use an old wooden cutlery box fixed to the wall to act as a miniature display case for small objects.

Short flowers: Use an old sauce boat as a vase for short-stemmed flowers.

Keeping the cats away: Chilli sauce makes an unusual cat repellant. To keep the cats off a surface, rub it with a little sauce then buff. (Don't try this with soft furnishings, only hard, washable surfaces.)

Battery corrosion: Fizzy drinks have all kinds of unusual uses. To remove corrosion where a battery has leaked, soak the affected area in a fizzy drink overnight, rinse and dry (see also page 29).

Corner dust: An old toothbrush, ready to be thrown away, is useful for getting dust out of awkward corners.

Rub off: If you haven't an eraser, try using a thick rubber band instead.

PARCEL POST

Avoid paper waste: The easiest way to cut just the right length of wrapping paper for a parcel is to wrap a piece of string around the parcel, cut this off and use this to measure the correct length of paper.

Safely tied up: Make sure your parcels stay done up properly. Before tying, dip the string in a little warm water. Tie the knot while the string is still wet. As the string dries it will contract making the knot extra tight.

Better safe . . . : When sending a parcel abroad, wrap and label it twice – then if the outer covering is damaged or lost, it should still reach its destination.

Cutting down on household chores

TIME SAVERS

Less leg work: When tidying the house, keep a basket in a strategic place, such as the foot of the stairs, so that as you go along you can put things in it that need to be taken up to the next floor.

Quick quilts: Use continental quilts, then you will find bedmaking quicker and easier.

Avoid ironing: If you smooth and fold clothes carefully when they come off the line, or out of the drier, you can keep ironing down to a minimum. You will not have to iron things like pillow cases, tea towels, sheets, etc.

Spread the work: Tidy up as you go along, it is much quicker than leaving it all to tackle at one time.

CLEANING AND POLISHING

Once a year: Furniture polish, applied to surfaces that do not receive wear, will last for a year and should therefore just need dusting from then on.

Wooden floors: Don't have hand-polished floors, they take time. Seal all wooden floors with a paint or wood sealer, so that they can be simply swept to keep them looking good.

Plastic pick up: As you go around the house, wear a small plastic bag tucked into your waist for picking up bits like drawing pins, hair pins, etc.

On the move: Keep a set of duplicate cleaning tools upstairs, to cut down on time. Have an extra long flex fitted to the vacuum cleaner, or use an extension cable, in order to let you go for a long period without unplugging.

Skirting dust: If you don't have a hose attachment to the vacuum cleaner and you want to clean near the skirting board, damp the fingers of your rubber glove and run them over the area. The dust should cling together into manageable lumps.

Clean as you go: Clean up stains and marks as you go. You will find they are much easier to remove immediately rather than later.

IN THE KITCHEN

Saves drying up: Invest in a good dish drainer, including a special cutlery basket, so that you don't have to do drying up after washing.

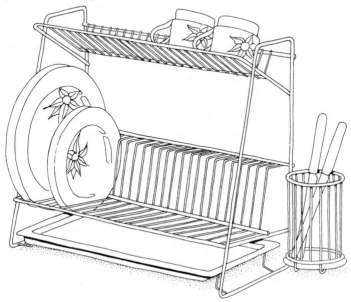

Wipe clean shelves: Cover shelf tops with stick-on wipe clean plastic covering, then they are quick and easy to clean.

Oven clean: When cooking roasts, place kitchen foil loosely over the joints. It cuts down on grease spatters and you won't have to clean the oven afterwards. Or, try cooking meat in special plastic roasting bags as they cut down on basting too, and cleaning the tins.

Non-stick: Use non-stick pans, whenever you can, to make washing up quicker and easier.

Out of sight: A dishwasher not only cuts down on washing up, but makes the kitchen tidier, since dirty plates are stacked out of sight immediately.

Scrape away: Use a plastic windscreen scraper for cleaning excess food off plates before washing up.

Warm whisk: A whisk, warmed by dipping in boiling water, will help to melt fat which is too cold to cream.

No last minute washing up: Use paper picnic cups and plates which you can throw away when you have your last meal before a weekend away or a holiday. This saves last minute washing up.

Quick wipe clean: When putting jam jars, sauce bottles, etc., away, wipe their bottoms to prevent them marking the shelf they stand on.

Keeping tastes apart: Use one side of a chopping board for onions and smelly chopping, and use the other for lemons and other items to avoid tainting. (See page 186 for how to get rid of smells.)

Contain those crumbs: Line the bread bin and other drawers that will contain crumbly things with foil or paper to help cleaning up afterwards.

Instant rubbish disposal: When preparing a lot of food in one go and therefore accumulating a great deal of rubbish, hang a carrier bag as near to the work surface as possible; on a floor unit door, for example. You can then sweep the peelings, crumbs, etc., into it straightaway, thus clearing up as you go along.

Oven shelves: If your oven shelves have badly burnt-on food, remove them and soak them in a bowl of biological washing powder and water overnight. They will be much easier to clean the next day.

Kitchen planning: One day, keep a careful watch on your movements in the kitchen to see how often you need to walk from one side to the other. If this seems to be too often, you will need to rethink your storage systems. Keep all much-used items, such as tea and coffee-making equipment, together and electrical appliances near the sockets.

THREE GOOD THOUGHTS

Better bikes: Put a thin coat of petroleum jelly on bicycles that are left out in the rain, to protect them from rust.

Powder container: To save making a mess when applying talcum powder on your feet, put a little into an old shoe box instead and step into the box.

Hairbrush care: Don't wash hair brushes with soap, instead use the same shampoo you use for your hair. It is much easier to rinse out afterwards.

Money savers

WASHING UP

Clean to dirty: To conserve water and detergent, always wash from the cleanest items to the dirtiest, whether it is clothing or crockery, pots and pans.

Too strong: Most people tend to use more washing-up liquid than they need – dilute yours to half strength with water whilst still in the container and save money.

Soap scraps: Save scraps of soap left over from bars to make into useful liquid soap. Combine 250 ml ($\frac{1}{2}$ pint) of scraps with 250 ml ($\frac{1}{2}$ pint) of hot water and 3 ml ($\frac{1}{2}$ teaspoon) of borax. Mix well and leave to cool before using. (See also page 289.)

SHOPPING FOR FOOD

Bulk buying: Large amounts of goods usually work out cheaper, but don't lose your head; if the product is perishable and is likely to lose its flavour before you use it, don't buy.

Dented tins: Do not buy fruit or vegetable cans that show signs of leakage, or that look in very bad condition. Never buy damaged or dented cans of meat or fish.

No bargain: Some 'bargains' are not what they seem, such as jams that look as though they are 450 g (1 lb) jars but are, in fact, only 350 g (12 oz). The answer is always to check the weight on the label.

Hungry shopping: Don't shop when you're hungry or you'll find you've bought a lot more than you need.

Share the bulk: Buying in bulk really does mean buying huge quantities, for example, 4 litre (7 lb) jars of jam. So the best way is to form a co-operative and share the load a bit.

Supermarkets save: Large supermarket chains are almost always cheaper for groceries because they buy in bulk and package their own brands.

FRUIT AND VEGETABLES

Open markets: The cheapest places to buy fruit and vegetables are open markets. As long as you are prepared to bargain, you should get good quality, too. Don't accept inferior fruit from the back of the stall.

Go for fresh first: Fresh vegetables in season are almost always much cheaper than those that are frozen, tinned or dried.

POULTRY, MEAT AND FISH

Lean turkey: There's more lean meat on a turkey – 54% in fact, compared with 42% on chicken. Duck has more fat and only 33% lean meat.

Clean bones: Mince cooked chicken bones, both to clean the mincer and to provide the dog with cheap meal. Use the finest disc on the mincer and add bread to the bones as they go through.

More fish for less: Buy filleted fish – although it seems more expensive, it means you are not getting any wastage. The bones and head of most fish weigh surprisingly heavy.

Better bacon: Smoked bacon is more expensive than green but lasts longer. Buy bacon loose. Look for shops selling bacon bits, they are often a good buy. (See also page 88.)

Low fat mince: There are no regulations governing the amount of fat in mince. If you are worried, then select a piece of meat and have it minced for you or mince it yourself.

Home-made burgers: Most frozen burgers have only 80% meat content and are expensive; it is much cheaper to make your own.

Pork versus beef: Pork sausages have to contain 56% pork, so are more expensive than beef sausages which contain only 51% beef. The beef are less nutritious but very filling.

No cheap cuts: Buying cheap cuts of meat is often a false economy as they take more fuel, because they need longer cooking and often shrink a lot in the cooking.

Check on chickens: Fresh chickens may look more expensive to buy initially but contain 10% less water than frozen ones. Take this into account when comparing prices. Remember when calculating weight, only half of the chicken's weight is made up of meat. The other half is bones, giblets, etc.

Bacon for quiches: When using bacon in quiches, etc., don't use cut whole rashers. Buy bacon offcuts instead. These are perfectly good, they're just too small, or the wrong shape to be made into rashers. (See also page 87).

FUEL SAVING

Cheapest fuel: Check with the Solid Fuel Advisory Service as to which is the cheapest fuel for your appliance. Buy as much as you can store in one go, out of season, when it is cheaper.

Maximum comfort: Set the time clock so that the heating comes on half an hour before you get up, and goes off half an hour before you go to bed. This provides maximum comfort at less cost.

Central heating: Gas or solid fuel central heating is cheaper than electricity.

Expensive to run: Storage heaters are very expensive to run although cheap to install.

Buy in summer: Buy heaters and other winter items in the summer when they are on special offer.

Save 8%: By turning the heating down by one degree Centigrade all year, you will save 8% of your yearly bill.

PREVENT HEAT LOSS

Foil the heat: Most radiators give off a fair amount of heat direct into the outside wall. You can make them much more efficient by sticking metal foil to the wall behind them.

Loft insulation: You can lose 40% of your heat through windows, floors and other gaps. Make sure that your loft is insulated – if not, see if you can get a government grant.

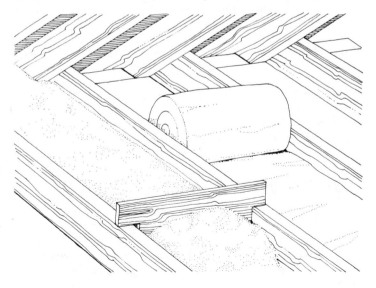

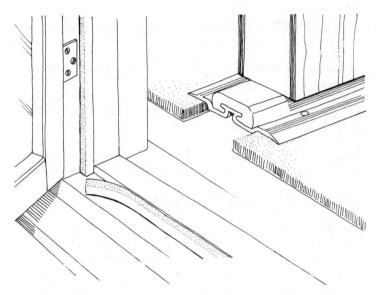

Stop that draught: Cut down on heat losses, use draught excluders around doors and windows – use thin plastic strips from ironmongers. Use a sausage type excluder at the bottom of the doors.

Flap a gap: Cover the gap in the door where the letter box is with a flap of material to cut out draughts.

Cover old fireplaces: If you do not use old fireplaces, then cover them with hardboard to keep the room warmer. Fit the hardboard out of sight in the chimney throat and drill a few holes in it for ventilation. Remember to remove it, though, if you change your mind and decide to have a fire.

AVOID WASTING HOT WATER

Hot running tap: Do not wash anything under a hot running tap with the plug out of the basin. It wastes money.

Bowl is better: Use a bowl for washing up, instead of the sink, and save on hot water. (See also page 166.)

Take a shower: A shower uses 29 litres (6½ gallons) of water compared to a bath which uses 90 litres (20 gallons).

Once a day: Reduce the amount of hot water you use by not doing the washing up after every meal. Stack it neatly in the corner of the sink, and tackle it once a day.

CAREFUL COOKING

Saucepans should fit: Make sure that the saucepan covers the electric ring, or that the flames of the gas are not licking around the edge of the pan, otherwise you are wasting energy.

One ring not two: Steam faster-cooking vegetables over slower vegetables – put them in a colander with a lid over a saucepan containing the slower-cooking vegetables. This saves using a second ring.

Less for pressure cookers: Use your pressure cooker whenever you can, it takes less fuel than conventional methods.

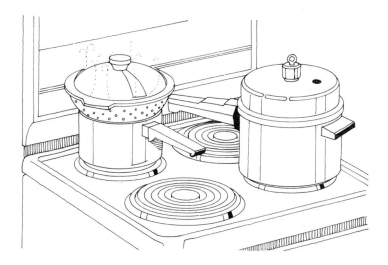

All together now: When you use the cooker, prepare as many dishes as possible to go in the oven together. Save up your baking so that you do a week's worth at one time, or get together with a neighbour and use each other's ovens in turn.

Just enough water: Never boil more water than you need in a kettle, but always make sure you cover the element with water in electric ones. Excess boiled water can be tipped into a vacuum flask to keep hot for the next cup.

One cuppa: If you only want one cup of tea, it is cheaper to boil the water on a gas ring than to use an electric kettle.

Early turn off: You can save energy when cooking a dish in the oven, for which the exact cooking time is not critical, by turning off the oven 15 minutes before you intend to serve.

SIMPLE SAVERS

'Log' fire: If you have an open fire, don't throw away old newspapers; not only can they be used for starting the fire, you can make them into 'logs' by rolling them up tightly and tying the ends with string.

Candle lighters: Save waxed milk cartons and the stub ends of candles. They make good fire lighters.

Foiled again: Kitchen foil can be washed after use with a little hot water and detergent, smoothed out, left to dry, and used again.

Restringing a necklace: Nylon fishing line is ideal for restringing necklaces – it's very strong and rigid enough to be used without a needle.

Long distance: Save money on long distant telephone calls by setting a time for the call on a kitchen timer before you start. Also make a list beforehand of any special things you want to say.

Cleaning windows: Don't waste money on special window cleaning preparations – old newspaper dipped in warm water works just as well (see page 268).

Line with wallpaper: Use leftover wallpaper to line drawers and cupboards.

The last trace: You will find it easier to get out the last traces of toothpaste if you warm the tube before squeezing it.

Half a load is not better than none: Do not use dishwashers when they are only half full as this is a waste of water and money. Wait till you have a full load – items can usually be pre-rinsed while they wait.

Cooking for one: Save the foil containers in which some convenience foods are wrapped. They are a handy size for cooking small portions.

"The Proof of the Pudding Is In The Eating"

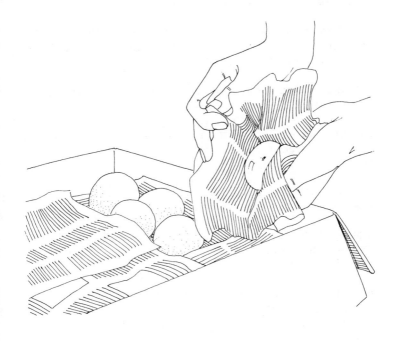

Hints about food

Storing food

VEGETABLES, FRUIT AND HERBS

Onions: To store half an onion, rub the cut side with butter, it will keep fresh longer and smell less.

Towel for artichokes: Artichokes can be kept for almost a week in the refrigerator if you wrap them, unwashed, in a damp piece of towelling and store in a plastic bag.

Vegetable stock: Save water in which vegetables have been cooked to add to stock for soups or sauces.

Storing lettuce: Store washed lettuce, watercress or parsley in a loose plastic bag in the refrigerator and it will keep for a week.

Carrot tops: Before storing carrots, cut off the tops. They keep moister that way.

Storing small amounts: Leftover concentrates like tomato purée from the tin, can be frozen in the ice-cube tray and stored for future use.

Strawberry fair: To store strawberries successfully in the refrigerator before use, put them in a sieve or a colander to allow the air to circulate around them.

Lemon juice: To save lemon juice, pierce one end of the fruit with a wooden kebab or cocktail stick and squeeze out what you want, then plug the hole with the stick again. It will store well that way.

Ripe pears: To ripen pears, place them in a paper bag with a ripe apple.

Ripe peaches: Ripen peaches quickly by putting them in a box and covering them with several layers of newspaper.

Lemon fresh: Keep whole lemons in a plastic box in the refrigerator. That way they will stay fresh for weeks.

Grated rind: Grate leftover orange or lemon rind and add to caster sugar, store in a screw-top jar and use for flavouring cakes and puddings.

Banana store: Do not store bananas in a refrigerator. It turns their skins black in time.

Store in the dark: Green tomatoes will ripen better and keep their moisture longer, if you wrap them in newspaper and keep them in a cool, dark, dry place, like a drawer.

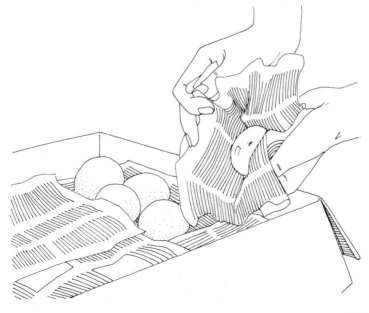

T'ain't worth it: Never store melon or cucumber in the refrigerator unless they have been securely wrapped in cling plastic. Otherwise they will taint other food, especially dairy products.

Flies beware: Basil, grown in a pot on the kitchen window sill, helps to keep flies away.

Keeping flavour in: Dry fresh bayleaves well away from the sun. Warmth and light will take away their flavour.

Green mint: Before drying mint for winter use, wash it in a solution of 30 ml (2 tablespoons) of bicarbonate of soda to 250 ml ($\frac{1}{2}$ pint) of water. This keeps it looking green.

BREAD, CAKES, BISCUITS AND SWEET THINGS

Storing a decorated cake: When storing a decorated cake, place it on the lid and invert the tin over it. It is much easier to take the cake out this way, and less likely to damage the icing.

Stay crisp: Keep two sugar lumps in the biscuit tin to make sure your biscuits stay crisp. The sugar absorbs moisture.

Moist fruit cake: Add a slice of apple to the tin when storing a fruit cake. It will keep it moist.

Non-stick sweets: Sprinkle sticky sweets with icing sugar to stop them glueing together.

Fresh bread: Put a stick of celery in the bread bin, it will keep bread fresher for longer. It will need to be renewed at least once a week or as soon as it goes limp and brown.

Vanilla sugar: Make your own vanilla-flavoured sugar by storing a packetful of caster sugar together with a vanilla pod in a jar. Keep the jar away from the light.

Break a seal: If you are sealing a jelly preserve, such as redcurrant or mint jelly, with paraffin wax, first place a circle of waxed paper over the jelly, then lay a piece of button thread across it, before pouring on the paraffin wax. Then, when you want to break the seal, all you need do is pull on the cotton.

Jam seals: Save waxed paper from cereal packets to cut into circles to seal the top of home-made jam.

Cool jam: Allow home-made jam to cool and thicken a little before you put it into jars. This stops the fruit from sinking to the bottom.

CHEESE

Foil, not plastic: Always remove the plastic wrapping from cheese and replace it with kitchen foil before storing. Plastic makes the cheese become sweaty.

Free from mould: To keep cheese fresh and free from mould if it is not being stored in the refrigerator, place a lump of sugar on it to absorb the moisture.

Tasty finish: Save leftover crumbs from the bottom of cereal packets in an airtight jar. They are useful to scatter over meat or fruit stews to give a crispy topping.

EGGS

Keep fresh: To preserve eggs for up to a month at a time, smear the shells thickly with glycerine when they are very fresh. Store them small end upward.

Storing yolks: Store egg yolks by covering them with water and putting them in the refrigerator. They will keep for several days that way.

Storing whites: Store egg whites in an airtight container, a plastic box or a jar with a lid. Leave them in the refrigerator until you need them. They should last a week.

Onions into eggs will go: Never store eggs alongside onions. Egg shells are porous and the eggs will taste onion-flavoured when you cook them.

POULTRY, MEAT AND FISH

Nutritious stock: Keep bones from poultry and joints. They can be boiled up in a pressure cooker to make meat stock, which can be stored in your freezer until needed. Alternatively, if you do not have the time to make the stock straightaway, store the bones in the freezer.

Extra flavour: Save bacon rinds. Dice, then added to stews and casseroles they give them an extra flavour.

Stop rashers sticking: Roll up plastic packs of bacon and store that way, it stops the rashers from sticking together.

OIL, VINEGAR AND PEPPERS

Out of sunlight: Always strain oil after use and keep out of direct sunlight. It will last longer that way.

Olives for flavour: Store your salad oil with a few olives in the bottom of the jar. It improves the flavour, particularly in the case of cheap corn oils.

Bottled dressing: Keep French dressing in a bottle with a screw top. It is then easy to shake and mix before use.

Long life oil: Olive oil can be kept longer if you add a pinch of sugar to the bottle and then keep it in the refrigerator.

Peppercorns to pepper: Add a few peppercorns to your pepper shaker. It keeps the holes from clogging and adds a fresh taste.

Rice to salt: Add a few grains of rice to your salt shaker. It will take up any moisture and stop the salt from clogging.

Avoid humidity: Store items like paprika, red pepper, cayenne and chilli in a dark, cool place, otherwise they are easily affected by heat and humidity.

Unusual holder: A scooped-out green or red pepper makes an unusual holder for salad dressing or mayonnaise.

Wooden servers: Always use plastic or wooden salad servers, not metal ones. These tend to bruise lettuce leaves and turn the edges brown.

WINE AND SAUCE

Damp corks: All wine should be stored in bottles placed on their side. Otherwise the corks dry out in time and air can get at the wine.

Prevent a skin: When storing sauce, cover the surface with dampened greaseproof paper. This prevents a skin forming.

Freezing
and refrigerating

GENERAL TIPS

Power cut: If you have a power cut, keep your freezer door firmly shut. Provided the freezer is well stocked, food will stay frozen for 8 hours at least, and possibly up to 24 hours. To help keep conditions cool, open the windows, so that the room is well ventilated. However, if you're in any doubt at all, then throw the food away.

Cool milk: If your refrigerator is full, milk bottles can be kept cool in a washing up bowl of cold water. Cover the bottles with a clean cloth allowing the ends to dip into the water. Add an ice cube or two from time to time in hot weather.

What's available: Keep a list of available foods on the inside of the door of your freezer or refrigerator, to remind you what you can serve for supper.

Space saving soup: When making soups for the freezer, save space by adding only half the amount of liquid. Leave out the milk in creamy soups, this can be added later when the soup is defrosted.

Individual cubes: Spray ice-cubes wth soda water before storing them in polythene bags. It stops them from sticking together.

Netted in: To stop small items from slipping through the grid of a freezer basket, line it with a piece of netting. It allows the air to circulate and keeps the food in place.

Soft ice cream: If a block of ice cream has become too soft to eat, cut it into portions or use an ice cream scoop to turn it into servings, before returning it to the freezer. It will re-freeze much more quickly that way.

Keeping cool: If you need to remove frozen food temporarily from the freezer, wrap it in several layers of newspaper. This will help to keep it cool.

Keeping small fruits apart: Open-freeze fruits and small items spreading them out on trays before you put them in boxes or bags. That way they will stay separate from each other.

BE PREPARED

Freezing pancakes: Make pancakes in advance. Place them between sheets of greaseproof paper and freeze. They can be defrosted on a warm griddle or under a low grill as needed.

Cream in a hurry: Boil an unopened can of evaporated milk in water for 20 minutes, then chill and store in the refrigerator. It will whip up to at least double its size and can be used in an emergency instead of cream.

Frozen pulse: Soak pulses, such as peas and beans, then freeze, for a quick addition to casseroles and stews.

Emergency toast: Freeze individual slices of bread for emergency toast. They can be taken straight from the freezer into the electric toaster.

Sandwich lunch: Make sandwiches for packed lunches in weekly batches and freeze in packets for individual days. Take them out the night before and they will defrost in time for lunch the following day.

'Chopped' chives: Store chives and parsley in a freezer. Once frozen they won't need chopping before use because they will be brittle and can be grated or crumbled straight over dishes.

Separate pieces: Use sheets of greaseproof paper between cutlets and/or pieces of fish before you freeze them. They are easier to separate when you want to thaw them.

Fancy cubes: Freeze pieces of herb like sprigs of mint, borage and small pieces of lemon too, in ice-cubes (detach from the ice-tray and store in plastic bags) to add to summer drinks.

PASTRY AND CAKES

Ready-to-bake cake: Fill patty tins with cake mix, freeze, then decant into a plastic bag. You then have ready-to-bake cakes to hand for unexpected visitors. The same can be done with biscuit dough, by spreading portions on a baking sheet before decanting and freezing.

Trifles: Save leftover oddments of cake and store them in the freezer. When you have collected enough they can be made into a trifle.

Frozen flan: If you are making an uncooked flan for the freezer, brush over the pastry with melted margarine or butter, then add the cooled filling. The fat will stop the pastry from becoming soggy when you take it out of the freezer for baking. If you freeze the flan in a baking tin, dust it with flour first so that it will slip out easily.

Quick to thaw: Slice fruit cake and sponges and wrap individually before freezing: or cut pieces of greaseproof paper between the segments. They will then thaw much more quickly.

Freeze separately: Freeze the sponge layers and the fillings of cakes and gâteaux separately. They will thaw out more quickly that way.

CHEESE AND FRUIT

Fresh cottage cheese: Store cartons of cottage cheese upside down in the refrigerator. They will remain fresh longer.

For full flavour: Never store cheese unwrapped in the refrigerator. Cover it with kitchen foil. Take it out an hour before you want to use it for the flavour to be restored.

Fresh fruit: Line the salad container in the refrigerator with paper towelling before you use it. This will take up any excess moisture and keep fruit and vegetables fresher for longer

Cooking tips

VEGETABLES

Asparagus tips: Cook fresh asparagus in the cleaned container part of your coffee percolator, the stems stand upright this way and the tips steam perfectly at the same time.

White mushrooms: Add a teaspoonful of lemon juice to the butter when you are frying mushrooms. It will keep them white and firm. Shake the pan frequently to stop them from steaming rather than sautéeing.

Whole onions: To keep onions whole when you are cooking them, cut a small cross at the stem end, as if you were preparing Brussels sprouts.

Red beetroot: To keep beetroot a good red colour, cook them whole and leave an inch or so of stem on them. Also, add a little vinegar to the cooking water.

White cauliflower: Add a little milk to the water when cooking cauliflower, it keeps it white.

Better corn: Use the green leaves from corn on the cob to line the bottom of the pot while they cook. The corn tastes better that way.

Retrieving herbs: Use an individual tea-making ball to house herbs like cloves or bay leaves, when you use them in stews and other dishes. That way they are easy to retrieve at the end of the cooking time.

Crushed garlic: Home-made garlic salt is easily made if you crush a clove of garlic on to a board heavily sprinkled with salt. Store in an airtight jar.

Two at a time: Cook two different vegetables at a time in one pot by wrapping each in aluminium foil before you put them into the water.

On the boil: A matchstick put between the lid and the saucepan lets out enough steam during cooking to stop the water from boiling over.

Keeping cabbage red: Always add a little vinegar to the water when you are cooking red cabbage, it stops it from turning purple.

Holding shape: Baked stuffed tomatoes (and peppers and apples) hold their shape better if you stand them in cake patty tins.

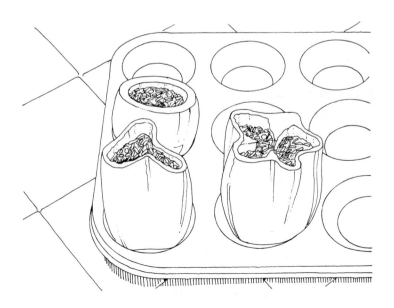

Superb flavour: Add a pinch of sugar to tomatoes when you cook them. It brings out the superb flavour.

Broccoli tip: Make an X incision in the stems of broccoli from the end towards the top before you cook it: it will then cook as fast as the top.

Peas in their pods: Try cooking peas in their pods. When they are done, the pods will open and float to the top, where they are easy to remove. The peas taste better this way and you save the chore of shelling them.

Fried onions: To fry chopped onions without burning them, cover with water, add a little butter. Boil them until the water has evaporated, then lower the heat and continue until they are golden. If you want them to brown more quickly, add a little sugar to the pan at this stage.

Flavour for artichokes: A few drops of lemon juice or vinegar, added to the water in which artichokes are cooking, brings out their flavour.

Onion taste: Grated onion makes a softer tasting substitute for garlic. Use it in salads or soups.

POTATOES

Crisp answer: Roast potatoes will be crisper if you dredge them with a little flour halfway through their roasting time.

Doubly crisp: To crisp up potato chips, fry them twice. Cook for a few minutes, lift out of the fat and bring the oil back to boiling point. Plunge in again and cook until they are golden brown.

Extra texture: Add a whisked white of egg to purée potatoes to improve their texture.

Butter adds taste: Rub a little butter over the skin of a potato before you bake it, to improve the taste.

Potato saver: Overcooked potatoes can be puréed. Add a little dried milk powder to them and beat, or a little powdered instant potato mix.

Quick roast potatoes: To do quick roast potatoes, boil them until they are almost done, drain the water off, leave for a moment, then shake the pan until their outsides become fluffy. Then put them to roast round the joint in the normal way.

Get rid of grease: Shake freshly-cooked chips in a clean paper bag for a moment before serving. It helps to rid them of excess grease.

Old into new: To give old potatoes a new look, cut into new potato-sized pieces, stand in cold water for $2\frac{1}{2}$ hours. Cook in boiling salted water with a few drops of vinegar added, then drain. Put back on the heat for a few minutes, shaking from time to time to avoid sticking.

Wrapped up: Bake items such as potatoes, whole onions and apples, wrapped in kitchen foil. They cook quicker that way and are easy to serve as they will keep hot longer.

Add dressing to hot potatoes: Always add the dressing to potato salad while the potatoes are still piping hot, so that it penetrates the pieces.

Reheat potatoes: To reheat baked potatoes successfully, dip them first into hot water, then bake them in an oven at 180°C, 350°F, Mark 4 for 25 minutes.

Quick jacket potatoes 1: Speed up potatoes in their jackets by boiling them first for about 10 minutes. Finish them off in a very hot oven.

Quick jacket potatoes 2: To bake potatoes in their skins quickly, cut a thin slice off each end first. Or, leave them whole and insert a large, clean, galvanized nail or skewer into each to convey the heat to the centre quickly.

SOUPS

Extra flavour: Finely grated raw carrot, added to a soup just before serving, gives it a rich colouring and adds extra flavour.

Herb dumplings: Steam extra dumplings for soups or stews in an egg poacher. Add a pinch of dried herbs to the mixture for an extra special taste.

Good thickener: Instant potato powder makes a good thickener for soups and stews.

Potato thickener: Save leftover purée potatoes to use as a thickening for soups and stews.

Sugar to the rescue: Too-salty soup can sometimes be improved if you add a little sugar.

Dried herbs: If you are using dried herbs rather than fresh herbs in a recipe, halve the amount that is indicated.

Home-made taste: Add a dash of sherry to tinned soups before you serve them. It makes them taste home-made. This works particularly well with lobster or crab bisque.

Egg shell clear: Two or three pieces of egg shell added to a home-made stock or consommé will clear it.

Mince for soup: A little mince added to a bouillon gives it a better flavour, especially if you have used stock cubes. Strain before using.

STEWS

Off with fat: Blot the top of a casserole, or a stew, with kitchen paper to remove surplus fat. Or, in an emergency, pour off the liquid and drop several ice-cubes into it. The fat will congeal around them and they can both be lifted out easily.

10 minutes for safety: Always reheat stews and casseroles by bringing slowly to the boil and cooking at that heat for at least 10 minutes, to make sure that no bacteria survive.

Cure for too much garlic: If you have put too much garlic into a sauce or a stew, add some chopped parsley to tone down the flavour.

Saving a burned casserole: If you have burned a casserole or a stew, at the end of its cooking time, turn it (in its pan) upside down over another container. The food that comes away from the pan will be perfectly edible. Do not be tempted to scrape the bottom of the pan.

Cold plunge: If a stew is burning half-way through its cooking time, plunge the pan quickly into cold water, turn out into another saucepan and continue. Add more stock if necessary.

Vinegar makes it tender: Add 15 ml (a tablespoonful) of vinegar to a beef stew when you put it on to cook. It will make the meat more tender and brings out the flavour in the gravy.

Rich colour and flavour: Leftover beer gives casseroles and stews a rich colour and flavour.

Cook with marigolds: Use marigold (calendula) petals instead of saffron to colour food, i.e. the Old English or Pot Marigold not the African or French kinds. They make a casserole's liquid a dark golden brown. They can also be sprinkled fresh over salads.

Marble stops burning: Put a large, clean marble into a slow-cooking sauce or stew after it has thickened. It will stir the sauce for you and stop it from burning.

Absorbing salt: Add a few pieces of peeled, raw potato to a stew if it has become too seasoned. As it cooks it will absorb the excess salt.

111

Burned fat: Drop a raw peeled potato into the frying pan if you suspect the fat has burned. It will take away the taste.

Subtle garlic: Use a whole clove of garlic in soups or stews for a milder flavour. Thread on to a piece of cotton for easy retrieval. Remove before serving.

SAUCES AND SUCH

Lump-free sauce: To make a lump-free white sauce, mix flour and fat in the usual way, add cold liquid, then bring to the boil, whisking as you go. Or, combine the ingredients in a blender first, then bring carefully to the boil, stirring with a balloon whisk.

Shake away lumps: An emergency cure for a lumpy sauce is to pour it into a bottle, screw on the lid and shake it like a cocktail. The lumps should disappear.

Lighter pancakes: To make a lighter pancake or Yorkshire pudding mixture, separate the egg, beat in the yolk, then lightly whip the white and fold into the mixture last of all.

Ready-to-serve pancakes: Stack ready-cooked pancakes on a plate placed over a saucepan of boiling water and cover with a tea-towel. This will keep them warm for some time.

Making batter smooth: Add milk very gradually when making batter to avoid lumps. Or make it up in a food processor or blender. Remove lumps from batter or sauce by beating with a wire whisk. Alternatively, put the lumpy batter into a blender or food processor.

Gloss to a sauce: Give a gloss to white sauce, if you are using it as a coating, by adding 15 ml (a tablespoonful) of cream at the last moment and beating well.

Better batter: To make light, crisp, fritter batter, add just under 5 ml (a teaspoonful) of baking powder to the batter before you use it.

Save a sauce: Save a curdling Hollandaise sauce by pouring it into a cold bowl and whisking it. Return to the pan and reheat gently.

EGGS

Yellow yolks: Plunge hard-boiled eggs into cold water immediately after cooking to stop the yolks from becoming blackened.

Well scrambled: Add a tablespoonful of top of milk to an egg as you scramble it. This will stop the egg overcooking. Or, take scrambled eggs off the heat when they are three parts cooked, stir, cover and put on one side. They will finish cooking in their own heat and the pan will be easier to clean afterwards.

Prevent curdling: When adding egg to a creamed butter and sugar cake mix, add a little of the flour at the same time to prevent curdling.

Pierce the shell: Stop eggs from cracking while they boil by piercing the shell with a pin.

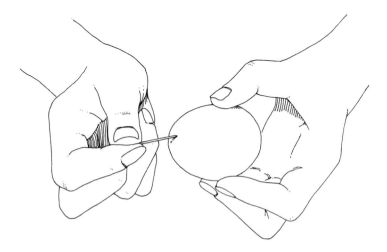

Rich glaze: Add a pinch of salt to an egg yolk glaze on pastries to give it a rich golden-brown colour.

Poached eggs: To keep poached eggs while waiting to serve them, put them into cool water the moment they are cooked. When you want to serve them, reheat for a minute in hot water.

Yolks in the middle: Turn eggs over in the water while they are boiling. This will keep the yolks in place in the middle of the whites. Alternatively, stir the water well with a spoon before adding the first egg, so that the 'whirlpool' keeps the white and yolk together.

Avoid cracking shells: Never take eggs straight from the refrigerator and put them into boiling water, they will crack. Instead, put them into lukewarm water and bring them to the boil.

Boiling a cracked egg: Eggs that are already cracked can still be boiled – simply wrap them tightly in aluminium foil before putting them into the water. It is a good idea to rub salt into the crack first as an added precaution.

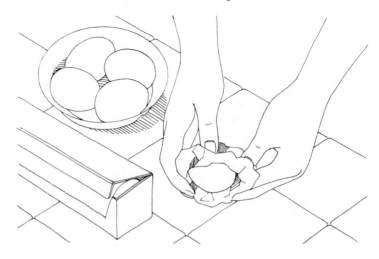

Stop that crack: If the egg does crack, add some salt or a little vinegar to the water to seal up the white and stop it from coming out of the crack.

Keeping the white in shape: Add 15 ml (a tablespoonful) of vinegar to the water, when you are poaching eggs. It helps to set the white of egg in good shape.

Lighter and fluffier: Add a splash of soda water to eggs you are using for an omelette or scrambled eggs. It makes them lighter and fluffier.

Meringue top: When making a meringue to top a pie, beat up the egg whites over a pan of hot water; this will warm them slightly and stop the meringue from 'weeping' when it comes in contact with the contents underneath.

MILK AND FATS

Stop milk boiling over: If the milk is boiling over in a saucepan, take it away from the heat and set it down with a bump. It will save the milk from going over the top.

Add salt: To remove the burnt taste from milk, try adding a pinch of salt.

Cool the fire: Cool a fiery curry by stirring in some natural yogurt just before serving. Don't let the mixture boil.

Preventing a skin: Sprinkle the surface of custard with icing sugar to stop a skin forming. Stir it in before serving.

Quick sandwiches: If you are making large batches of sandwiches, first cream the butter and the filling together in a food processor. Spreading will be much easier and quicker.

Potted cheese: Grate end pieces of cheese, mix with a little butter, beat in a little dry sherry and store in jars covered with melted butter to serve as potted cheese.

More cream: To make whipped cream go further, fold in some stiffly whisked egg white just before serving.

Sour cream: Make your own sour cream by adding 15 ml (a tablespoon) of lemon juice to each 300 ml ($\frac{1}{2}$ pint) of fresh cream.

Oil is ready: Drop a cube of bread into cooking oil when you have heated it. If it browns within a minute, the oil is ready to use.

Less likely to brown: Add a little cooking oil to butter when you are using it for cooking. It is far less likely to brown.

Single into double: If you haven't any whipping cream, spin out double cream for large dishes by using single cream instead for half the quantity. Add a little caster sugar and beat in the usual way.

Prevention is best: A knob of butter run over the still hot surface of jellies, puddings and sauces will stop a skin from forming, if you want to leave them before use.

Stop fat spitting: Turn a metal colander upside down over the frying pan when you are cooking spattery foods. It allows moisture to escape but reduces fat splats.

Pure dripping: To clarify dripping, pour boiling water over it, leave, then chill. The fat will have floated to the top and can be skimmed off.

Sour milk: In an emergency, a pinch of baking powder added to sour milk, can make it taste drinkable.

PIES, PASTRY AND MERINGUES

Stop over-browning: Cover the edges of pies and flans with a strip of kitchen foil to stop them from over-browning in the oven. Remove the foil just before the pastry is fully cooked.

Boiling juice: Pieces of drinking straw or macaroni placed upright in the vent of a fruit pie, should stop the juice inside from boiling over. Remember to remove them.

Small baking tray: Use the smallest baking tray possible when using the oven, it allows the heat to circulate more evenly.

Sweet crust: Paint the pastry around the edge of fruit tarts and pies with beaten egg white. Sprinkle with caster sugar to give a sweet crisp crust.

Better shape: Leave the air vent uncut in a pie until halfway through the cooking time; the pastry lid keeps its shape better that way.

Fluffy meringues: Add 5 ml (a teaspoonful) of cornflour to every 112 g (4 oz) of sugar when making meringues, it stops them from turning into a sticky, toffee consistency.

Whiter meringues: Cook meringues with a wooden board placed under the baking tray. It absorbs discolouring smoke and keeps them whiter.

Freshen up buns: Dip stale buns in milk, then heat in a slow oven to revive them. Serve hot with plenty of butter.

Repairing pastry: Save one or two scraps of pastry to repair cracks in flans that are being baked blind.

Cool before cooking: Always cover pastry and put it in a refrigerator to rest before rolling out. Leave it for about a quarter of an hour. When rolling out pastry, never stretch it, as it will shrink back again when it is cooking in the oven.

Pastry mix: Make your own pastry mix – rub the fat into the flour, then store in a jar in the refrigerator for future use.

High rise: Help flaky pastry to rise high by putting it on a dampened baking sheet.

Brown top: If sweet pastry refuses to brown, brush it quickly with a sugar and water syrup; put back into the oven for a few moments only.

Self-raising: Make your own self-raising flour by adding 25 ml (5 level teaspoons) baking powder to 500 g (1.1 lb) of plain flour. Sift the mixture well.

Golden sheen: Mix a small amount of custard powder with the milk you brush over scones or pies; it gives them a golden brown sheen.

Biscuits from scraps: Make leftover pastry scraps into biscuits – press grated cheese, desiccated coconut, or chip chocolate into the pieces and bake until crisp.

Lighter pastry: Add a little lemon juice to pastry when mixing it with water, this makes it lighter.

CAKES AND SPONGES

Removing cakes from tins: Leave large cakes to rest for 5 minutes before turning them out of the tin. They will come away from the sides more easily then.

Turning out a sponge: To decant a sponge cake, place the tin on a damp cloth, leave for a minute or two, then gently turn out.

Cake saver: If a cake sinks disastrously in the middle, cut out the centre and fill with fruit and whipped cream.

Emergency rack: Use an oven shelf as an emergency cooling rack for batches of cakes or pies.

Melting chocolate: The easiest way to melt chocolate for cooking is to make a cup of aluminium foil, butter it slightly, put the squares of chocolate in that. Put it into the oven when it is pre-heating and the chocolate will melt and slide out of the foil without sticking.

Whisk test: To check whether a sponge mix has been whisked enough, lift the whisk out of the mixture, it should leave a trail behind.

Fruitier and nuttier: Carefully sift 1.25 ml ($\frac{1}{4}$ teaspoonful) of dry mustard into every 225 g (8 oz) of flour when making a rich fruit cake. It gives it a fruitier flavour and a better colour. Also, 15 ml (a tablespoonful) of crunchy peanut butter will give it a nuttier taste.

Cake test: To see if a cake has cooked, press it with your finger. If it leaves a mark, the cake is not ready. Otherwise use a skewer. If it comes out clean, the cake is cooked; if mixture is clinging to it, it needs more time.

Too much rise: If the centre of your cake is rising too high in the oven, place another smaller cake tin on top to hold it down.

Instant pattern: Put a quick, instant pattern on the top of a sponge cake by placing a patterned paper doily on top and sifting sugar over it. Lift the doily off carefully.

ICING

Icing cup cakes: Instead of pouring icing over cup cakes, dip them into the icing mix, twirl and stand up the right way.

Perfect icing: For perfect cake icing with marzipan underneath, brush excess crumbs off the surface of the cake, cover with a very thin coat of icing. Allow to dry, then cover with the main batch of icing.

Turntable: To ice a cake, place it on a large plate, put upside down on top of an upturned basin. You can then move the plate round as you ice, using it as a turntable.

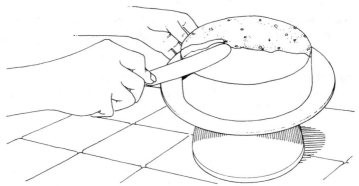

Stop layers slipping: When icing a cake, stop the layers from slipping out of place by pushing two thin skewers or kebab sticks through them. Make sure you remove these before the icing starts to set.

Substitute marzipan: To make a substitute marzipan, cream together 112 g (4 oz) butter and 112 g (4 oz) caster sugar and 15 ml (a tablespoonful) of almond essence. Knead in 450 g (1 lb) sponge or madeira cake crumbs.

Royal icing: Add 5 ml (a teaspoonful) of glycerine to each 450 g (1 lb) of icing sugar if you are making royal icing. It makes it easier to work.

Spread icing: Put a spoonful of icing on fairy cakes when they are still warm from the oven and put them back inside. The remaining heat in the cooling oven will cause the icing to spread itself over them.

Hot knife: Before using a knife to spread icing, dip it in boiling water. This will prevent the icing from clinging to the knife and will give a smoother finish.

Flat icing surface: To get a flat surface for an iced cake, cut a slice off the top and turn the cake upside down.

SWEET IDEAS

Speedy setting: Speed up the setting of a jelly by using ice-cubes. Melt the jelly with half the amount of boiling water specified. Then add ice cubes to bring it to the full amount.

Well set: Add a knob of butter to boiling jam to stop a scum forming. If your jam won't set, reboil it with 30 ml (2 tablespoonfuls) of lemon juice added to each 2 kg (4 lb) of fruit.

Fruity marmalade: Give a different flavour to marmalades and jams, by replacing some of the water with fruit juice.

Darker shade: Use brown sugar instead of white for a darker marmalade.

Added spice: Put spices, such as cloves and chopped cinnamon, into an individual aluminium tea infuser when making pickles or chutneys. They are easier to retrieve that way.

Mocha flavour: Next time you make a cup of hot chocolate, add a teaspoonful of instant coffee for a mocha flavour.

Meringue top: Use marshmallows for a meringue-style topping to puddings. Put them on top of the mixture about 15 minutes before baking time is over.

BREAD

Crusty finish: Brush over home-made bread with a little salty water to give it a crusty finish. Do this half way through the baking, when the top is firm.

Melba toast: To make easy Melba toast, cut the crusts off some pieces of ready-cut loaf, roll out the slices with a rolling pin, using heavy pressure, then bake them in a low oven until they have just turned colour.

Reviving and reheating: Revive stale bread by wrapping it in foil and putting it in a hot oven 230°C, 450°F, Mark 8 for 10 minutes. Leave to cool in the foil before unwrapping. To reheat rolls, leave them unwrapped, put in a low oven 120°C, 250°F, Mark ½ for a minute or so.

Bread to mince: An emergency measure for making mince go further is to add a little one-day-old bread, first soaked in milk, then squeezed out. (See also page 124.)

Crumb topping: Use leftover buttered bread to add a crisp finishing touch to dishes. Turn into crumbs in a blender, then scatter over cauliflower and potato dishes.

Rising dough: If you are making bread, put the dough to rise in a greased plastic bag. The dough will rise faster, will not form a crust, and won't stick to the plastic.

RICE

Whiter rice: Add a few drops of lemon to the water when you are cooking rice, it keeps it white.

Absorbing a burnt taste: If you have burned a saucepanful of rice, tip the rice into a clean saucepan and place a fresh crust of bread over the top and cover. It should absorb the burst taste. If you have burned the rice before it has finished cooking, transfer to a clean saucepan, put in some more water and add the bread crust.

Self-cook pudding: To make a rice pudding overnight, put the sugar and rice into a wide-necked vacuum flask, add the boiling milk, shake and leave until morning. It will cook itself.

PASTA

Pasta cooking: To save fuel when cooking pasta, put it into boiling water, bring back to the boil. Turn off the heat, then cover with a layer of aluminium foil and the lid for an extra tight fit. (See page 153.) After 15 minutes the pasta should be ready to eat.

Reheat spaghetti: Reheat ready-cooked spaghetti by dipping it for half a minute in boiling water. Then drain and serve quickly.

Keeping spaghetti long: There is no need to break up spaghetti to fit the pan. Just poke one end into the boiling water and coil it round as it softens, until it is all under water.

Easy lifting: Put a frying basket, or large mesh strainer, in the pan first when you are cooking spaghetti, macaroni and all kinds of pasta. It makes them easy to lift out when they are cooked.

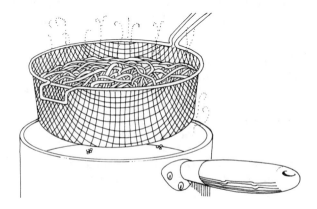

Keeping pasta apart: Pasta that has become glued together in cooking can often be loosened if you bring it back to the boil again. Avoid this problem another time by rinsing it well before cooking to remove excess starch.

No boiling over: To stop spaghetti from boiling over when cooking, add a small knob of butter or 5 ml (a teaspoonful) of oil to the water. It will also stop it from clogging together.

MEATS, POULTRY AND KIPPERS

More meat: To make roast meat go further, place it on a rack in the roasting tin. It shrinks less than if it comes in contact with the tin itself.

More mince: To bulk out mince dishes, add 30 ml (two tablespoonfuls) of porridge oats to each 450 g (1 lb) of mince. (See also page 122.)

Marrow bone: A ring of chopped marrow bone makes a good funnel for a savoury pie and adds extra flavour.

Minced filling: To make cold cooked meat or fish go further in sandwiches, put it through the coarse blade of the mincer first, before spreading.

Care when carving: When carving a joint, place the carving board on a damp towel to stop it slipping on the working surface.

Getting rid of salt: To de-salt gammon or bacon quickly, put into a pan, cover with cold water and bring to the boil. Discard the water and repeat, then cook in the usual way.

Browned sausages: Slow-cooked sausages brown better if you roll them in flour before frying.

Tastier pork: Soak pork chops in boiling water for two or three minutes before cooking them. Blot dry, then grill or fry. They will taste better.

Cocktail bacon: Crisp up bacon rings in 2.5 cm (1 inch) lengths in a tray in the oven. They make good cocktail snacks.

Quick hamburger: Poke a hole through the centre of a hamburger with a skewer to speed up the cooking. By the time it is cooked, the hole will have closed up again.

Let a roast rest: Do not slice a roast joint immediately you bring it out of the oven; let it rest for a minute or two. It will slice better.

Bacon stops sticking: Put a slice of streaky bacon in the bottom of a dish in which you are cooking meat loaf or shepherds pie, to stop the mince from sticking.

Cooked stuffing: If you can't get all the stuffing into the vent of a chicken or turkey, moisten the remainder, wrap in a parcel of aluminium foil and place in the roasting pan.

Easy-turn sausages: Spear two sausages together side-by-side before grilling or frying them. They are much easier to turn over.

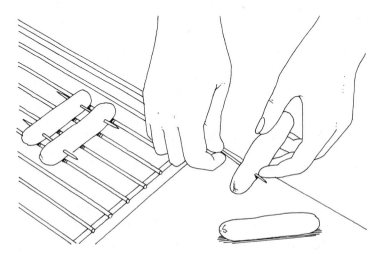

Apple for goose: Place an unpeeled apple inside a goose or a duck before you roast it to absorb excess fat. Discard after use.

Moist kippers: Add a little boiling water to the pan when grilling kippers. It stops them from becoming dry.

Boil, don't fry: Save time and washing up on cooking kippers. Run a skewer through their tails and hang them up in a pot full of boiling water. They will cook this way and you won't have a frying pan to clean up afterwards.

SOME EXTRA IDEAS

Crushed crisps: Use crushed potato crisps, instead of breadcrumbs, on escalopes or fried fish. Empty the crisps into a polythene bag, then crush them with a rolling pin.

Pop corn: When popping corn in a saucepan, empty it into a deep fat frying basket afterwards. The unpopped pieces will drop through.

Crisp cornflakes: To crisp up cornflakes and other breakfast cereals that have become soggy, spread them on a baking sheet and put them in a warm oven for about 10 minutes.

Warning rattle: If you're steaming something in a double saucepan for any length of time, put one or two pebbles in the bottom saucepan. If the water evaporates to danger level you will hear them rattling.

Re-use coffee grounds: Coffee grounds can be re-used if you spread them on a baking tray in the oven for 30 minutes at 180°C, 350°F, Mark 4. Use them half and half with freshly ground coffee when making the next pot.

Clean aluminium: Add a slice of lemon or some apple peel to the contents of an aluminium pan if you are steaming food in it. It will stop it from discolouring.

Less acid rhubarb: Cook rhubarb in cold tea to reduce its acidity.

Cooking pulses: Add a pinch of baking powder to the water when cooking large pulses like haricot beans, it stops them cracking and becoming mushy. They should be salted at the end of their cooking time, not at the beginning.

Crumbs: For dried or baked breadcrumbs, it is quicker and easier to crumble the bread slices roughly first, then crisp them in a hot oven. The crumbs can be made finer afterwards.

Oil for frying: Groundnut oil is a cheaper substitute for olive oil. If you are frying with it, add a knot of butter for an enhanced flavour.

Rock salt: Untreated pure rock salt is more expensive than table salt but has a more concentrated flavour, so you don't need to use as much. It is also tastier.

Preparation and serving

VEGETABLES

Revive asparagus: Uncooked asparagus that has become limp can be revived this way: stand it upright in a jug containing a little water and cover with a plastic bag. Leave it in the refrigerator for half an hour before cooking.

Tender stalks: If the lower stalks of asparagus look tough, take off the outer layer with a potato peeler before cooking.

Careful preparation: Be sure to wear rubber gloves if you are preparing artichokes, that way you won't prick your fingers as you handle the leaves.

No aluminium: Don't use aluminium or iron pots when cooking artichokes, they will turn the inside grey.

No discoloration: Stand artichokes in cold water with a dash of vinegar for an hour before cooking. It stops them from discolouring.

Baked aubergines: To improve the flavour of baked aubergines, drop them into salted water as you peel; pat them dry, then cook.

Stuffed cabbage: To prepare the leaves easily for a stuffed cabbage recipe, put the whole cabbage into boiling water for a minute or so. Remove and pull off the leaves that are softened. They are now more pliant and will not tear. Bring the water back to the boil and repeat until you have all the leaves you require.

Insects: If you suspect there are insects in your cabbage or lettuce, soak it before cooking, in cold water, with a little salt or vinegar added.

Crisp beans: Flaccid, wilted beans can be made crisper if you chill them in the refrigerator in a polythene bag.

Blanching vegetables: Use a cleaned deep fat fryer to blanch quantities of vegetables for freezing. Part fill with water, heat to boiling point, then plunge in the vegetables, using a chip basket. Alternatively, use a salad shaking basket and a saucepan of boiling water.

Defrosting: Pour boiling water over blocks of frozen vegetables before you cook them to rinse away the frost. That way they retain their flavour better in cooking.

Skinning garlic: To skin a clove of garlic, pound it with the side of a heavy knife, or steak hammer, and the skin will slip off easily.

Mushroom slicer: Use an egg slicer to slice mushrooms for soups and sauces.

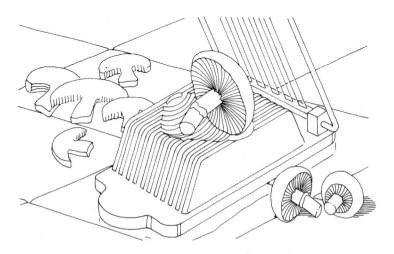

Wipe mushrooms: Never dip mushrooms into water when cleaning them; they will absorb too much water and will be difficult to fry. Just wipe them over with a damp cloth. If you have washed them, they can be used straightaway in a stew, but must be allowed to dry in a colander before frying.

Leek grit: Wash leeks after slicing them, not before. It is much easier to remove dirt and grit that way.

Skinning peppers: Skin large peppers by blistering the outside quickly under a hot grill. Plunge into cold water and the skin will rub off.

Removing seeds: Use an ice-cream scoop to take the seeds out of marrows or melons.

Yellow corn: Add a teaspoonful of lemon juice to sweetcorn before cooking it to keep a good yellow colour.

Celery flavour: Discarded celery leaves first dried, then rubbed to a powder and stored, make a good celery-flavoured addition for soups, stews, etc.

Peeling tomatoes: To peel tomatoes easily for soup or chutney, gather them up in a piece of clean sheeting, plunge them into a large saucepan of boiling water for a minute or two then lift out. The skin will split readily when pierced.

Skinning carrots: To skin carrots easily, drop them as they are into boiling water, leave for five minutes. Drain and drop into cold water; the skins will slip off without the aid of a knife.

Removing silk: A clean, damp toothbrush, stroked downwards on the corn cob, will remove every strand of silk.

Buttering corn: Use a pastry brush to spread melted butter over a corn on the cob. A little goes much further that way.

Soften dried herbs: If you are using dried herbs in a recipe in which they will not get much cooking, you can soften them by steeping in a spot of boiling water for a few minutes before using (see also page 110).

Mint sauce: Sprinkle sugar over mint before you chop it for sauces, it makes the job easier.

POTATOES

Softening the skin: Soak new potatoes in water with a tablespoonful of salt added. It softens the skins and makes them easier to peel.

New potato scraper: Use a nylon pot-scourer for scraping the skins off very new potatoes.

Overnight soaking: If you are peeling potatoes which are to be left in soak overnight, add a drop or two of milk to the water. It stops them from going mushy. Change the water before you boil them the next day.

Extra flavour: When mashing purée potatoes, heat the milk and beat in half a chicken stock cube or bouillon cube before mixing in with the potatoes, for an extra tasty flavour.

Soak chips: Leave chipped potatoes to soak in cold water before cooking. Blot dry with a clean tea towel.

Skin cold potatoes: Boil new potatoes first before skinning them if you are serving them cold. The skins will peel off easily after cooking.

Stop jackets bursting: Prick jacket potatoes all over with a fork to stop them from bursting.

Revive raw potatoes: Raw potatoes that have become flaccid can be revived if you put them in iced water for a minute or two before peeling.

ONIONS

Skinning shallots: Skin pickling onions and shallots by plunging them first in water that is almost on the boil, then in cold water. The skins will come off easily.

Without tears: Try these ways of peeling onions without tears: refrigerate first for an hour, or peel under a cold running tap. Cut the root end off last of all.

Easy peeling: Plunge spring onions into boiling water for a minute or so; they will peel more easily after that.

Chopping with a processor: Chop onions in a food processor, or blender, by adding a little cold water. Switch on for a second or two, then drain off the water and use. Always hold the root end of an onion when you slice it, to stop it from disintegrating.

SALAD VEGETABLES

Firm tomatoes: Always slice tomatoes vertically, not horizontally. They stay firmer that way.

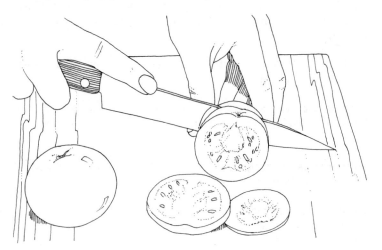

Soft tomatoes: Soft over-ripe tomatoes will become firmer if you place them in a bowl of salted water in the refrigerator for about an hour.

Cleaning celery: Use an old, clean toothbrush for cleaning celery or rhubarb.

Limp lettuce: Smarten up a limp lettuce by placing it in a bowl of cold water with a little lemon juice and some ice-cubes added. Leave for an hour in the refrigerator. Or, place it in a pan of cold water and add a few slices of raw potato. This trick works for celery, too.

Celery curls: To make celery curls, cut 12.5 cm (5 inch) strips into narrow slivers, stopping just short of the end, drop in iced water for half an hour.

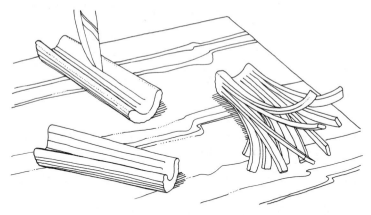

Greener cucumber: To make sliced cucumber look greener and to render it less indigestible, plunge it into boiling water and bring back to the boil. Strain off the hot water immediately and fill the pan with cold water instead. Drain and pat dry with a clean towel.

Digestible cucumber: To make cucumber less indigestible, slice it, sprinkle with salt and leave to drain. It is the liquid that causes indigestion.

Avocado mix: Put the stone back into an avocado mix to stop it from discolouring before you use it. Cover the basin with plastic cling film too.

Ripe avocados: Avocados can be ripened more quickly if you bury them in a bowl of flour.

Radish flowers: To make radish flowers for a garnish, trim off the root and leaves, cut lengthwise almost to the base, six times. Put in a bowl of iced water and leave in the refrigerator for an hour or so.

Limp celery: To freshen up limp celery, wrap it in newspaper and stand upright in a jug of cold water.

Dry lettuce: If you want to dry a large quantity of lettuce, put it into a clean pillow case and whirl it for half a minute in a spin drier.

Crisp lettuce: Break, rather than cut up a lettuce, it is less likely to wilt.

Clean lettuce: Dunk lettuce, head downwards, in water when washing it. The movement will suck out the dirt.

Large salads: Toss a large salad with dressing in a clean washing up bowl. It makes the job much easier.

FRUIT

Grated orange: Frozen oranges and lemons are much easier to grate. Put them in a freezer for an hour or two before you need them.

Warm juice: Before squeezing oranges and lemons, warm them in the oven, or stand in almost boiling water for a minute or so. That way you get more juice from them.

Easier cutting: Roll a grapefruit between your hands or over a table, before preparing it. It will be easier to cut into segments.

Flavoursome strawberries: Pour the juice of an orange over a bowl of strawberries before you serve them. It brings out their flavour.

Keeping a good colour: Squeeze lemon juice over sliced apples and bananas to stop them discolouring.

Apple peeling: Apples can be peeled much more easily if you pour boiling water over them first and allow them to stand a minute or two.

Apple sauce: Use a potato masher to crush items like cooked apple for apple sauce.

Stoning apricots: To stone apricots successfully, cut them in half lengthwise, then twist the two halves in opposite directions. The stone can be lifted out of one half with the top of a knife.

Peach peeling: To peel a peach, drop it in a pan of boiling water for 15 seconds and remove.

Removing thin skins: Thin-skinned fruit that needs peeling, such as plums or tomatoes, can be speared with a fork and held over a gas flame for a moment or two until the skin cracks. It will then come away easily.

Reducing acidity: To reduce the acidity of a fresh pine-apple, sprinkle a pinch of salt over the slices.

Sweeter rhubarb: Soak rhubarb for an hour in a solution of 5 ml (1 teaspoon) of bicarbonate of soda to a saucepanful of water. It will make it less acid and it will need less sugar.

Tailing gooseberries: Scissors are the easiest tool to use to top and tail gooseberries.

To core a pineapple: Use a small round pastry cutter to stamp out the core of the pineapple slices.

Iced lollies: Use leftover fruit juice, mousse mixes, or fruit drinks as ice lollies. Once almost frozen they can be dipped into cake decorations like grated chocolate.

CAKES

Double tin: To prevent the outside of a rich cake burning, place the cake tin inside another larger tin before you put it in the oven.

No-run icing: If you are just icing the top of a cake, sprinkle a little flour all over the cake first, to stop the icing from running down the sides.

Fat-free cake: If you are baking a cake without any fat in it, a sponge for instance, dust the tin with flour. Do not grease it or it will stick.

Hungry children: If you are making a large cake and the children are clamouring for a taste, decant some of the mix into small cup cake tins and bake separately. Give these to the children rather than risk cutting the cake before it has cooled.

Plastic scraper: Use a plastic scraper to get every possible amount of cake mixture out of a bowl.

Even coverage: Stir icing sugar gently in a tea strainer and move over the surface of a sponge cake to give it an even coverage.

Several layers at once: Cut several layers of greaseproof paper when lining a cake tin; store the rest for use next time around.

Cake lift: If you don't have a cake tin with a detachable base, slip a long strip of folded foil into the tin, with the ends dangling over each side, to help lift out the cake when it is cooked.

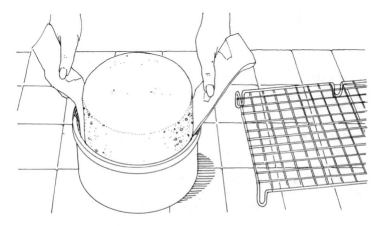

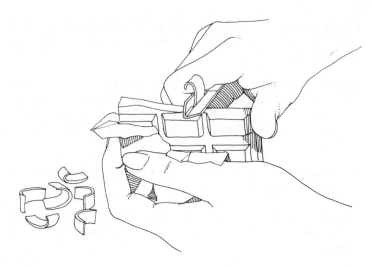

Chocolate curls: Use a potato peeler to make decorative chocolate curls, making sure that the chocolate block is well chilled first.

Smooth chocolate: If melted chocolate becomes too dry, add a little butter to improve its consistency.

Flat top: To ensure a flat top to a cake, make a slight hollow in the centre of the mixture before baking.

No tears: Use a lightly buttered knife to cut sticky cakes and meringues. The butter will stop it from tearing them.

Quick mixing: Warm the mixing bowl first when creaming a butter and sugar mixture. It softens the fat slightly and makes it easier and quicker to work.

Butter wrappings: Keep the wrappings off butter to grease a cake tin, or to line it. Store them in the refrigerator.

No bubbles: Eliminate air bubbles in icing that has been made in an electric blender by leaving it in the refrigerator overnight. Cover with cling film or it may form a hard crust.

Fluffy chocolate cake: For a fluffier effect, add 5 ml (a teaspoonful) of vinegar to the raising powder when making a chocolate cake.

Almond paste: Always allow several days rest after putting almond paste on to a fruit cake before topping it with icing. Otherwise, oils from the paste may mix with the icing and discolour it.

Icing sugar: To make your own icing sugar, put the equivalent weight of granulated sugar plus a little cornflour into a liquidizer and process.

Chocolate sponge: When baking a chocolate sponge, dust the tin first with cocoa instead of flour to give it a darker appearance.

Baking powder: 30 ml (two tablespoons) of cream of tartar, 15 ml (one tablespoonful) of bicarbonate of soda and 15 ml (one tablespoonful) of cornflour, sifted together, makes a substitute for baking powder.

Emergency icing bag: Use a paper bag, or a polythene bag, with a corner snipped off as an emergency icing bag. Polythene bags can also be used in this way for puréed potato.

Cherry cake: To stop glacé cherries sinking to the bottom of a cake, rinse them under cold running water to remove the syrup, then pat a little flour into them before adding to the mixture.

Greasing a cake tin: Always use vegetable fats when greasing cake dishes. Animal fats contain water and salt and may cause sticking.

Short of an egg: If you are one egg short for a cake recipe, substitute 5 ml (1 teaspoonful) of cornflour or 5 ml (1 teaspoonful) of vinegar. Add 45 ml (3 tablespoonfuls) more liquid.

PASTRY AND BISCUITS

Save mopping up: Put fruit pies on a baking tray, or a layer of tin foil, when they go in the oven. This saves having to mop up spillages.

Biscuit shapes: Never lift biscuits off the baking tray when they are still soft or they will go out of shape. Instead, stand the tray on a damp cloth and leave for a minute or so. The biscuits will then slide off easily.

New flavour: Substitute peanut butter for fat when making pie crust for a sweet pudding to give a new and exciting flavour.

No sticking: Put a rolling pin in the freezer for a moment or two before sprinkling with flour and using. It stops the pastry from sticking to it.

Trimming a pie: To trim a pie dish, run a rolling pin along the edge and the surplus pastry will drop off.

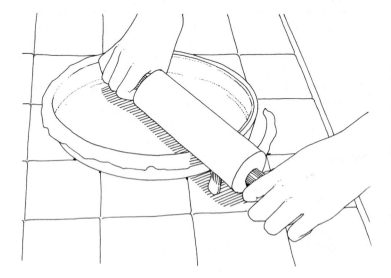

Hand cover: Keep a polythene bag by you when making pastry. You can then slip your hand into it if you have to answer the telephone or open the door, thus avoiding floury marks.

Oil moulds: Oil wooden moulds, such as those used for shortbread, before use. This makes it easier to turn out the contents when cooked.

Substitute cutters: Use an inverted wine glass to cut pastry rounds if you don't have a cutter of the right size. A saucepan lid can be used too, for pizza-sized rounds.

Rolling out: If you are rolling out pastry that contains a high proportion of fat, or mixes, such as shortbread, cover the rolling pin with a layer of cling film to stop the fat from sticking to it.

Trouble saver: When rubbing fat into flour, chill it, then grate it into the mixture to save time and trouble.

Baking blind: Brush a pastry case with egg white before baking it blind. This will prevent it from going soggy when the contents are added.

Cooking fairy cakes: Use a curved grapefruit knife to coax fairy cakes and small individual tarts from their patty tins.

Handling pastry: Roll out pastry on greaseproof paper. You can then handle the paper, rather than the dough, when working with it and it is less likely to tear.

Lighter pastry: Use soda water instead of tap water when mixing short pastry. This makes it lighter.

EGGS

Peeling eggs: To peel hard-boiled eggs perfectly, plunge them in cold water, then roll between your hands before removing the shell.

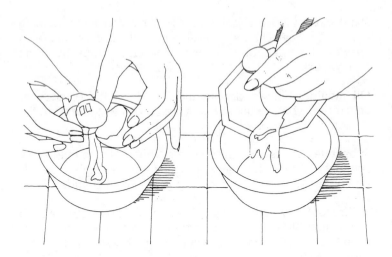

Separating yolks and whites: To separate the yolk of egg from the white, crack the shell in half and pour the yolk from one shell to the other, letting the white drop through. Or break the egg into a saucer, put a small glass upside down over the yolk and drain off the white.

No stick omelette: To stop the frying pan from sticking when you cook an omelette, heat it dry, then add a knob of butter, tilt to cover the pan, then add the eggs.

Fresh eggs: To test eggs for freshness before cracking them, place them in a bowl of water. Fresh eggs sink, stale eggs float.

Egg slicer: If you do not have an egg slicer, cut hard-boiled eggs with a hot knife to stop them from crumbling.

Bad eggs: Always break eggs individually into a cup before adding them to a mixture in case they are bad.

Eggshell scoop: Egg whites cannot be beaten stiff if there is a trace of grease or a trace of egg yolk in the mixture. Remove egg yolk using a piece of eggshell as a scoop.

Extra egg white: Run a cut slice of lemon round the inside of a bowl before whisking up egg whites, it makes them bulk out more.

Cream of tartar: Add half a teaspoon of cream of tartar to every four egg whites you whisk. It will stop them from separating.

HELP FOR THE COOK

Easier handling: Warm up the spoon first if you are measuring syrup or treacle. This will help the treacle slip off the spoon more easily to give an accurate measure.

Stone removing: To remove the stones from plum or damson jam, cook the fruit until it has become soft. Cool, then pick out the stones by hand.

Chill cream: Cream can always be whipped more quickly if it is chilled, together with the basin, beforehand.

Reviving dried fruit: Raisins, sultanas or currants that have dried out can be revived if you place them in a bowl, sprinkle a little water over them, then place them in the refrigerator for 30 minutes.

Fun ice-cubes: Save the plastic shapes from around chocolates in a box. They can be filled with water for fun party ice-cubes.

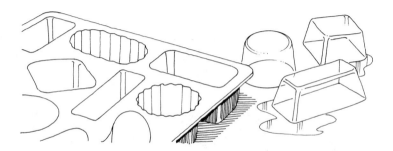

Home-made caster sugar: Make you own caster sugar in an emergency by grinding down granulated sugar in a liquidizer. Keep an eye on the process, if left on too long it will turn into icing sugar instead.

Stop syrup sticking: To stop honey or syrup sticking to the sides of a liquid measure, oil the inside first with cooking oil, then rinse in hot water. Syrups will then slide out of it easily.

Soften peel: Candied peel or angelica that has become sugary and hard is easily softened if you soak it in hot water for a minute or two.

A good turn out: To turn out a jelly, stand the mould for a few seconds in a basin of hot water. The jelly will slip out easily. Dip the serving plate beforehand into cold water so the jelly will slide into place without difficulty.

Family ice-cubes: When serving up fruit drinks at a party, pre-freeze some of the liquid to make flavoured ice-cubes to go with them. Ordinary ice-cubes would tend to dilute the taste.

Party butter: Squeeze softened butter through an icing bag in decorative whirls on to a baking sheet and refrigerate for party servings.

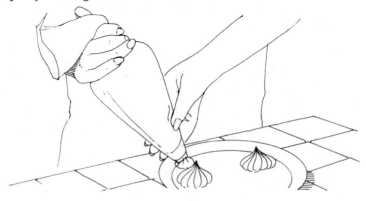

Warm fruit: Sticky fruit such as dates and raisins, can be separated easily if you warm them through first in the oven.

Quick defrost: To defrost frozen fruit juice quickly, put it into the food processor or blender and switch on for a minute or two.

Yogurt for a dieter: Plain yogurt makes a good low calorie substitute for sour cream.

Fruit yogurt: Make your own fruit yogurts by stirring jam into plain yogurts instead.

Cider apples: Soak dried apple slices in cider before using to give an extra flavour.

Soften honey: Warm hardened honey by standing the jar in a bowl of hot water. It will regain its original consistency.

Pie juice: Mix a level tablespoonful of cornflour with the sugar when adding it to a fruit pie. It will thicken the juice.

Toffee making: If you are making toffee or caramel, add a little lemon juice to stop it hardening in the pan.

CHEESE

Cheese taste: Strengthen the taste of grated Cheddar cheese by beating in a little dry mustard.

Easy cutting: If the cheese you are cutting shows signs of crumbling, dip the knife in boiling water before you continue.

Warm cheese: Always serve cheese at room temperature; take it out of the refrigerator for at least 45 minutes before the meal (see also page 99 for how to store cheese).

Easy grating: Put cheese in the freezer for about a quarter of an hour before grating. It makes the job easier.

145

Welsh rarebit: Save leftovers of cheese sauce for a Welsh rarebit topping for toast. They can be kept in a refrigerator for a week. Add more grated cheese, spread on the toast, and heat under the grill.

MEAT, FISH AND POULTRY

Diced bacon: One thick rasher of bacon dices into small pieces more successfully than several thin rashers.

Moist mince: Try adding grated raw potato to the mince when you are making a meat loaf, it helps to keep it moist.

Quick mince: Cut meat into chunks and freeze it slightly before putting it through the mincer. It makes the whole operation quicker and less messy.

Straight bacon: To stop bacon rashers from curling, dip them in cold water and blot before frying. Snip the rind at intervals with kitchen scissors.

Bacon bits: One cut across the end of a pack of rashers will give you several bits of bacon with the minimum effort.

Crisp crackling: Rub pork rind with oil and coarse salt before roasting for a crisp crackling.

Easy to slice liver: Slice liver with ease by pouring boiling water over it first. Leave for about 1 minute, then drain.

Cool first: Chill canned food, such as corned beef, in a fridge before using. It will come out of the can more easily and slice without breaking.

Coat well: To coat meat in flour before cooking, put both items in a paper or polythene bag and shake well.

Non-stick food: Dampen your hands before shaping meat balls and other similar mixtures. The food is less likely to stick to them.

Tender steak: When tenderizing steak with a steak hammer, put a piece of greaseproof paper between the two to save having to pick pieces of meat fibre out of the hammer afterwards.

Kitchen scissors: Use kitchen scissors to cut up cooked pork crackling into manageable pieces.

Whole sausages: Dip sausages for a minute or two in boiling water, blot well and then dry. The skins are less likely to split.

Crisp lamb: Sprinkle the outside of a joint of lamb with flour before roasting, for a crisp finish. Season the flour first.

Avoid tough meat: Always marinate meat before barbecueing or cooking it on kebab skewers. It will then taste better and it avoids toughness.

Tender steak: Rub a little French dressing over a steak before you fry it and leave it to stand for two hours. It makes the meat more tender and more flavoursome.

Defrosting a chicken: To defrost a frozen chicken in a hurry, place it in a bowl of cold, *not hot*, water. Leave for an hour or so, but renew the water if it becomes slightly warm.

Removing giblets: Always remove the giblets from a chicken before you freeze it. It will defrost faster without them inside.

Removing feathers: Plunge poultry or game into boiling water for a moment before plucking. This opens up the pores and makes the feathers easier to remove.

Crisp batter for fish: Add a spot of vinegar to the batter you use to coat fish. It makes the covering extra crisp.

Getting rid of salt: Fish that is too salty can be improved if you soak it in vinegar before cooking.

147

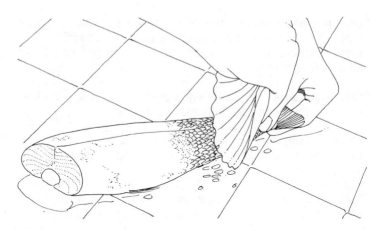

Removing scales: Use a scallop shell to remove scales easily from fish. Always work from the tail towards the head. Dip your fingers in salt first for a firm grip.

New coating: Equal quantities of custard powder and flour make a good coating for fried fish – instead of the usual egg and flour.

Fish full of flavour: Defrost frozen fish in a dish of milk, it improves the flavour. Use the milk to make a sauce to go with it.

Fish soup: Ask your local fish and chip shop for fish trimmings. They can be bought very cheaply and make a marvellous fish soup. Cook them with milk, season well.

SAVOURY IDEAS

Sweet and sour: Save the sweet and sour vinegar from bottles of dill pickle to use when making a salad dressing. It gives a subtle difference to the flavour.

Touch of garlic: Rub the inside of a salad bowl with a cut clove of garlic for a delicate flavour, or rub the clove over a cube of dry stale bread, toss with the salad, then remove.

Soaking time: Bring dried pulses, such as beans, to the boil in plenty of water, then leave to soak for 2 hours. This method cuts down on overnight soaking time, as they should then be ready to cook. Remember that red kidney beans, after soaking, must be boiled rapidly for at least ten minutes and then cooked until soft, whatever dish they are being used in.

Curry flavour: Warm curry powder slightly before using it, this brings out the flavour.

Fresh mustard: Add a pinch of salt to dry mustard before making it up. It gives a better flavour and stays fresh longer.

Less salt: Anchovies are less salty if you soak them in milk for 30 minutes before you use them.

Fried bread: Moisten bread with a little milk before frying it. It cooks better and needs less fat.

Even spread: If you are adding mustard to a sandwich, mix it in with the butter before spreading so it is more evenly distributed.

No soggy sandwiches: Don't spread mayonnaise on the bread in the salad sandwich. It will make it soggy. Instead, spread it over the lettuce leaves.

Savoury moulds: Use lime or lemon jelly instead of more expensive aspic for savoury moulds.

Dark gravy: Equal quantities of sugar and water, heated in a heavy pan until the water evaporates and the sugar begins to brown, makes a good emergency way to darken gravy.

Winter soup: Put leftover vegetables through a food pro-cessor or liquidizer and boil up with some chicken stock cubes. This makes an excellent winter soup.

Time
and trouble savers

HELP AROUND THE KITCHEN

Thumb protector: Use a thimble to protect your thumb when grating cheese or vegetables.

No finger stains: Cut the fingers off discarded rubber gloves and slip them over your thumb and forefinger when cleaning or scraping vegetables. This will stop your fingers from becoming stained.

Plastic protects: Slip your hands into plastic sandwich bags when handling any fruits or mixtures that might otherwise stain your fingers.

Dropped egg: If you drop an egg on the floor, sprinkle it heavily with salt which will absorb most of the liquid and make it easier to scoop up.

Prevent rust: Every so often, when you switch on the oven, leave the door open for the first five minutes or so. This helps to prevent rusting of the metal inside.

Colour dropper: An eye dropper that has been washed out thoroughly, is an ideal tool to dispense just the right amount of food colourings and essences into food.

Emergency board: If you need an emergency cutting board, cover several layers of cardboard or a thick magazine with heavy duty foil. It can also be used as a base on which to put hot saucepans.

Pizza cutter: Use a pair of kitchen shears to cut up portions of pizza. It's less likely to crumble or break that way.

Quicker crushing: Speed up the work when crushing items in a pestle and mortar, by adding some coarse salt, or some granulated sugar, according to the recipe you are using.

Blunt grater: If your kitchen grater has become blunt, sharpen it by rubbing it over with coarse sandpaper. Wash well afterwards.

Easy-clean saucepan: Rinse out the saucepan with cold water before heating milk in it. It will be easier to clean afterwards.

Small beating: Use one beater only in your hand-held electric mixer if you are only dealing with small quantities. That way you can use a smaller bowl, too.

Bottle neck: Can't get the ketchup out of the bottle? Push a drinking straw right down to the bottom and then take it out again. That should put in enough air to get it flowing.

Salad bowl care: Never wash a wooden salad bowl unless you really have to. Wipe it with kitchen paper instead, then rub a little oil into it. Store upside down to keep out dust.

Eye level: For accuracy, read the scale on the side of a measuring jug when holding it at eye level.

No fur: Pour off surplus water after using the electric kettle, it will help to stop it from furring.

Outdoor food: If you are barbecuing food out of doors, line the base and the sides of the pan with kitchen foil to speed up cooking. It helps food to cook right through.

Quick defrost: Place a bowl of hot water in the refrigerator or freezer when you want to defrost it. It speeds up the process.

Non-stick wrap: Store plastic wrappings and bags in the freezer. It stops them from sticking to themselves and to each other.

Oil dispenser: A sewing machine oil-can, once empty and thoroughly cleaned, makes an ideal dispenser for salad or cooking oil in small quantities.

Cooking tongs: Invest in a pair of cooking tongs. It makes turning over food in a frying pan or moving it on to a dish quicker and easier.

Pan base: If you have burned food in a pan, clean it thoroughly (see page 168), then grease the base with a little butter to stop food from catching again.

Emergency funnel: If you need an emergency funnel for dry items, such as sugar, you can cut the corner off a large brown envelope and use that.

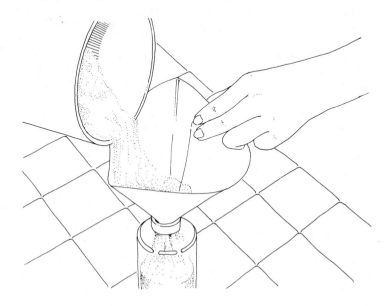

Add a fizz: A fizzy drink that has gone flat can be revived if you add 5 ml (a teaspoonful) of bicarbonate of soda to it.

Flour puff: Keep a clean powder puff in your flour bin. It is very useful for dusting flour on to pastry boards or rolling pins.

Extra work surface: Need temporary extra space in the kitchen? Pull out a drawer and put a baking sheet on top of it to serve as an emergency work surface.

Baking tins: Wash baking tins immediately after use and put them into the oven while it is still warm to dry them off.

New pan: Pour vinegar into a new frying pan and bring to the boil to prevent foods from sticking.

Oil a pastry tin: Keep some oil in a bottle with a sprinkler top – a disused vinegar or soy sauce bottle, for instance. It can be used to sprinkle oil on pastry tins before using them. Finish spreading the oil with a pastry brush or a cloth.

Close-fitting lid: Use kitchen foil to make a saucepan lid fit more closely. Sandwich a piece between the lid and the pan, especially if you want to steam cook the contents. (See also page 123.)

French dressing holder: A baby's feeding bottle, which is no longer needed for milk, makes a good holder in which to mix French dressing. Use the calibrations on the side to measure the oil and vinegar in the correct proportions. However, leave it out of your child's reach, otherwise he or she may drink it thinking it is still milk.

Griddle test: Test a cooker top griddle before you use it for heat. Sprinkle a little flour on the surface. If it turns light brown in 2–3 minutes, the griddle is ready to use.

Opening canned asparagus: Always open canned asparagus from the bottom of the tin to avoid damaging the tops.

Protect a table: Sandwich a piece of foam plastic between the clamp of mincers or bean slicers and the table top you fix them to. This stops the surface from becoming marked.

Emergency corkscrew: For an emergency corkscrew, insert a large long screw into the cork of the bottle, tie a piece of string round its head and pull in a sharp upward direction.

BREAD AND BISCUITS

Warm slices: Use your electric toaster on its lowest setting to quickly defrost, but not toast, slices of frozen bread.

Bread as a cleaner: Pass a piece of stale bread through the mincer to clean the blades and the discs. Process some stale bread in your blender or food processor too, if you have been chopping meat. It makes washing up cleaner and easier.

Crushed biscuits: To crush biscuits for cooking, put them in a polythene bag and seal. Then run a rolling pin over them.

Rolled bread: To curve slices of bread successfully, around asparagus for instance, first roll them out with a rolling pin, then butter. It stops them from splitting.

Fresh bread: Chill very fresh bread before you slice it. It is less likely to split or break.

Stop that crumble: Use a hot, but dry, knife when cutting still-warm bread; this stops it from crumbling.

Buttering biscuits: To butter crumbling water biscuits without breaking them, stack, butter the top biscuit and place at the bottom of the pile. Repeat until they are all done.

Easy-spread butter: To warm up a packet of butter straight from the refrigerator, ready for spreading sandwiches, grate it while still ice cold with a coarse grater, then put into a warmed butter dish.

NUTS

Nut cracking: Put nuts in a freezer for one day before you intend to crack them open. They are more likely to come out of their shells whole and are easier to tackle.

Walnut crusher: Walnuts can be opened without a nutcracker if you crush two together in your hand.

Skinning is easy: Hazelnuts are easily skinned if you put them under the grill until the covering splits, then decant them into a polythene bag and rub them vigorously against each other.

Almonds: Blanch almonds by pouring boiling water over them. Leave them like that for 3 minutes, drain and put into cold water immediately. The skins then rub off easily.

Brazil nuts: Put Brazil nuts in a saucepan of cold water, boil for one minute, then plunge into cold water and drain. Dry thoroughly and you will find that they are much easier to crack.

Nut chopping: To chop nuts the easy way, put them in a polythene bag, then crush them with a rolling pin.

No bursting: To stop chestnuts from bursting while grilling or roasting them, make a small nick in the skin with the point of a knife.

FRESH AND DRIED FRUITS

An easy way: To strip blackcurrants and red currants successfully, freeze them for a while, complete with stalks. Then give the container a shake before thawing and most of the fruit will drop off. Remove the rest by stripping off the berries with a fork.

Grape peeling: To peel grapes easily, plunge the bunch in almost boiling water. Then peel.

Pips out of grapes: Take the pips out of grapes with the loop end of a clean hair pin.

Fruit mesh: Never use a wire mesh sieve for straining fruit, it may discolour it or taint the flavour. Use a nylon mesh instead, or discarded nylon tights.

Crack a coconut: Put a coconut in the oven at 150°C, 300°F, Mark 2 for 25 minutes if you want to open it easily. Place it in a container in case there are any drips. It should crack by itself while cooking. Failing that, tap it with a hammer.

Orange grating: Dip the grater into cold water for a moment before you grate oranges or lemons. The peel will slide off the grater more easily.

Fresh ginger: Use a scouring pad to clean up fresh ginger roots.

Cutting sticky fruit: Use scissors to cut up sticky fruits like dates. Dip them in hot water from time to time as you do so.

Removing date skins: Squeeze fresh dates at the stem end to remove their tough skin.

Baked apples: Plunge the apple corer into a bag of brown sugar when you have cored the apples for baking, fill it two thirds full, then replace in the centre of the apple and tap. It's the easiest way to fill them without spilling.

BUTTER AND SUGAR

Butter curls: Use a potato peeler to make curls out of firm butter.

Softer sugar: Cover hardened brown sugar with a damp piece of towelling overnight to soften it.

Weighing butter: Keep foods, such as butter or margarine, in their paper wrappers when you weigh them out. The difference in weight is unnoticeable and the scale pan won't need cleaning afterwards. Or, lay a sheet of greaseproof paper on the scale first when weighing items.

MAYONNAISE AND SALAD DRESSING

Curdled mayonnaise: If mayonnaise shows signs of curdling, put 15 ml (a tablespoonful) of hot water in a bowl and slowly pour the mayonnaise on to it, beating as you do so. If necessary, beat in another 15 ml (tablespoonful) of hot water.

Light mayonnaise: To make mayonnaise lighter, beat the white of an egg and add to the mixture before serving.

Well balanced: Add an ice-cube to your French dressing when you are mixing it. Shake well, then remove the cube. It will make the ingredients blend more smoothly.

TEA AND COFFEE

Iced coffee: For a quick iced coffee, freeze cubes of coffee concentrate in the ice-making compartment of your refrigerator and use them as the basis for the drink.

Orange tea: Add a piece of dried orange rind to the tea caddy. It gives a delicious smell and taste to the tea.

Flavour for coffee: Sprinkle a pinch of salt on to damp coffee grounds before you make the coffee. It brings out the flavour.

Coffee filters: Paper towels can be cut and used as inexpensive filters for drip coffee machines.

"If a Job's Worth Doing, It's Worth Doing Well"

All about cleaning

Cleaning
room by room

GENERAL

Cover-up: Before you start your daily cleaning make sure that you are wearing protective clothing. Nowadays we tend to tackle household cleaning in whatever informal clothes we happen to be wearing – an old skirt and jumper, jeans and a T-shirt – but the good old-fashioned idea of covering up with an apron has a lot to recommend it. There are many attractive, vinyl-treated designs now available so the apron has lost the dowdy image it once had. Wear a large one with plenty of pockets, which will come in useful for picking up the odds and ends that you spot as you go about the house.

Rubber gloves: For any really filthy work or for when you are handling water, wear a good strong pair of rubber gloves. If you find them difficult to get on, then dust the inside with a little talcum powder. To dry them, stretch them over an empty milk bottle. This will prevent them from perishing, which they will do if they are left wet.

Hand creams: Protect your hands with hand cream after you have finished work. Some household cleaning chemicals are unkind to skin.

Daily chores: Daily chores should include washing up, making beds, and a thorough cleaning of the kitchen, including wiping all the surfaces clear of grease, and cleaning up the eating area. They should also include a general tidy-away of all rubbish and bits and pieces that have accumulated where they shouldn't.

Weekly chores: Weekly chores should include cleaning the floors of the most-used areas, and a thorough vacuuming of all carpets. Brush down the stairs, and change the bedroom linen.

Occasional chores: Wash the windows and wax the floors about once a month. At the same time clean the walls and ceilings of cobwebs.

Longer lasting: Carpets and curtains will last longer if they are cleaned at least once a year.

Behind the scenes: Clean behind the furniture at least once a year. You can make this job more pleasant for yourself by re-arranging the furniture at the same time.

Family help: Help the family help you to keep the house tidy. Create a box under the stairs, or in some convenient cupboard, into which you put anything that you find out of place. Once a month, or when necessary, threaten to take the stuff to the next jumble sale or the dustbin and see how quickly those things are reclaimed!

Soft mop: If the head of a sponge mop is allowed to dry out completely when not in use it will crack and break up. Make yours last longer by wrapping the head in a plastic bag before putting it away.

Better dusters: Your dusters will last longer and pick up better if, when they're new, you soak them in a solution of one part glycerine to one part water. Leave them to dry thoroughly before using.

Bag tidy: Before vacuuming, tape a small paper bag to the handle of the cleaner. Odds and ends, like paper clips, that the machine won't pick up can be dropped into the bag.

Dusting at the double: Instead of using a duster, slip an old sock over each hand when dusting and you'll get the job done in half the time.

THE LIVING ROOM

Shut the door: Close all the doors and windows, so that you have the room before you in its entirety and you can see the tasks that will lay ahead.

Out with the ashes: Clear out the fire of any old ashes, unless you intend to have a wood fire, in which case you will need the base of the ashes. Empty the ash trays.

Dust clouds: Vacuum the carpets first as this will raise large amounts of dust which must be dusted off later. (See also page 232 for how to deal with stained carpets.)

Work downwards: Now start to dust, beginning at the highest point, and working your way down to floor level.

Cleaning old radiators: Old fashioned radiators can be tricky to clean. The best way of removing dust and cobwebs is to hang a damp towel behind the radiator and blow from the front using a cylinder vacuum cleaner with the tube on the opposite end to normal or a hair dryer.

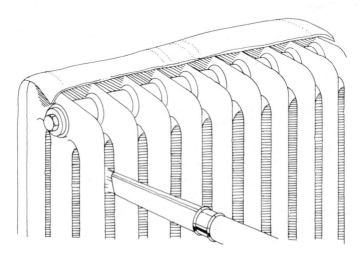

Damp cloth to the ready: Have a damp cloth ready for any dirt that needs damp mopping.

Feather duster: Check over the paintwork, particularly if you have a picture rail, and remove the dust with a cloth or feather duster.

Dust before polishing: Dust all furniture before you begin to polish it.

Clean heat: Dirty radiators give off far less heat than clean ones. Make sure yours are regularly dusted.

THE KITCHEN

THE COOKER
A wipe in time: Wipe the top over after every cooking session to save serious cleaning chores. Baked-on grease takes a long time to remove.

Clean the holes: Remove the burner on gas cookers and scrub well with hot water and detergent. Clean the holes with a pipe-cleaner. A build-up of grease will cut down efficiency and cause cooking smells.

Grease free: Keep reflector pans of electric cookers free from grease spots as these can cause fires. They are also more efficient when clean.

A quick mop: Mop up any spills that may occur, while the oven is still warm. For cleaning, see stains section.

Removing plastic: Plastic bags that have melted on to fires and other heating appliances can be removed with nail varnish remover. Make sure the appliance is cool before you start.

Salt to the rescue: If you spill something in a hot oven, cover the affected area with salt. When the oven cools the spill should just lift off.

Shining chrome: Go over chrome fittings on the cooker occasionally with metal polish to bring up the shine.

THE REFRIGERATOR
A wipe a week: Wipe a refrigerator over at least once a week. If the surface is greasy, dissolve some borax in a little hot water to shift it.

Regular defrost: Defrost the refrigerator, ideally, once a week before you do the main shopping trip. Speed up the process by filling the ice-tray with boiling water and putting it back in the ice-making compartment. Do not use detergent inside: wash the refrigerator inside and out with a solution of borax in hot water, including the shelves. Rinse with fresh water and blot dry with a piece of old clean towelling before you switch on again. A solution of bicarbonate of soda can also be used, instead of the borax. Use a handful of bicarbonate to a bowl of water.

WORKING TOPS AND SURFACES
Strong brew: Varnished woodwork can be cleaned with strong cold tea.

Cleaning the slats: Venetian blinds can be cleaned by soaking a pair of fabric gloves in soapy water, putting them on and sliding each slat between the fingers.

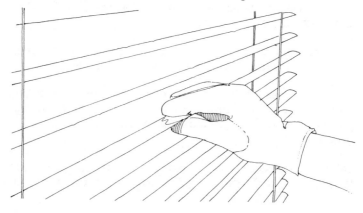

Bitter taste: Any equipment used to make coffee should be cleaned regularly. The coffee beans produce an oil which makes the coffee taste bitter, and this should not be allowed to build up.

Shine rejects: Kitchen ceilings should be painted with gloss, not emulsion paint. The shiny surface makes it much easier to remove the build-up of grease that is inevitable in a kitchen.

Top with toothpaste: To get a good, clean and shining surface on plastic-coated tabletops and work tops try rubbing a little toothpaste on to the surface and then buffing up with a soft cloth.

Away with spills: Laminates are not totally impervious to staining – liquids will be absorbed over a period of time so remove any spills straight away. (See page 274 for stain removal.)

Clean tops: Wipe down counter tops, and other surfaces used in the preparation of food, with hot soapy water after every meal, to make sure they are clean.

Wise chop: Be sure to cut bread, and chop vegetables, on a special board: the less that working surfaces are marred by knife marks, the easier they are to clean.

Wooden surfaces: Scrub wooden surfaces regularly with scouring powder. Build up a seal on the surface by rubbing in a little olive oil afterwards.

Watch the cracks: Check the cracks in the folding leaves of tables and where kitchen units join. Grime that builds up there can be removed with the aid of a knife.

Wax not: Wooden kitchen tables and cabinets should not be waxed when you are polishing them; this traps grease and damp and will soften the wood surface. Use a furniture polish that has no wax base to it.

WASHING UP

Be organized: Organize your washing up before you tackle it. Stack the items before you start to save time. Put on one side items that will need soaking.

Soak first: Soak dishes that have starchy food particles or egg in them in cold, not hot, water. Greasy food should be soaked in hot water with a little detergent added.

DELICATE CHINA AND GLASS

Sideways in: To prevent the heat from cracking it, put delicate glassware into hot water sideways not bottom first.

Sparkling crystal: Real crystal glass should be rinsed in a weak solution of vinegar to make it sparkle.

Precious glass: Use a plastic bowl to avoid smashing precious pieces of glass or china. Deal with non-greasy items like glasses first. Polish glass and china with a lint-free cloth.

No washing: China that is very fragile should not be washed – instead clean it with Fuller's Earth (see page 180).

China teapot: Heavy tea stains in a china teapot can be removed by soaking the pot in any type of washing powder and water overnight. Rinse thoroughly before using again.

Hand wash only: Decoration on top of the glaze surface of china (called 'on-glaze') will fade if it is washed repeatedly in a dishwasher.

POTS AND PANS

Non-stick: To clean non-stick pans, boil some water with a little bleach and a little vinegar in them, then rinse and wash normally. After using this treatment you will need to grease the pan lightly with cooking oil. (See also page 275 for stain removal.)

Cast iron rust: Don't be too zealous in cleaning cast iron pans – they need a thin coating of lard or cooking oil to keep them from rusting. Wipe with kitchen paper before you use it next. (See also page 271 for removal of burnt-on food from cast iron cookware.)

Biological solution: To remove really badly burnt-on food from any kind of pan, soak it overnight in biological washing powder.

CUTLERY
Cork on carbon: Carbon steel knives should be dried immediately to avoid rust. Clean any rust stains with a cork, dampened and then dipped in scouring powder.

Ivory handles: Never wet the ivory handles of cutlery. If the ivory is yellowed then rub clean with a cut lemon.

Egg stains: Don't throw away water used for boiling eggs – save it to soak cutlery stained with egg yolk.

TEA TOWELS
Lint away: If you rinse your tea towels in a weak starch solution after washing them, it will save them covering everything in lint.

MAINTENANCE

KETTLES
Prevent furring: To prevent kettles furring up, pop an oyster shell inside to collect any deposits. (See also page 274 for removal of fur.)

TEAPOTS
Bottle tops: Clean the inside of silver teapots by putting a little washing soda, dissolved in water, with a few milk bottle tops inside the pot. Leave for a few minutes and rinse out well.

Salt in the spout: To clean the spout of a teapot pack it with salt as tightly as possible and leave overnight.

Take a tablet: Clean the inside of a metal teapot with a tablet for cleaning false teeth. Leave overnight and the stains will disappear.

Teapot storage: A silver teapot that is not in constant use can impart an unpleasant flavour to tea when it is used. To prevent this drop a couple of sugar lumps in and prop the lid open before putting away.

SAUCEPANS

Bright lights: Aluminium pans can be brightened by rubbing with kitchen foil or with a mixture of wood ash and lemon juice.

Caring for aluminium: Avoid using aluminium pans to boil water as it discolours them, but if you want to use them for this purpose they can be cleaned with vinegar and hot water. Always make sure to clean aluminium pans straight after use as any food left in them will stain. (See also page 270 for stain removal.)

Prevention is ... : Line the bottom of saucepans with kitchen foil to prevent vegetables sticking to the bottom.

Burnt saucepans: Don't waste time trying to scrape off food that has been burnt on to a saucepan – you may scratch the pan badly into the bargain. Fill immediately with soapy water and leave to soak overnight.

SILVER, STEEL AND GLASS

Chalk it up: To keep silver dry, and so prevent it from tarnishing, put a few pieces of chalk in the drawer with it to absorb moisture.

Well-wrapped: Silver plate should only be wrapped in special acid-free paper – never use ordinary paper. The acid will damage the plating.

Polished steel: Stainless steel can be polished using old newspapers.

Don't bleach steel: Stainless steel is damaged by bleach – don't use it to clean cutlery or to remove stains from sinks. (See also page 277 for stain removal.)

Decanter cleaner: A glass decanter should be cleaned by chopping raw potato into small pieces and filling the decanter, adding some water and shaking well.

GENERAL APPLIANCES
Clean a blender: To clean out a blender, fill it to half way with hot water, add a few drops of detergent and switch on; then rinse with warm water.

Feed the jaws: Can openers can be cleaned by feeding a piece of kitchen towel through the jaws.

Vinegar against mildew: To prevent mildew appearing in a bread bin, wipe it with a cloth soaked in vinegar. Leave the bin open and do not store bread inside until the smell has completely gone.

In a vacuum: If a vacuum flask is badly stained inside fill it with hot water, add some raw rice and give it a good shake.

Stubborn meat: To remove stubborn bits of meat from a grinder, run some bread or raw potato through it before washing.

BEDROOMS

CUPBOARDS AND SHELVES
Silver lining: Line all the cupboard shelves and the drawers with sticky-backed plastic or old wallpaper offcuts. It will help when you come to dust out the drawers, as well as keeping the clothes clean.

Lack of drawers: If you find that you lack drawer space but have plenty of room in the wardrobe then put underwear and socks in a plastic bag and they can be hung with the rest of your clothes.

Tie hang: Stretch a piece of elastic across the back of the wardrobe door and secure it in position, then use it to hang ties and scarves.

Clean and re-arrange: After cleaning inside a chest of drawers, re-arrange the order in which you put the clothes back so that they all get worn equally.

PILLOWS
Washing feathers: Washing a feather pillow should be avoided if possible as it takes the natural oils out of the feathers. (See also page 233 for how to treat badly stained pillows.)

Care for polyester: Polyester pillows should be washed according to the care label. They cannot be dry-cleaned and must not be tumble-dried.

Buying test: When buying a pillow, hold it by one end and shake. If the bulk of the filling falls down to the opposite end, then the pillow will tend to go flat after a while.

MATTRESSES
Regular cleaning: To keep mattresses clean, turn them regularly and vacuum both sides with the nozzle attachment of the vacuum cleaner. The surface of the mattress should always be protected from sweat and dirt by an underblanket.

Weak spots: Avoid sitting in the same place on the edge of the mattress or it will be weakened in that spot.

Stop a spill staining: If you spill liquid on a mattress, then act quickly to stop the stain from spreading. Stand the mattress on its side, take up the excess liquid with a clean cloth, and dab away at the stain with a cloth dipped in cold water. Do not overwet the mattress or the damp will get into the filling. If the wet patch left is a very large one, then you can aid the drying process by playing a hair dryer over the area (see also page 233 for how to treat specific stains on mattresses).

BED LINEN
Spot a sheet: Mark all sheets in the corner with an 'S' for single or 'D' for double. This makes it easy to pick the right sheet out of a pile.

Wash a duvet: If the filling of a duvet is synthetic then it can be washed in the bath, following the manufacturer's instructions. Do not peg out on the line but hang supported from two lines to make sure that it dries in shape.

Call in the professionals: Feather and down quilts or eiderdowns should be professionally cleaned. Never attempt to clean one in a launderette-type dry cleaning machine (see page 233).

Air the blanket: Blankets can be dry-cleaned in a launderette, but must be aired well outside before you use them again. Suspend the blanket between two lines and pull into shape while it is hanging. Bring the pile up with a soft brush or shake well.

HAIRBRUSHES
Brighter bristles: To clean a bristle hairbrush, dissolve a little soda in warm water and stand the hairbrush up in it. Do not let the water touch the handle part of the brush. Dry the brush by standing it on its bristles. If the brush has an ivory back then shine this up with a cotton wool ball dipped in methylated spirits.

Stiffer bristles: A rinse in cold water will stiffen the bristles of a bristle brush.

JEWELLERY
Diamond rings: To clean diamond rings, add a few soap flakes or 5 ml (a teaspoonful) of soap powder to a cup of hot water, swish, then follow up with a few drops of ammonia. Immerse the jewellery in this for a second or two, then remove and put on a saucer to cool. Rinse thoroughly, then dip into an egg-cupful of white spirit, methylated spirit (or vodka!) and pat dry on tissue paper.

Gold, silver, semi-precious stones: These can all be washed in hot water with washing-up liquid but don't use very hot water or the settings on the rings may expand so that the stone will drop out. Polish afterwards with chamois leather. If something stronger is needed, toothpaste, applied with an old toothbrush, is good for getting into crevices. Rinse well afterwards.

Beads: A toothbrush dipped into dry sodium bicarbonate is excellent for cleaning these.

Pearls: Wash pearls in warm water with a few soap flakes (never add ammonia to it). Then polish with a chamois leather.

Separate storage: Keep things in separate boxes if you can, to stop them from becoming entangled. Wrap precious items in individual pieces of tissue paper.

String along with tape: If you are re-stringing a row of graduated beads, place some cellophane or masking tape, sticky side up, on the table and arrange the beads in the right order on that before you start work.

BATHROOM

THE BATH
Prevent steam: To prevent the bathroom steaming up and to reduce condensation on the walls when you run a hot bath, put the cold water into the bath first and then bring it up to temperature with the hot water.

Instant clean: Cleaning the bath is easiest when it is still warm just after use. Train those using the bath to realise this and to clean it just after they get out. If the bath is kept clean then this will prevent staining. (See also pages 270–1 for stain removal from different types of baths.)

No steel wool: Never use steel wool, bleach or loo cleaner on the enamel of the bath.

Don't get steamed up: To stop the mirror getting steamed up after you have had a bath, smear it over with some soap and then rub until clear.

Adding the salts: If you use bath salts then make sure that they are added while the water is running. If they do not dissolve properly then they may cause small scratches on the bath surface.

Save a mark: Use a capful of washing-up liquid in the bath with you. It will save having to wipe the bath out afterwards as it takes the tidemark with it.

Give it a shine: Porcelain and enamel baths and washbasins will keep their shining appearance if you rub them regularly with coarse salt.

LAVATORY
Chemical reaction: Never mix two kinds of lavatory cleaner as the chemicals may react violently.

Avoid abrasion: Never use an abrasive on the inside of the lavatory bowl as this will scratch the surface. This will, in turn, encourage the build-up of unpleasant scale which is difficult to remove. (See also page 274 for stain removal.)

SHOWER
Uneven spray: If your shower distributes water unevenly it is likely that the head is partially blocked. Take it off, and unplug the holes with a darning needle. If this doesn't work, try boiling it in a solution of vinegar for a little while.

Clean glass: Glass shower doors can be cleaned by rubbing with white vinegar. This will bring up a shine and remove white film caused by water.

SHOWER CURTAINS
Water softener: Clean soap build-up on shower curtains by soaking the curtains in warm water with water softener added to it.

Out with mould: Bleach can be used to get rid of mould from the bottom of shower curtains. Use a weak solution and rinse well afterwards.

Prevent mildew: You can prevent mildew from forming on the curtain. Soak the curtain in salt water before using it.

TILES
Shining tiles: Tiles can be shined by rubbing with a cloth that has been dipped in methylated spirits. Buff up with a soft dry cloth. (See also page 272 for stain removal from ceramic tiles.)

Clean the grouting: The grouting between tiles can be cleaned with an old toothbrush dipped in a solution of domestic bleach. If you have a large area of tiles to clean, put the solution in an old plastic washing-up liquid bottle and run it along the lines of grouting. Leave to soak for several minutes and then rinse clear.

CLEANING THE ACCESSORIES
Gleaming taps: Clean the taps after use with a rub from a bar of soap and a buff up with a clean cloth or old towel. Use an old toothbrush to clean up the more inaccessible areas around the tap base.

Shining chrome: Chrome-plated taps should be rubbed over with a soft cloth dipped in washing-up detergent solution. The shine can be brought up by using car chrome cleaning cream.

Scale on chrome: Neat ammonia on a cotton wool pad will remove scale staining on chrome taps.

Washing soda: Soap dishes can be cleaned by soaking for a few minutes in a mild solution of washing soda and water. The water should be very hot. Scrub the stains off the surface and rinse well.

Care for a bath mat: A bath mat will become mouldy if not kept well aired. Store it either flat over the towel rack or rolled and standing in the corner of the bath. If the mould has already taken a grip soak in a mild solution of bleach. Rinse well.

Sponge clean: To clean a sponge, soak it overnight in a solution of vinegar or lemon juice.

Boil once a week: Face flannels, sponges and loofahs should be boiled once a week in a solution of vinegar and water. Use half a cup of vinegar to a large saucepan of water.

Cleaning agents A-Z

ACETONE

This is usually bought as a non-oily nail varnish remover. It dissolves acetate materials, so use with care. It will remove lacquer and nail varnish from most surfaces and will remove some paints and glues, acting as a solvent to remove the stain. It is highly inflammable so remember not to smoke when using it. Store it out of the reach of children. When using, keep the room well ventilated and the acetone away from the skin, eyes and nose.

AMMONIA

This is an alkali and a grease solvent, which can be bought in liquid form and will remove such stains as grease, chocolate and blood. It should be used in a 10% solution. It has a slight bleaching quality. Use it to clean surfaces such as cooker tops, tiles, etc. Do not use it on paintwork, plastics or vinyl floors. Ammonia is *poisonous* and should always be used in a weak solution to keep it harmless. Always use it on its own, as it reacts with many other cleaning products to produce disastrous results. The fumes will harm your lungs, so if you are handling a strong solution wear a mask. Always use in a well ventilated room. Wear gloves and keep it well away from your skin. Wash your hands in plenty of cold water if they come into contact with it. If ammonia is taken internally, give plenty of water and contact a doctor or hospital. If it gets in your eyes then use this solution: 10 g boric acid per 400 ml of water (1 level teaspoon per pint). Bathe the eye in the solution and contact the doctor. If it gets on the skin, sponge with a solution of

25 ml vinegar per 500 ml of water (1 tablespoon per pint).

Use ammonia to remove perspiration stains from clothing. Just soak the affected area for a few minutes then rinse thoroughly. Check before you start that the ammonia won't bleach the material.

BICARBONATE OF SODA

This comes in powder form. It is an alkali which will cancel out mild acid stains, such as fruit juice. It will also remove stains from glass and is good for cleaning the insides of refrigerators. Used in solution, it will relieve itching and burning. The glass doors on modern ovens become stained quite quickly. A paste of bicarbonate of soda and water can be used to restore their original sparkle.

BLEACH

Always use bleach in dilute form. It will take the colour out of most fabrics, but will damage the fibres in a strong solution. Follow the directions for dilution on the side of the bottle. Use it on the kitchen surfaces in weak solution to disinfect them and remove tea stains. It will take most heavy staining off the inside of the lavatory bowl. It is, however, capable of removing the surface gloss from enamel, so check the side of the bottle for the Vitreous Enamel Council sign before you use on a lavatory. Never use on wool, silk or any fabric with a special finish. (To bleach these, use hydrogen peroxide.) Bleach is *poisonous*, it will react violently with some other cleaning products so never mix them. Try not to get it on the skin or inhale the fumes. If you splash your skin, then rinse it off with plenty of cold water. If taken internally, drink water followed by quantities of milk which will help to neutralize the bleach, *and* contact your doctor or a hospital. Store bleach in a safe, locked cupboard, along with the other dangerous chemicals listed here. Strong solutions will burn through some fabrics and will start to corrode some metals. A mild solution of bleach would be 10 ml of bleach to 300 ml of water. (One teaspoonful to $\frac{1}{2}$ pint.)

BLUE

This can be bought separately from washing powders although it is already in most powders. It gives white clothes a blue tinge which makes them appear whiter. Use according to the instructions on the packet.

BUILDERS

These are found in laundry soaps which will increase the cleaning power of the soap. Soap that contains builders should not be used on delicate fabric or to wash skin.

CARPET SHAMPOO

Now normally sold in a dry form, which is the best for home carpet cleaning, as it doesn't wet the backing of the carpet, and dries to a foam that has picked up the dirt in the fibres. It has then only to be vacuumed off. Follow the manufacturer's instructions; test first to make sure the carpet is colourfast (see page 227).

CASTOR OIL

This can be used for polishing leather, but only use it on clean leather, as it will seal the surface.

CAUSTIC SODA

This is a very strong alkali which will burn cloth, enamel, bristle, rubber and aluminium. It comes in crystal form. Caustic soda can be used for cleaning ovens, and is contained in most proprietary oven cleaners. It is recommended for unblocking drains, but there is a problem if the drain contains grease, because the soda will react to the grease and block up the sink rock hard. (For greasy drains, see Washing Soda.) Use caustic soda only on those drains that you can be sure do not have any grease in them. It is highly corrosive, so handle it only when wearing rubber gloves and follow the manufacturer's instructions for use.

Any small splashes should be rinsed with plenty of cold water. Do not inhale the fumes; always work in a well ventilated room. When diluting, put the crystals into the water, not the other way round.

DESCALING FLUID

Scale is a problem facing those in hard water areas. Many appliances which use water are prone to being affected by scale. Buy a proprietary fluid and follow the manufacturer's instructions.

DETERGENT

This comes in a variety of forms.

Soap powders come as normal washing powders and as soap flakes, which are recommended for soaking some materials, (see Stain Chart, pages 234–67). These are not synthetic and are good for washing delicate fabrics.

Synthetic powders have no soap in them and come in heavy washing powders to be used in machines other than front loaders.

Low-lather powders are specially formulated for automatic and front-loading machines which should not have any other types of powder used in them or they will overflow with soap suds.

Enzyme or biological powders come in many combinations and most of the powders listed above have their own biological powder attached to the particular group. Do not use them in water above 60°C, 140°F as the detergent and enzyme effect will not work at very high temperatures.

The manufacturer's recommendation on how much powder to use should be your guide, as too much or too little powder will effect the quality of your wash. Hard water areas need more than soft water ones. It is not necessary to have great amounts of suds to get the clothes clean. Most detergents contain builders, perfume and a bleaching agent. The beauty of modern washing powders is that they are dissolved quickly, either by hand or by the washing machine and they do not leave a scum behind.

FABRIC CONDITIONER

This is added to the final rinse. It must be used regularly to have the best effect. Use it on wool, towels and man-made fabrics. It will make soft fabrics softer, and it will reduce the static in many man-made fabrics. The conditioner should always be diluted before use. It will also prevent creasing.

FLOOR POLISHES

There are two types, wax-based and emulsion-based. Wax-based polish comes in a cream or a liquid form. It shines by building up a wax surface which can be buffed up. It does create a slippery surface, so do not use on areas covered by mats which will then slip very easily. Emulsion-based polish comes in liquid form and is applied with a mop. It dries to a high gloss finish. There is no surface build-up but these types of polish do tend to show water marks in the kitchen. Emulsion-based polishes are suitable for vinyl flooring and for sealed cork and wood. Wax-based ones are good for wood, cork and unglazed quarry tiles but should not be used on vinyl.

FULLER'S EARTH

This has great absorbent qualities. It will absorb grease-based dirt. It is convenient to use on items that cannot be washed, such as fur and embroidery. It is sprinkled on, left overnight, then brushed off.

FURNITURE POLISH

Use furniture polish to protect the surface of wood: it comes in wax, liquid and aerosol form and is very easy to use. Wax polish is the best, as it is the most penetrating and therefore is longer-lasting. However, it also requires the most elbow grease on your part. The liquid polish is much quicker to apply, as it spreads more easily. The aerosol form only gives a fine coating but is useful on surfaces already treated with an artificial polish.

GLYCERINE

This comes in a colourless liquid. It is good at removing stains from washable fabrics. It acts as a solvent and will soften old stains, so that it is possible to treat them. Never use it on non-washable fabrics.

HYDROGEN PEROXIDE

This comes in liquid form and in different strengths. For stain removal use the 20 vol. strength and dilute according to instructions (see Stain Chart, pages 234–67). A paste of hydrogen peroxide and cream of tartar will remove the very stubborn stains off enamel but only use if everything else has failed (see page 273). Hydrogen peroxide makes a good cleaning agent for marble and ivory. It will remove some scorching from fabric. Store it in a cool dark place. It is a *poisonous* substance, so keep well out of reach of children. If swallowed, administer drinks of water and contact the doctor or the hospital at once.

JEWELLER'S ROUGE

This comes in a red powder form, which is slightly abrasive and so is good to use on scratched glass, and for polishing jewellery. It can be bought in a hardware store. It is mixed with water or methylated spirits, according to instructions. It is possible to buy special cloths already treated with jeweller's rouge.

LAUNDRY BORAX

This is an alkali mineral salt. It loosens dirt and grease and will cancel out any acid stains. It has various household uses and will aid the action of cleaning agents, such as washing-up liquid by acting as a water softener. It is *poisonous*, so keep out of the reach of children. It can irritate the skin, so wear rubber gloves when dealing with it. If swallowed, administer plenty of water and ring the doctor or the hospital at once.

LAVATORY CLEANER

This comes in the form of powder in a puffer pack. It is an acid-based product. Follow the manufacturer's instructions, and do not use to clean any other surfaces. It is important that you do not mix lavatory cleaners with any other cleaners as they can react with one another and cause explosions. It must be left for several hours in order to work properly.

LINSEED OIL

This is an oil from flax. It has no taste and only a slight smell. Mix it in equal proportions with turpentine to rub the water marks out of wood. Use on oak to darken the colour of the wood. It is highly inflammable, so store it very carefully.

METAL POLISH

It is important that you use the right polish for the right metal, otherwise you are in danger of harming the surface of the metal. Once you have polished the metal, protect it with a proprietary brand metal tarnish retarder. Store polished metal properly, most tarnish comes from exposure to water, acid or chemicals. Always store silver in special acid-free tissue paper.

METHYLATED SPIRIT

This comes in liquid form and is dyed a purple colour. It is derived from a low grade alcohol made from sugar cane. Use it to remove grease stains from fabrics (see Stains Sections pages 234–67). It will remove ballpoint pen marks, chocolate, coffee, and grass stains from non-washable fabric. Used undiluted it will polish glass and mirrors, jewellery and ivory. Used with paraffin (see page 269) it will polish chrome and paintwork. Outside storage (e.g. in the garden shed) is the safest, as it is highly inflammable and *poisonous.* Keep in a locked cupboard out of the reach of children.

OVEN CLEANER

Oven cleaner should not be used on the self-cleaning oven
linings. It comes in a variety of forms in aerosol cans and in
cleaning pads. The latter are easier to use on really dirty
ovens. Clean the grease off the oven (after you have used
the oven and while it is still warm) with ordinary soapy
water before using the oven cleaner. The proprietary oven
cleaners are often highly caustic, so protect your hands by
wearing rubber gloves while working with them. Follow
the manufacturers' instructions, both on the package and in
the manual for your oven.

PAINT BRUSH CLEANER

On emulsion paint use soapy water. The recommended
thinner for other paints will be the best brush cleaner: for
gloss paint use white spirit, for cellulose paint use a
cellulose cleaner, for varnish and enamel paint use
turpentine.

PARAFFIN

Paraffin is a colourless solvent for grease. It is highly
inflammable.

SADDLE SOAP

It is used for cleaning leather. Buff it well with a soft cloth to
get a polished finish.

SOAP

Soap comes in the form of bars or powder (see Detergent)
and is made from animal fat or vegetable oils. In laundry
soap there are added builders, which will harm the skin, so
do not use laundry soap for washing yourself. It is
excellent for removing stubborn stains on work clothes,
etc., before they are put in to a boiling wash. Toilet soaps
have added perfume and no builders.

183

SOLVENTS

Many materials act as solvents which will dissolve grease and thus release the dirt that is trapped in the grease. Solvents are also found in proprietary spot removers and dry cleaning fluids. (See below.)

SPRAY LAUNDRY PREPARATIONS

These usually come in aerosol cans for spraying on to any stains that the manufacturer says it will treat. They work quickly – normally in less than a minute. They are particularly good at getting rid of food and grease stains and collar and cuff dirt. After treatment, put the item into the wash at the right temperature for the material.

STARCH

This comes either in powder form or in an aerosol can. Use the powder type starch in your wash. It will often strengthen old fibres, will make the wash look fresh and feel good, particularly on white cotton. It will also form a surface on material, which will resist staining and make dirt removal easier. For a medium stiffness use 30 ml to 2.2 litres (1 heaped tablespoon to half gallon) of water. Do not starch children's clothes as children are often slightly allergic to the finish. If you wish to starch selective areas, such as just the collar of a shirt, use the aerosol when ironing.

TURPENTINE

This is a liquid with a very strong smell. It works as a grease solvent as well as a solvent for wax and paint. Store turpentine away from sunlight and heat, and away from children. It is highly inflammable, so store out of the house if possible. Do not smoke when using it.

VINEGAR

White vinegar is commonly used around the house for

many purposes. It will soften water as it is slightly acid. It will remove stains on upholstery and carpets as well as many other surfaces. Do not use it on acetate or tri-acetate fabric, as it will dissolve the surface. Malt vinegar is not recommended for fabric as the brown colour may affect certain of the fabrics; but it is fine for use on scale caused by hard water on baths, etc., and on brickwork.

WASHING SODA

This comes either as a powder or as crystals. Although it is a mild alkali, it is quite strong as a remover. Protect your skin with rubber gloves when using it. It will act as a water softener but will take time to have an effect in cold water. It acts as a grease solvent in clearing drains. It is also very good as a silver cleaner. Some surfaces do not like it, so never use it on aluminium, which it stains badly and corrodes. Do not use it on wool, silk, sisal or vinyl.

WASHING-UP LIQUID

This is a liquid detergent. It is not necessary to have a lot of lather to clean with it. Most washing-up liquids are just as effective if you dilute them before you use them, by adding an equal quantity of water.

WATER SOFTENER

This should be used in hard water areas to prevent the build-up of scale on appliances that run on water. Washing soda will soften the water but a proprietary water softener will work for longer. It will make detergent go further by making the water seem very sudsy.

WHITE SPIRIT

This is most useful as a cheap alternative to turpentine. It acts as a grease solvent. It will act on paint, varnish and can be used on carpets and upholstery in the same way as turpentine. It is very inflammable and *poisonous*, so store in a locked cupboard.

Removing unwanted smells

CIGARETTE SMOKE

Lavender oil: A mixture of household soda, a few drops of ammonia and some lavender oil infused with boiling water should get rid of stale tobacco smells. If the smell persists, dilute a few drops of ammonia in some water and leave in the room overnight.

Absorbing vinegar: A small bowl of vinegar placed in the room while people are smoking will absorb the smell of the smoke.

In a damp spin: To get rid of lingering smoke spin a damp towel around the room.

COOKING AND KITCHEN SMELLS

Lovely lemon: When cooking cabbage, put a little fresh lemon juice in the water with it – this will stop the cooking smells from spreading, without affecting the taste of the vegetable. Or, add a slice of stale bread, it takes away the smell and can be skimmed off the surface easily afterwards.

On the board: Chopping boards tend to absorb the smell of foods. These can be difficult to get rid of by washing. Rub a paste of bicarbonate of soda into the board, rinse and wash as usual.

Salt removes onion smell: To eradicate the smell of onion from a wooden chopping board, rub it over with coarse salt then rinse with cold water.

Boiling white vinegar: Smells will disappear from a saucepan if you boil a little white vinegar in it.

Absorbing thought: If you are cooking something with a smell that you do not want to travel all over the house keep a saucer of vinegar at your side. It will absorb most of the smell.

Into the fire: Coffee grounds can be used to get rid of unpleasant odours in rooms. Boil some up in a saucepan, or throw some into an open fire.

Onion and garlic on hands: When you have onion or garlic smells on your hands, the trick is to wash them as quickly as possible in cold water. Hot water seals the smell into the skin. If the smell persists, rub your hands with lemon juice or vinegar and wash with soap and water.

Bleach out: Vinegar will remove the smell left when you have been washing with diluted bleach. Just rub a little over your hands.

Fishy thoughts 1: If silver cutlery has a fishy smell clinging to it, add a drop of mustard to the washing-up water. A little vinegar added to the water will remove fish smells from china.

Fishy thoughts 2: To get rid of the smell of fish from a frying pan put salt in it and add boiling water then leave to soak.

Fishy thoughts 3: A few pieces of celery dropped into the cooking oil will help to disguise the smell of fried fish.

Garlic on breath: Chew a piece of fresh parsley or, if you can bear it, a coffee bean, to relieve garlicky breath.

PETS

Litter tray: Make sure that used litter is removed daily and use an air freshener.

Accidents: If your cat or dog has been sick on a carpet, a quick squirt from the soda syphon will help to get rid of the smell, once you have cleared up.

REFRIGERATOR

Stubborn smells: Smells very often linger in the refrigerator and are difficult to get rid of. They can be absorbed by one of these substances: charcoal, cat litter, baking soda, or crumpled newspaper. A small amount of any of these should absorb smells. If the smell persists then wipe the inside of the refrigerator with a solution of sterilizing fluid used for babies' bottles. Do not use on metal. Rinse the inside of the refrigerator and leave to dry before you switch it on again.

Make a paste: A paste of baking soda smeared around the inside of the refrigerator will also get rid of lingering odours.

SHOES

Baking soda: A little baking soda in shoes will absorb any smells. Sprinkle it into the shoes and leave overnight before removing.

CUPBOARDS

Bath salts: Put a saucer full of bath salts on the floor of a little-used cupboard. It will keep clothes fresh and dispel musty smells.

Charcoal: Activated charcoal will eat up musty smells in small cupboards.

BATHROOM

Strike a match: Unwanted smells in the bathroom will disappear if you strike a match and let it burn down. Do not leave the room until you are sure the match has gone out.

GLOVES

Lavender for gloves: Keep gloves smelling fresh by putting a lavender sachet in the drawer with them.

NEW PAINT AND CHEMICALS

A bowl of salt: Leave a small bowl of salt in a newly painted room overnight. This will get rid of paint smells.

Onion and water: A peeled onion in a bucket of water will remove very strong chemical smells.

DUSTBINS

Fly off: Putting mothballs in the bottom of a dustbin will make it smell better and deter flies.

NICE SMELLS

Oranges and lemons: If you have an open fire, throw orange and lemon peel on to it. The room will soon be filled with a very pleasant smell.

Household pests

GENERAL PREVENTION

Many of the pests listed below are attracted to our houses in search of warmth and food. So with this in mind there are several things you can do to prevent pests from bothering you in your general housekeeping.

1. Make sure that you wipe up food crumbs thoroughly after each meal.
2. Make sure that pet food is taken up once the pet has finished with it, so that flies do not lay their eggs in it.
3. Make sure that your dustbin is always covered with a lid, otherwise you will find that flies will use it as a breeding ground.
4. Regularly clean the drains out and make sure that they are not blocked.

SAFE PROCEDURES WITH PEST REPELLANTS

Read and heed: There are many proprietary products on the market which deal with most sorts of pests but it is essential to follow a few safety rules. Read the manufacturer's instructions and cautions fully.

Poisonous waste: If you have some of the poison left over then make sure that you either put it back into the correct container or that you dispose of it safely. Many liquid products can be flushed down the drains, but follow this with copious amounts of water to ensure that it gets right down the system.

Wash your hands of it: Always be careful when handling the products. If you do splash your skin, then wash off immediately. Wash your hands well after you have been using the poison.

Careful spraying: Aerosol treatment should only be used in a well-ventilated room, making sure that all pets and food are right out of the way. Do not breath in the vapours from these cans, as they are very often *highly toxic*. Do not smoke while spraying and do not work near naked flames.

ANTS

Ants are mostly likely to bother you during the summer. They are attracted into the house by sweet, sticky things, fat and grease. Black ants are the most common type to come into the home. Watch them to find out where there nest is located and then destroy it with a kettle of boiling water poured down the entrance hole. If they  continue coming in, try to find their point of entry and stuff it with cotton wool soaked in paraffin. There are many proprietary products on the market for getting rid of ants. Some will be taken back into the nests and thus kill a whole colony, others are more localized.

If you are really desperate about getting them out of the house but cannot obtain any insecticide, use small sponges soaked in sweet water to attract them and to keep them busy. When there are a number collected together on the sponge pick it up and pour boiling water over it. This will kill them outright.

Protect food from attack by putting it on a table and then standing the table legs in bowls of water. The ants will not be able to cross the water.

If you are sure that the children and pets will not get hold

191

of it, make a solution of 2 cups of borax with 1 cup of sugar and sprinkle outside around the house. This will both attract ants and kill them.

BEDBUGS

Bedbugs are wingless, minute brown insects that live almost anywhere in old houses and furniture. They are active at night and leave a small itchy bite. They may have been resident in the cracks of the floor and in the wallpaper for some time or they may be brought in with mattresses and old furniture.

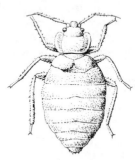

In order to rid the bed of them it is necessary to spray all the parts including the iron work with a suitable insecticide. Spray the mattress as well but be sure not to saturate it. If you have an idea where bedbugs may be lurking, such as the skirting boards, then spray those too. In severe cases, the local health authority will help.

BEES AND WASPS

Most bees and wasps can be paralysed by a quick squirt with hair spray. It will make their wings sticky so that they are unable to fly, then you can quickly put them out of their misery. If there is a wasps' or bees' nest near the house, then it is in your interests to destroy it. Contact your local health authority for

advice. If a swarm has settled in your house, then it will need a professional to shift it. Call the local health authority for help. Do not disturb the nest under any circumstances.

BOOK LICE

These are off-white insects that feed on mould and damp in books, paper, cardboard and plaster. They do not like dry, warm conditions so expose the area to the highest temperature possible or spray with a preparation for crawling insects. Do not keep up the heat, however, as it is bad for book bindings.

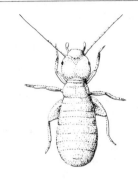

CARPET BEETLES

It is the grubs of this insect, rather than the insect itself, that are the pest. They will feed on carpets, feathers and wool. They may come from birds' nests in the attic and will travel to a warm area wherever there is food. You will find that they leave small holes in the fabric. Treat with a proprietary insecticide.

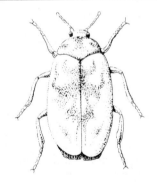

COCKROACHES

These come out at night and eat food, starch, fabric and paper. They are carriers of food poisoning and will infect any food or surface that they have walked across. They can be very difficult to get rid of. Spray the roaches themselves with an insecticide and then their haunts and any

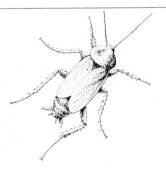

routes that they use. If you find the problem is getting worse and you are unable to get rid of them then contact the health authorities who will come in and fumigate the house.

To prevent cockroaches reappearing, sprinkle boric acid powder along the areas where they appeared before. The acid acts slowly but does eventually kill the roaches. Use it with caution (see Silverfish entry).

EARWIGS

These look unpleasant, but do no damage. They do not live naturally in the house but sometimes are found in quite large numbers. They have probably been brought in from the garden. If necessary squirt with an insecticidal powder and then brush them up.

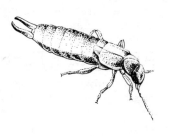

FLEAS

These are a common pest in homes where there are either cats or dogs. Cat fleas will actually infest human beings. Dog fleas tend to stick to dogs. Dog fleas carry the eggs of the tapeworm, so if the dog eats the fleas it will become infected. The fleas' bites cause areas of irritation, formed around a red spot.

They are spaced wider apart than mosquito bites and are often in a long series. Check your pet for fleas. You should be able to see them running about in the fur. It may also be infested with the eggs, which look like dandruff. It is at this point that you should spray the pet with a proprietary product. Follow the manufacturer's instructions, avoiding the pet's eyes. Give it a flea collar once it has been treated as this will make sure that it will not get re-infested. Treat bedding and furniture as well.

It is not a good idea to de-infest young kittens. Wait until they are at least three months old.

Vacuum thoroughly after you have treated the carpets and furniture for fleas as the eggs may well lay dormant for two months. Destroy the cleaner bag after use.

FLIES

Flies really are the most un-pleasant of the household pests. They trail about in rotting meat, and in dung and then, if allowed to settle, will regurgitate on to food or any surface. They carry over thirty different diseases, and lay their eggs at an alarming rate during the summer. Prevention is the best remedy to 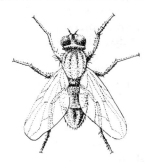 the fly problem. Keep general hygiene high in the kitchen.

Do not leave food around to rot. Crumbs are also an attraction, as is pet food.

Keep the lid firmly on both your outdoor dustbin and your indoor one.

If flies are swarming around your dustbin, wash it down with some warm water, allow to dry and then sprinkle soap powder in the dustbin.

Mothballs placed on the outside and inside of your dustbin will discourage flies and other insects from showing an interest in its contents.

Keep any garden manure well away from the house as flies are attracted to it and will swarm around it.

Use insecticides carefully as some strips should not be placed in a room used by elderly people or young children. Read the instructions.

Rub the flies' settling points with oil of lavender as they find this smell repellant.

Many herbs from the garden will act as insect repellants around the house. They can be made up as an alternative to lavender bags. Use cloves, chamomile, rosemary and dried orange peel.

Bay leaves in the larder will discourage flies and last for a year or more. Leave them on the branch and then use them for cooking when you need them.

MICE

Mice can be dangerous pests as they carry salmonella and if allowed to reach your food can infect it. They can be heard scratching around in the woodwork, or you may see their small, brown drop- pings around the house. They have very sharp teeth which they need to keep that way, so they will chew through  most things including electricity cables, packets and newspapers. They breed at a great rate and it is not long before a minor problem becomes a major infestation, so get rid of them as quickly as possible. Your local health authority will be able to help. Sometimes the smell of a cat will get rid of them. Try borrowing a friend's pet. If this fails, then either trap them or put down rodenticide. Try using a trap first as rodenticide is *poisonous*.

If you do use a rodenticide follow the manufacturer's instructions *to the letter*, and try, if possible, to isolate the area that is being treated by locking up the room, so that pets and children are really safe.

Put anything other than cheese in a mouse trap as they do not particularly like it. They are much more fond of chocolate, nuts and peanut butter.

Mice do not like the smell of fresh mint. If you have sprigs of peppermint in the garden, scatter them around the areas affected by the mice; or use oil of peppermint. Saturate paper with it, and place in mouse-affected areas.

MITES

There are a variety of mites in the house, mostly so small they are seldom seen, unless they catch your eye when they move. The house or furniture mite may be found in old upholstery, especially if it is damp. Treat as for book lice. Dust mites are ubiquitous. Though harmless, some people are allergic to them.

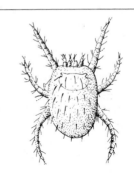

MOSQUITOES

These breed in stagnant water. If you can get them while they are still breeding, drop a spot of paraffin into the water to kill the larvae. If mosquitoes are annoying you outdoors, light a cigarette or a couple of candles as they do not like smoke. Nor do they like basil so keep a pot of it in places they frequent.

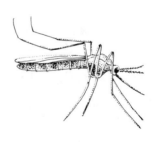

MOTHS

It is the moth larvae that actually do the damage to cloth. They are most often found in the folds of the cloth and are surrounded by a fluffy substance. The first thing to do is to brush the larvae off the material. They attack natural fibres, especially wool, and are cap-

197

able of eating the wool out of a wool and synthetic mix.

If you find the larvae eating the carpet, the best way to destroy them is to steam them to death with a warm iron and a damp cloth. Once you have removed the larvae treat the carpet with an aerosol preparation that will protect the carpet from further damage.

Never put anything away with greasy stains on it, as moths will be attracted to the grease.

If you find that clothing is being attacked by moths, remove the larvae, bearing in mind that they may be tucked under pocket and collar flaps. Then clear the drawer, checking everything else for damage. Wipe the inside with a paraffin rag to prevent any further infestation. Line drawers with newspaper so that the larvae cannot get back in through the bottom of the drawer.

Epsom salts sprinkled among garments in long storage will help make sure that the clothes are not attacked by moths.

If you are winding knitting wool for long-term storage then wind it around a central ball of camphor.

PLASTER BEETLES

Found in damp plaster in either new or old houses: they are a dark colour and about 2 mm ($\frac{1}{10}$ inch) long. They feed off the mould that grows on the damp plaster and should disappear when the mould dries out. They may be a sign of a damp spot you didn't know about.

RATS

Rats represent a grave health risk as they carry many diseases. They are encouraged to appear where there is food or rubbish left lying around which they will use to make nests with. There are two types of common rat – the sewer rat and the water rat. They are larger than mice, have longer tails and can grow to 23 cm (9 inches) or more. There are many poisonous rat baits available but they must be used with great care.

If you are unable to deal with the problem yourself then get in touch with the health authorities. They will come and get rid of them. If you do succeed in killing a rat, make sure that you either bury it deep in the garden or burn it.

SILVERFISH

They appear in damp areas of the house; usually around the bathroom. If they come from other areas this may indicate a problem with damp that you do not know about. They are small, wingless insects with cigar-shaped bodies that move quickly. They feed off starch and glue that they find around the

house and can be harmful to books. Use an insecticide, or sprinkle boric acid mixed with a little sugar, around the places they come from. However, do not use boric acid if there is a possibility that children or dogs will touch it.

SPIDERS

These are much maligned as they do no harm and in fact will rid your house or crawling insects as well as flies. If you do not like touching them but still wish to remove them, open the window or door in readiness, and use a long-handled mop or broom. Once the spider has crawled on to the end, take it to the outside and shake. Alternatively, you can use a piece of paper in the same way, if you don't mind coming close to a spider. Or, place a glass over the spider once it has crawled inside, cover the bottom of the glass with a piece of paper, then take it outside, uncover it and leave the spider to crawl out.

WEEVILS

These are small beetles with long noses. Some eat food, others live on wood (see Woodworm). Those which are food-eating may be found in flour or bread although they are not very common. Any products affected should be returned to the shop. Then spray all round with an insecticide.

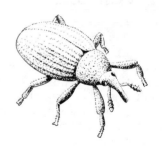

WOODWORM

These are the grub of the furniture beetle and will appear accompanied by holes and piles of fresh sawdust. They attack any kind of wood, new or old, so check wood floors and furniture when you are cleaning. Small areas can be treated with a proprietary fluid from hardware or DIY

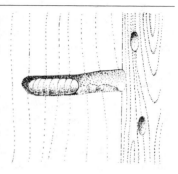

stores. Follow the instructions that come with the fluid. Do not inhale the fumes and do not let it splash on the skin. If possible work in the open air and wear overalls to protect your clothing.

If you find that the infestation is in structural beams of the house or that it covers a large area, then it is essential that you call in professional help. Use someone well known, who will be around to keep to a guarantee, which will usually last about twenty years.

As a precaution, check any second-hand or antique furniture that you bring into the house for signs of fresh woodworm activity.

"Cut Your Coat According To Your Cloth"

Hints on
fabrics and fabric care

Cleaning labels and codes

CARE LABELS

It's the law: Manufacturers must, by law, label all garments and state the type of material they are made from. Many manufacturers also add the care labels which correspond to internationally agreed washing and care symbols. This should mean that it is possible to understand the care of foreign-made clothes as well as British clothes. It is as well to understand these labels as they provide information about fabric care and how to keep the material in its best condition. This is important, as many fabrics must be washed at the recommended temperature to get them really clean.

This symbol gives the recommended washing instructions.

This symbol means do not machine wash.

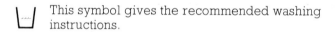 The figure above the line indicates the machine code that the fabric should be washed at. This may correspond with your washing machine. These are also shown on the side of the detergent pack. The temperature shown below the line is a guide for water temperature.

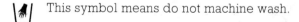 This indicates that the article must not be washed.

This indicates that the article can be bleached with chlorine bleach in solution.

Do not use bleach on garments bearing this sign.

The circle indicates that the garment should be dry-cleaned only.

The letter inside the circle indicates the kind of dry cleaning fluid that should be used on the garment (see below). This will not concern you unless you are attempting to clean it in a laundrette dry cleaning machine, in which case you should check that the symbols correspond with fluid in the machine you are using (see page 206).

This symbol provides you with a guide to ironing the garment.

One dot means use a cool iron on such fabrics as acrylic, nylon, acetate, polyester and viscose.

Two dots mean use a warm iron. This should be used on such fabric as polyester mixes and wool fibres.

Three dots indicate a very hot setting which should only be used on cotton and linen.

This indicates that the article should not be ironed because it would harm it to do so.

This symbol indicates the drying instructions.

Tumble dry.   Line dry.

Drip dry.   Dry flat.

(A) If the dry cleaning symbol has an A in its circle then any type of dry cleaning fluid can be used. This is useful if you want to use the laundrette dry cleaning machine.

(P) **in the circle** means that many dry cleaning solvents can be used, i.e. you can use a laundrette machine. Both these symbols mean that any dry cleaner can cope with the garment.

(P) **in the circle and a line underneath** means do not use a laundrette machine and that cleaners should be made aware of the symbol as certain precautions have to be taken.

(F) indicates that only a certain number of cleaners will be able to deal with this. It usually appears on a delicate fabric. When you take a garment into a cleaners bearing this sign, point it out to the cleaner and ask if he has the chemical. It indicates that solvent 113 should be used on the garment.

Aftercare: After either dry cleaning the clothes yourself, or having them cleaned, make sure that they are well aired before they are put away as the fumes are quite poisonous. Articles you should never dry clean yourself include padded materials, duvets, or anything that is likely to house the fumes for a long time.

FABRIC CARE

Wash programmes: There are nine basic wash programmes. Most modern automatic washing machines are designed and labelled to cope with them. You will also find these symbols on most packets of washing powder. The temperature in the tub symbol indicates the water heat for machines. Corresponding details for washing by hand are also given. Codes 8 and 9 are later additions, usually only seen on foreign clothes. The codes are part of the International Textile Care Labelling Code.

Wash code	1 95°	2 60°	3 60°	4 50°	5 40°	6 40°	7 40°	8 30°	9 95°
Machine Washing	Very hot to boil Maximum wash	Hot Maximum wash	Hot Medium wash	Hand-hot Medium wash	Warm Medium wash	Warm Minimum wash	Warm Minimum wash	Cool Minimum wash	Very hot (95°C) to boil
Hand Washing	Hand-hot (50°C) or boil	Hand-hot (50°C)	Hand-hot (50°C)	Hand-hot	Warm	Warm	Warm Do not rub	Cool	Hand-hot (50°C) or boil
Agitation	Maximum	Maximum	Medium	Medium	Maximum	Minimum	Minimum Do not rub	Minimum	Medium
Rinsing, spinning, wringing	Spin or wring	Spin or wring	Cold rinse Short spin or drip-dry	Cold rinse Short spin or drip-dry	Spin or wring	Cold rinse Short spin Do not wring	Spin Do not hand wring	Cold rinse Short spin Do not wring	Cold rinse Drip-dry
Suitable fabrics	White cotton and linen fabrics without special finishes	Cotton, linen or viscose fabrics without special finishes and colour-fast at 60°C	White nylon; white polyester/cotton fabrics	Coloured nylon, polyester special finish cotton and viscose; acrylic cotton; coloured polyester/cotton	Machine washable wool, cotton, linen or viscose fabrics with colours fast at 40°C, but not at 60°C	Acrylics; acetate and triacetate, including mixtures with wool; polyester/wool blends	Wool, including blankets and wool mixtures with cotton or viscose; silk	Silk and printed acetate fabrics with colours not fast at 40°C	Cotton articles with special finishes capable of being boiled, but requiring drip-drying

A-Z of fabrics and fabric care

ACETATE

Normally used for lining other fabric. Looks silky, but can come in other textures. Washing instructions depend on what fabric the acetate is lining. Acetate itself can be washed on wash code 6 or 8. Wool lined with acetate mixtures should be hand washed carefully. Use warm water with a cold rinse and a short spin. It myst not be wrung.

Iron while still damp but re-soak the whole garment if it gets too dry. Do not sprinkle water on it or the finish will be blotchy.

Acetate is dissolved by solvent stain removers, and by vinegar, so never use them in an attempt to remove stains.

ACRYLIC

Usually used to simulate fine wool. It is a synthetic material; soft and durable and easier to wash than wool. Follow the care label on the garment – it can usually be machine washed on code 6. Beware, however, of using too high washing temperatures, anything above 40°C/104°F will set in creases that never come out.

It is sensible to wash acrylic garments often, and well, before the dirt becomes impregnated. To wash by hand (some acrylic/wool mixes need treating this way) use warm water, but be careful in handling while wet. Do not twist or agitate too much.

A cold rinse will help to stop any creasing in acrylics, but be sure either to do a very short spin, or to treat as wool and lay between towels and then roll, or you will put fresh creases in.

Do not hang up to drip-dry, or the garment will be lengthened by its own weight. Dry as for wool, flat.

Never iron acrylic when it is slightly damp, otherwise it will stretch out of shape. Wait patiently until it is completely dry. If the fabric is pleated, then rinse in warm water and drip-dry. Do not bleach.

ANGORA

Rabbit fur wool, has a very fluffy appearance. It is often mixed with other materials to give it strength and to make it easier to care for. Wash as for wool.

BATISTE

A very lightweight fabric used to make underwear, linings and shirts. It is made from a variety of fabrics usually cotton, silk or viscose and must be washed according to the material from which it is made.

BOUCLÉ

This has a bobbly surface made up of loops of fibres, and is often used in knitted garments. It can also come in fabric form, and in a variety of materials, such as wool, cotton and synthetic fibres. It should, therefore, be washed according to its care label for the fabric used. If you are unsure of its treatment, dry clean.

BRAID

Braid trimmings should not be washed. If you want to wash the garment they are on, then first remove the trimmings. Silver braid can be cleaned with dry bicarbonate of soda. Make sure that the powder gets well into all the crevices. It will take some time to absorb the dirt so leave on for as long as possible. Take off again with a stiff brush, or an old toothbrush. To clean gold braid, use a mix of dry cream of tartar and stale breadcrumbs. Leave on as before, then remove with a stiff brush.

BROCADE

The raised surface on this decorative border material makes it difficult to wash successfully. It is woven from several different fibres, some silky, so it must be dry-cleaned.

BRODERIE ANGLAISE

Most broderie anglaise is used as a border on cotton material. Unless it is very delicate it can be washed with other cotton garments. Check first that the material it is attached to is cotton. If it is very delicate, wash by hand.

BUMP

This cotton curtain lining material cannot be washed as it is not of very high quality. Dry clean.

CALICO

Calico is usually made from pure cotton, but, on occasions, can be mixed with synthetic material. It is uncoloured and has a slightly rough texture to it. Wash as for cotton when it is a synthetic mix. If you need to whiten calico, do so in the first wash by adding a drop of white spirit to the water.

CAMBRIC

Cotton fabric with a smooth appearance. Wash as for cotton and starch to restore its slightly stiff appearance.

CANDLEWICK

This is used for making bedspreads and dressing gowns because of its warmth. It comes in a variety of colours and the tufts make a variety of patterns. Used to be made entirely from cotton, but now, to reduce the price, it is often mixed with synthetic fibres. Wash according to the more delicate fibre. Shake well after washing to restore the pile.

CANVAS

Canvas is a very strong fabric mainly used for making bags and for upholstery. It has a slightly rough finish and is usually left in its natural colour. Wash with detergent and warm water. Scrub with a nail brush to remove stubborn marks. Now made from a variety of fibres including cotton and synthetic.

CHALLIS

An expensive but beautiful fabric made from wool. Wash as for wool but by hand only.

CHEESECLOTH

A fabric that was not much used for clothing until it became fashionable a few years ago. Very lightweight and loosely woven. Made from cotton, or cotton mixture, it must be hand washed to keep its shape. Do not wring but use towels to absorb the moisture. Iron while damp, stretching into shape as you do so.

CHENILLE

This is used for heavy curtains and tablecloths; can be pure silk or synthetic. Clean according to the fibres used to make the chenille. It has a raised pile and often comes in very plush colours, which may run in the wash so wash sep-arately at first. If the chenille is very old, the material is often rather delicate, so it is preferable to wash carefully by hand or dry clean.

CHIFFON

A very soft, sheer fabric made from silk or synthetic fibres. If it is made from viscose or silk, it is best to have it dry-cleaned; otherwise wash according to the fibre type. Iron while still damp. This will give you an opportunity to ease the fabric back into its original shape.

CHINTZ

This is cotton with a glazed finish on its right side. It is traditionally printed with flowers and used for furnishings. Old chintz should be dry-cleaned. Modern fabric can be washed, but should be treated carefully when still wet. Do not rub or twist. Do not treat with starch. The final rinse must be cold to prevent excessive creasing. Iron while still damp.

CIRÉ

Ciré is a synthetic material, often made from nylon, and has a shiny finish. It should be hand washed.

CORDUROY

A very hard wearing fabric with a soft, velvety raised pile. It is used for upholstery and for garments. Made from a cotton or a cotton mix. Best washed by hand according to the mixture. Rough treatment when wet will harm the pile. Do not wring or twist. While the material is drying, smooth the pile in the right direction with a soft clean cloth. Shake well. Iron on the wrong side while still slightly damp using a warm iron.

COTTON

A versatile fabric, strong and easy to care for. Comes in such a variety of weaves and finishes that it is essential to follow any instructions that come with the material. Used for almost anything – upholstery, clothing, fabrics, curtains – it also comes in a variety of mixes with synthetic fibres. Can have special finishes to make it waterproof or flameproof.

White cotton can be boiled to keep it white.

Most colourfast cottons will stand a hot water wash. However, even colourfast cottons sometimes bleed slightly at every wash so it is safest to wash them separately. If the cotton does bleed then wash it separately in warm water. Some cottons do tend to shrink, particularly jeans, unless they are pre-shrunk. Any special finishes should be washed according to the care label. Detergent, not soap, should be used on flame-resistant finishes. Most cottons can be ironed with a hot iron on the wrong side. Glazed cotton should be ironed on the right side to make it shine.

CRÊPE AND CRÊPE DE CHINE

Crêpe is usually thin with a wrinkled, bumpy texture and is made from a variety of fabrics. Some crêpes have to be dry cleaned, so follow the care label. Otherwise wash in warm water by hand. Crêpe must be ironed on the wrong side while still damp. Crêpe de Chine is of lighter weight with a slight shine. Made from silk or synthetic fibres. Treat according to the fabric, iron on the wrong side when damp.

DAMASK

A fancy fabric with a design woven into the fabric in shiny thread. Made from a variety of fibres including silk, and synthetic materials. Treat according to fabric.

DENIM

Usually made from cotton, although it does now appear in synthetic mixes, with white warp thread and coloured, usually blue, weft thread. Hard-wearing but it does shrink in the wash. Tends to wear in patches and the colour fades. Wash on its own as the colour never really becomes fast. Iron while still damp.

DRILL

This has a slightly raised surface, but is useful for clothes that get a lot of use, as it wears well. Wash as for cotton.

FELT

Made from matted fibres of thick wool. Felt cannot be washed as it shrinks very easily. Dry clean only.

FLANNEL

This is usually a woollen fabric with a choice of finishes that are either smooth or slightly raised. Anything large or precious should be taken to the dry cleaners; otherwise wash very gently as for wool.

GABARDINE

This fabric is used mostly for raincoats and outdoor coats. It is a woven fabric, often made of a blend of fibres. Often treated with a water-resistant finish. Should only be dry-cleaned.

GINGHAM

Old-fashioned checked cotton fabric, but can now be made from a fibre mix. Wash accordingly. Iron back into shape when still damp.

HESSIAN

A rough fabric made with an open weave. Hard-wearing and made from natural fibres, it has a variety of uses. It can even be used as a wall covering. This material must be dry-cleaned.

JERSEY

This fabric has a knitted surface and stretches. It is made from a number of different fibres, including expensive wool, which must be dry-cleaned. Viscose jersey should also be dry-cleaned. Synthetic types should be washed according to the label. Do not twist. A short spin will not do it any harm. Dry as wool.

LACE

Lace can be made from a variety of materials, some are synthetic. If it is not delicate, then wash as for the fibre it is made from. If it is old and delicate, protect it by washing it inside a pillow case or a small bag. Press the lace according to the type of fibre, but be careful in your handling at this stage as it is easy to catch the lace and rip it. Press under a cloth if necessary. The lace may need to be ironed and pulled back into shape.

LAWN

A very fine soft cotton or cotton and synthetic mix. Wash by hand and spin gently. Can be ironed while still damp on the wrong side.

LEATHER

Coats and jackets – treat with washing-up liquid in a solution of 1 part liquid to 5 parts lukewarm water. Do not saturate the surface but leave for a few minutes before wiping off again. It is best to test this method first on an inconspicuous part. If the colour begins to come out of the leather, use a weaker solution. Ballpoint pen marks will often come off if you treat them immediately with milk, or rub them very gently with a little white spirit. For other marks always have leather clothing dry cleaned. Never use home dry cleaning fluid on leather, it will damage it.

Gloves – wash according to the type of leather, using a proprietary glove cleaning shampoo. It is best to wear them while you do this. Hang them out of the sunlight or away from intense heat. Put them back on your hands for a moment or two before they are completely dry so that they are a comfortable shape.

Shoes – soften leather with castor oil, polish with proprietary shoe cleaner and the correct colour for the shoes, buff up with a soft cloth. Shoes that are soaked through with water should be left to dry away from heat. It may take some time, so be patient. Trying to speed up the process by placing them near a fire or heater will crack the leather. Stuff them with newspaper to absorb the moisture and help to keep their shape while they are drying. Replace the newspaper as it becomes damp. Use shoe trees on leather boots to help boots last longer. There are many preparations for protecting leather from the weather, and from wear, so investigate these.

LINEN

An expensive fabric, as it is made from natural fibre flax, linen is very strong and hard-wearing and is used for table cloths and napkins as well as garments. It is possible to wash colourfast linen on codes 1 or 2 but check the care label. If you want to hand wash, use hot soapy water and treat as cotton. Linen can be boiled to restore its whiteness, but it may shrink. Iron with a hot iron on the wrong side when still damp, as this is the only way to get the creases out. Once the fabric is dry, creases are impossible to remove.

MOHAIR

This fibre comes from the angora goat. It has to be washed as for wool, although some mixtures may take other treatment. Check care label for details. Do not wash mohair jumpers too often as it is difficult to prevent them from furring badly.

MOIRÉ

Moiré is usually made from silk, although demand has meant the introduction of other fibres. The fabric is water-marked in great swirls with a raised surface. It can only be dry-cleaned.

MUSLIN

Originally used in the dairy for straining cheese, it is now used as a fashion material. It has a large open weave and is usually slightly sheer. It should be hand-washed as cheesecloth. Iron while still damp.

NET

An open mesh fabric with many uses, though principally as curtaining. Comes now in a variety of fibres, usually synthetic. Net curtains should be shaken well before washing as the dirt tends to get stuck in the holes. If net curtains are made from synthetic fibre then wash accordingly, but do not machine wash as it is too rough on the net. Squeeze gently, do not wring.

Some cotton net tends to shrink, so allow for this when buying. Leave a good length hem. The easiest method of drying is to drip-dry until damp, and then put a stair rod in the bottom seam and rehang the curtains. This way the curtains will not need ironing. If you have to iron them, do it very carefully while the net is still damp. Dress net must be washed by hand in soap flakes and warm water.

NYLON

A synthetic fibre which is strong, tough and versatile. Used in clothes. Follow the care label. Most nylon can be machine washed at code 3 for whites, and 4 for coloureds. Wash by hand in hand hot water. Make sure that the water is not too hot otherwise white nylon starts to take on a greyish tinge. Never use bleach on nylon. Use a cold rinse to ensure that you get a crease-free finish. If treated properly nylon should not need to be ironed. If it is necessary, then iron with a warm iron while still slightly damp.

OILSKIN

Used for rainwear and for tablecloths, it is treated with oil and has a shiny surface. Clean by wiping with a damp cloth.

PIQUÉ

A strong cotton or synthetic material with a raised design. Wash according to fibre, shake to raise the pile, and then iron on the back on a thick clean cloth to protect the pile from flattening.

POLYESTER

A synthetic fibre, though sometimes blended with natural fibres, it is easy to care for and very versatile, lending itself to woven or knitted textures. Machine wash according to the label. Most polyesters will machine wash at code 3 for white and 4 for coloureds. Hand washing should be done in hand hot water. Water above that temperature will damage the fibres. Never boil. A cold rinse and a short spin will ensure that there are few creases. Some fabrics, especially those with pleats, are best drip-dried – study the care label. A cool iron will get rid of any creases when the fabric is dry.

POPLIN

Usually a cotton fabric, woven with a fairly smooth finish, now produced in synthetic fibres too. Must be washed according to the fibre type. See under fabric heading.

SAILCLOTH

A very strong cotton or cotton mix fabric. Wash according to the fibre.

SATIN

A luxurious, smooth, shiny fabric, originally made from closely woven silk fibres, but now more often, and more cheaply, made from synthetic fibres. Dress satin can usually be washed according to the fibre it is made of. The heavier upholstery satin must be dry cleaned. Iron with a cool iron on the wrong side while still damp to restore the shiny finish.

SEERSUCKER

A cotton or cotton mix with a bumpy crinkly finish to it, it comes in very bright colours and stripes. Wash according to the fibre content. There is no need to iron.

SERGE

A very strong hard-wearing fabric, principally used for clothes, such as uniforms, that need to last a long time. Originally serge was made from pure wool, but now it is mixed with cotton or synthetic fibres which give it a longer life. Study the care label. It should be dry-cleaned.

SHANTUNG

Originally the name for wild silk material with bobbly threads, giving a very uneven surface. Now imitated with synthetic fibres. Wash according to the fibre content. Iron on the wrong side when completely dry.

SILK

A delicate natural fibre with a beautiful feel and appearance. Must be hand washed to prevent damage. Do not boil or soak. Wash in hand-hot water, squeezing the soap through the material as you do for wool. The temperature of the rinsing water should be the same as for washing. Put the silk between two towels to absorb the moisture. Do not wring. Iron while still slightly damp on the wrong side.

Do not allow silk to become heavily soiled; perspiration stains are almost impossible to remove. Do not rub silk while wet, as this is when it is in its weakest state. Anything that is badly stained should be dry-cleaned before the stain is set. Also dry clean taffeta, ties, scarves, non-colourfast items and highly decorated silk. If the garment has become too dry to iron then dampen it entirely, otherwise small water marks appear. Do not wash in enzyme detergents as they will harm the delicate fibres.

SUEDE

Always follow the manufacturer's instructions. Some suedes can be washed by hand in soap flakes but only if the label says so. Chamois leather can usually be washed successfully. If in any doubt, dry-clean.

TAFFETA

This is traditionally made from silk but now more often produced in synthetic fabrics. If the taffeta is made from silk then send it to be dry-cleaned, or treat according to the label. Most man-made taffeta can be washed but must be handled gently. Use a mild detergent and warm water, squeezing the soap through the material. Use a cold water rinse and hang up to drip-dry. Iron while still damp on the wrong side.

TOWELLING

This is usually 100% cotton with a looped weave designed to have high absorbency. It can be machine or hand-washed according to the care label. If you are washing towels in the machine, reduce your normal washload, since towels need more room to ensure adequate rinsing. Deep colours have to be washed separately, as a rule, at least for the first few washes. They can be spun or wrung dry. Terry towelling used for nappies should be washed at a very high temperature and thoroughly rinsed. Fabric conditioner will keep them soft.

TWEED

This material is traditionally made with wool, usually used for suits, coats or skirts. If it is woollen then it must be treated according to the care label or dry-cleaned. If it is made from synthetic fibres it should be possible to wash carefully according to the fibre content. Check with the care label.

VELOUR

A velvety fabric, now widely used for dresses, it is lighter and more flexible than velvet, but with the same rich appearance. It is made in a variety of materials both natural and synthetic. Treat according to the care label. If it is crushed, treat as for velvet.

VELVET

An expensive, but luxurious, fabric which is now available in many fibres, some of which are easy to care for. Cotton velvet and silk velvet should be dry-cleaned, especially if you are unsure of its fibre content. If the care label indicates that it is washable, follow the instructions and drip-dry. If it is necessary to iron velvet, then do so over a number of thick towels to avoid crushing the pile; or, even better, hang the garment in the bathroom while someone is running a bath. This should straighten out any creases. If the pile becomes crushed, then hold the fabric over a steaming saucepan or kettle for a few minutes. This should perk it up again.

VISCOSE

This is used extensively to imitate natural fibres cheaply. It must be handled with care. Treat as for wool, squeezing the detergent through the material. Avoid wringing or rough handling. Iron while still damp on the wrong side. Do not press along the seams or marks will be left on the surface.

VIYELLA

This is a brand name for a soft cotton and wool mix and must be washed very gently by hand and treated as wool. Iron while still damp on the wrong side.

VOILE

A floaty, sheer fabric which can be made from synthetic or natural fibres. Treat according to the care label or according to the fabric. Do not wring, but roll up in a towel to get rid of the moisture. Iron very gently while still damp.

WOOL

This requires great care in its handling and in its washing in order to preserve its special qualities. It is the warmest and the softest of all the fabrics available, and is widely used in the manufacture of every type of garment. It is very versatile and can be knitted or woven and it is also used in conjunction with other fibres.

Some wools can be washed in a machine – check the label carefully. These should be laundered according to the care label or on code 5 or 7. However most wool needs hand washing. Each article should be given individual attention. It is best if the article is washed in a soapless detergent, or one that is specially designed for wool. If you are using a general washing powder, read the instructions on the pack for washing wool. Try not to rub the garment too much or pull it about.

If you suspect that the garment may lose its shape badly, draw around it when dry and then you will be able to reshape it to this pattern when the washing process is over. When you have diluted the detergent to its correct strength, put the garment in the water and squeeze the liquid through the fabric. Handle the wool very gently at this stage otherwise you will find that the finished garment is badly felted.

To reduce the risk of shrinking, wash and rinse wool in water of the same temperature. As you remove the garment from the water, lift gently, making sure that no part drags, or it will stretch.

It is possible to spin dry some types of wool (check the care label). To make sure that it comes to no harm, wrap in a towel and spin for short while only. Otherwise, to get rid of moisture, wrap up in two towels.

All wool must be dried flat and away from artificial heat, at room temperature. Do not tumble dry or it will felt.

When the wool is still slightly damp it is possible to iron using a cool temperature setting.

Hang woollen garments over the bannister, or the back of a chair to give them extra ventilation. It is also possible to suspend a lightweight woollen article over the bath on a net. Stick the net to the bath with suction cups and then lay the woollen article flat on the net. This way the wool dries more quickly. (Not suitable for heavy articles.)

Oiled wool must be washed in well-dissolved soap flakes

to avoid taking the oil out of the yarn.

Never soak wool, and never bleach it.

If you have washed an item and it has shrunk badly, try soaking it in tepid water mixed with a little hair shampoo. It may soften the fibres so that you can pull it back into shape.

Add a little olive oil in the final rinse of woollen blankets to soften them.

White or light-coloured wool clothes must not be dried in the sun otherwise they will tend to turn yellow.

Add a teaspoon of glycerine to the rinsing water of woollen garments to help keep them soft.

Wool cellular blankets may be better dry-cleaned than washed ordinarily. If this is the case, it will be shown on the care label.

WINCEYETTE

This is a brand name for a soft fabric with a slightly woolly finish, made most commonly in cotton, wool and viscose. It should be treated as wool.

"It's No Use Crying Over Spilt Milk"

How to deal with all types of stains

Stains

FIRST AID

Speed is the secret of success in dealing with stains. The faster you tackle them, the more likely you are to be successful. Old stains are far more difficult to remove than new ones, so instant action pays dividends.

Soak **non-greasy** stains in cold water if the fabric is washable, sponge them with water if it is not. Squirt soda from a syphon on to carpets for quick emergency action.

Sprinkle talcum powder on to **greasy stains** to keep them under control while you hunt for the solvent. You can also use French chalk or Fuller's earth for this purpose.

Pour salt over **highly coloured liquid** stains, those from fruit, red wine, beetroot and blood, for instance. This will absorb the moisture and, with it, some of the colour. Do not sprinkle salt on to a carpet, however, as it tends to stay in the pile, attract moisture and create permanent damp patches. Blot up as much of the stain as possible with paper tissue or kitchen paper towelling, as soon as it is discovered. If the garment is particularly delicate, or valuable, then don't risk treating it yourself – take it straight to a dry cleaner. It pays, in this case, to consult a professional. This also goes for anything that has a special finish, or is not colourfast.

SAFETY CHECK LIST

1. Find out whether the fabric is washable or not. Most non-washable items need to go to a dry cleaner, though straightforward grease marks can often be removed with a proprietary solvent or an aerosol dry cleaner.

2. Check that the fabric you are tackling can take the chemical that you plan to use. Hydrogen peroxide must not be used on nylon or fabrics with a special finish – flame-proof ones, for instance. Acetate fabrics – and that includes tri-acetates – cannot take vinegar, methylated spirit or commercial solvents.

3. **The colourfastness test:** To make sure that the fabric is colourfast before you apply the stain remover, find a patch that will not show should it turn out not to be colourfast: for instance, a piece of hem turn-up, a seam allowance, wrist or neck facing or pocket backing. Then apply some of the stain remover to it and lay it on a piece of clean white cloth. put another piece of white cloth over the top and press gently with a warm iron. If the colour comes out, take the garment to a dry cleaner, don't tackle it yourself.

4. Read the instructions carefully, particularly on any packets or bottles of chemicals, proprietary cleaners or general cleaning materials you plan to use. Biological detergents, for instance, will not be effective unless the water is at the right temperature, as given on the manufacturer's instructions (see page 179).

5. Many of the items used in stain removal are highly toxic and should always be handled with the greatest of care. Store them well out of the reach of children and away from food. Never decant them into other containers, leave them in their original packets or boxes and label them clearly as dangerous. Most of the solvents used are inflammable and vaporous. When using these, open the windows and doors for safe ventilation and keep them well away from naked flames.

6. If you use a dry cleaning solvent on a garment or piece of bedding, hang it out of doors before using, until you are sure that all the solvent has evaporated (see also pages 232–3 for treatment of bedding).

7. Use proprietary grease solvents, methylated and white spirits with caution on rubber-backed carpets and upholstery as permanent damage could be caused to the rubber or foam filling. Do not use too much liquid and blot dry thoroughly once the stain is loosened.

GENERAL TIPS

When using a solvent on a stain, be sure to lay a piece of clean white cloth underneath to catch the dirt, otherwise you are simply pushing it around the fabric.

When you are using a solvent as a second or third stage in stain removal, or if the stain is caused by preparations like tar, paint or nail varnish, work from the back or underside of the fabric, not from the front. You are much more likely to be successful because you are pushing the stain back up to the surface of the fabric, not working it through. When tackling a spot stain, work from the outer edge towards the middle, not vice versa. This stops it from spreading further and avoids that tell-tale ring effect.

Don't rub at a stain, dab at it, rubbing may damage the fabric and spread the mark.

Always use a piece of white cloth for stain removal (stockpile pieces of old sheeting for the purpose). Using a coloured cloth could spell disaster, as the dye could bleed. Call in the professionals if you don't succeed. Dry cleaners have all sorts of specialized solvents available which are not on sale in the shops.

Renew the pad, cottonwool or piece of fabric you're using on the stain frequently, otherwise if it becomes grubby you run the risk of pushing the mark back into the material again.

STAIN REMOVERS FOR YOUR STORE-CUPBOARD

Ammonia is a useful stain removing aid and should generally be used in a diluted form – 1 part ammonia to 3 parts water is the most usual one, though some remedies call for just a few drops of ammonia to be added to washing or rinsing water. Fabric is prone to bleeding when it is treated with ammonia, so be sure to do a colourfast test (see page 227) before you start. Ammonia gives off unpleasant fumes and can burn the skin if it comes into contact with it in an undiluted form, so handle it with care (see page 176).

Amyl acetate is very like nail varnish remover, but it is safe to use on acetate fabrics. It will dissolve some paints and glues and, of course, nail lacquer. It must be used with great care as it is inflammable.

Biological detergents (also known as enzyme detergents) are specially designed to digest protein based stains such as egg, blood, milk (see also page 179). If you are tackling a bad stain of this type, it is useful to soak the item for some time in biological detergent, but follow the instructions on the packet about water temperature. The colder the water is, the longer the soak needed. For bad stains, it is a good idea to soak through the night. Do not soak wool, silk, or anything that has a special finish in this type of detergent as it is very strong. And do not put anything with metal on it (buttons or clasps, for instance) into biological detergents as it may cause the metal to stain the garment.

Bleach is useful for stains on white cotton or linen. It should always be used diluted – neat bleach could damage the fabric irreparably. The ideal dilution for dabbing on to small stains is 5–10 ml (1–2 teaspoons) of bleach to 1 litre (2 pints) of water. If there is a large area to cover, mix 10 ml (2 teaspooons) of bleach to 10 litres (2½ gallons) of cold water. Soak the item in the solution for up to an hour. Always rinse the item well after dabbing or soaking. To prevent the stain from being bleached lighter than the surrounding fabric, immerse the whole garment in the solution. Thorough rinsing is vital, otherwise there is a danger that the traces of bleach will continue to act on the fabric and damage it badly (see also page 177).

Bleach cannot be used on synthetics, delicate fabrics like wool or silk, or anything with a special finish.

Borax (domestic) comes from the chemist in powdered form. It works well at neutralizing acid stains such as those made by wine and fruit, and it can be used on most fabrics. However, it will start to bleach the colour out of some materials after about 15 minutes, so it should be used with some care. The usual dilution is 10 ml (2 teaspoons) to half a litre (1 pint) of warm water. In some forms of stain removal, particularly on white fabrics, it is sprinkled on to the stain, then the material is stretched over a basin and the stain is flushed out with boiling water.

Eucalyptus oil is a highly effective, highly pungent oil that deals efficiently with tar stains. Worth having in stock if you are liable to encounter tar.

Glycerine softens stains and is useful if the stain is already set before you discover it. Glycerine should be used diluted in equal parts with warm water, though in certain circumstances it is applied neat.

Hydrogen peroxide is a milder form of bleach and can be bought from a chemist. It is suitable for getting stains off the more delicate fabrics, such as wool and silk, but it must not be used on nylon or on fabrics with special finishes. Hydrogen peroxide generally comes in 20 vol. strength and this is usually diluted to a strength of 1 part hydrogen peroxide to 6 parts of water. White garments can be safely soaked overnight in this solution, but coloured fabrics could start to bleach out after about half an hour, so keep a wary eye on them (see also page 181).

Lemon is useful for first-aid on stains such as iron-mould.

Methylated spirit will very often take the residual colour out of a stain after it has been treated in other ways. It is also useful for treating non-washable items. Use it neat and always apply with a clean white cloth. Do not use methylated spirit on acetate or tri-acetate fabrics. Remember that it is poisonous and very inflammable (see page 182).

Proprietary grease solvents and dry cleaners come in liquid, dab-on, paste or spray versions and you should ideally have one of each. Always follow the manufacturer's instructions carefully and avoid inhaling fumes. Proprietary solvents can dissolve some plastics, rubbers, etc., and may be harmful to the skin, so use them with caution. They are very efficient at removing all forms of grease, but be selective as to which solvent you use for which stain.

Salt removes blood and perspiration stains from most materials and is useful for absorbing fruit stains, etc.

Washing soda is useful for removing greasy stains in some circumstances. It is inclined to be caustic, so use it with care.

White spirit is useful for removing some items, paint stains, for instance. It is very inflammable and poisonous.

Stains:
special cases

BLANKETS

Check the care label to see if the blanket is washable and make sure you can get it into your washing machine – remember it will weigh considerably more when it is wet. It may pay you to take it to the launderette instead, as many of them have heavy duty machines. Otherwise it is possible to wash a blanket in the bath, but you will need help in wringing it out. Small stains on synthetic blankets can generally be treated with detergent, followed by a wash. Other types of material and synthetic blankets with large stains on them should be taken to the dry cleaner.

PILLOWS

Do not attempt to wash a stained pillow unless you have a large efficient spin dryer as they take a very long time to dry. Never put pillows into a tumbler drier because of their weight and do not use a coin-op dry cleaning machine for fear of toxic fumes.

Any stains that you cannot spot-remove should be tackled by a professional; if the pillow is foam-filled and the stain has penetrated to the foam, wash the whole pillow in warm soapy water, squeezing it gently, not rubbing, as this will harm the texture of the pillow. Run fresh water through it until it runs clear, and dry it flat at the top of an airing cupboard. Use the same method for feather pillows, but they should be dried on the washing line and they will take a long time to dry. Pillows with synthetic fillings usually bear the manufacturer's washing instructions. They must never be dry-cleaned.

MATTRESSES

Blood and urine are two frequent stains on mattresses. A bloodstained mattress should be tipped on to its side, then sponged carefully with cold salt water, rinsed and then treated with upholstery shampoo. Urine stains should be sponged off with washing-up liquid in cold water, with a little disinfectant added to the rinse.

DUVETS

Stains should be mopped up as quickly as possible. If the filling is feather or down, it is important to isolate the stain; shake the feathers well away from it and tie them up out of the way. Then treat the stained area according to whatever type of stain it is.

Duvets with a synthetic filling can usually be washed, but check, as with blankets, that your machine will take them. Never attempt to clean a feather duvet in a coin-op dry cleaning machine, as there is a danger that you may be overcome by fumes when you take it back home. Take it instead to a specialist dry cleaner. Avoid further stains by using a washable cover on the duvet.

CARPETS

In an emergency, blot up any liquid spillages with tissues, then try squirting the stain with a soda syphon, it is very efficient at saturating the pile quickly. But take care that you do not get the carpet backing sodden, or it may be damaged. If the carpet becomes too wet, blot it with a cloth and put some newspaper underneath or prop up to allow the backing to dry. Then treat the stain with a carpet shampoo, and if possible, shampoo the whole area in order to give a good even finish.

Always keep a spare scrap of carpeting by you – if it is rubbed into the stained area when it is still damp, it will restore any colour that may have come out of the carpet pile through treating the stain.

A-Z
of stain removal

ADHESIVE

There are so many different kinds on the market that, for some of the more unusual kinds, the only solution is to ask the manufacturer's advice. However, try these methods on washable fabrics, furnishings and carpets or, if the material is non-washable, take it to your dry cleaner.

Clear adhesives: (e.g. Bostik 1, UHU) Use non-oily nail varnish remover or acetone, except on anything made of acetate. Check before you do so for colour bleeding or other problems.

Contact adhesives: (e.g. Bostik 3, Evostick) These can be washed off with cold water if you catch them before they dry. Otherwise try methylated spirit.

Epoxy adhesives: (e.g. Bostik 7, Araldite) consist of a glue plus a hardener that you mix together and they set with alarming speed. Once hard, there is no way you can tackle them. But it you catch them before they harden, the glue will come off with methylated spirit.

Animal or fish-based glues should come out in cold water. If they don't then apply household ammonia and rinse. If some stain persists, then soak in a biological detergent.

Latex adhesives: (e.g. Copydex, Cow Gum) These can be removed with a cloth soaked in water while still wet, or scraped off if they have dried. If the stain persists, send for the manufacturer's special solvent or try paint brush cleaner on it, but use with caution. An ammonia solution (see page 176) sometimes works. Latex glue on the fingers or on a hard surface can be simply rubbed or rolled off.

Model aircraft cement: Manufacturers sometimes make their own solvent, if so, use this. Otherwise remove the cement carefully with a cloth (be careful not to spread the adhesive around). Then dab at the remainder with liquid stain remover. Alternatively try using acetone on any fabric that is not made out of acetate. If the cement is stuck on wooden surfaces, try rubbing the area with sunflower oil.

Superglues: (e.g. Loctite Superglue) stick in a matter of seconds. If you get some on your skin, your clothes or on furnishings, act immediately – hold a pad soaked in water over the spot and it will gradually unstick.

ALCOHOL (see also **Beers** and **Wine**)

This is not found simply in drinks, but also in perfume and skin tonics and even some medicines.

Washable items: Sponge with warm water, then wash in the usual way.

Non-washable items: Spot treat with warm water and a little liquid detergent, then sponge with warm water and blot.

Furnishings, carpets: Sponge over with warm water and blot with tissues or paper towels, then follow up with carpet or upholstery shampoo if necessary.

ALES (see **Beers**)

ANIMAL STAINS

Speed is the essence here – all messes should be cleaned up as quickly as possible. First scrape off anything solid with a knife. Blot up the liquid with paper towels.

Washable items: Soak in biological detergent for as long as possible, then rinse thoroughly. If a stain remains, then treat with liquid detergent in warm water with 5 ml (1 teaspoonful) of 20 vol. hydrogen peroxide per 500 ml (1 pint) stirred in. Rinse well, then wash as usual.

Non-washable items: Blot or scrape, take to the dry cleaner.

Furnishings, carpets: Sponge with lukewarm, clean water. Blot the stain dry, then use a proprietary pet stain remover. On carpets, use diluted carpet shampoo first. Don't let the pile get too wet. If the stain persists, then loosen it with a solution of 1 part white distilled vinegar to 3 parts water, blot dry.

ANTI-PERSPIRANTS

Washable items: Apply a paste of bicarbonate of soda and salt to the area and leave for a quarter of an hour, then soak in biological detergent and wash in the usual way.

Non-washable items: Treat with bicarbonate of soda and salt as above, then take to the dry cleaner.

BALLPOINT PENS

Washable items: Soak spot in methylated spirit, then soak in biological detergent, rinse.

Non-washable items: Treat with methylated spirit if the mark is small, otherwise take to dry cleaner.

BEERS, ALES AND STOUTS

Washable items: Sponge immediately with clean water, then treat the stain with white distilled vinegar in a solution of 1 part vinegar to 5 parts water. Do not use this on acetate fabrics. Rinse well, soak in biological detergent and rinse again. If this does not work, then use a solution of 1 part 20 vol. hydrogen peroxide in 6 parts cold water, but test a piece of the fabric first to make sure that this doesn't take out the colour from the fabric. Old stains can sometimes be removed with methylated spirit. Finally, wash in the highest temperature the fabric can take.

Non-washable items: Treat with the vinegar solution as above.

Furnishings, carpets: Blot dry, try vinegar solution. First aid for carpets: try flushing with a syphon of soda, then use a carpet shampoo with 5 ml (1 teaspoonful) of wine vinegar to each 500 ml (1 pint) of water.

BEETROOT

Washable items: Soak immediately in cold water, leave for as long as possible, rub liquid detergent into the mark, unless the fabric is woollen. If this does not remove it, soak in biological detergent, sprinkle borax on the stain, pour over boiling water, then wash in the usual way.

Non-washable items: Sponge with cold water to lessen the stain then take to a dry cleaner.

Furnishings, carpets: Treat furnishings as for non-washable items. Squirt carpet with soda syphon or sponge with cold water and blot with tissues or paper towels, follow up with carpet shampoo.

BIRD DROPPINGS

Washable items: Scrape, sponge with salt water and soak in warm biological detergent.

Non-washable items: Mix 30 ml (2 tablespoons) household ammonia in 1 litre (2 pints) of water and soak stain, then dab with white vinegar. If the bird has been eating berries, then it may be necessary to bleach white fabrics to remove all the stain, but this can only be done with cottons. Blot, dab with a solution of detergent, spot rinse then blot dry.

237

Furnishings, carpets: Scrape up anything that is on the surface then wipe clean with warm water or use a proprietary dry cleaning spray.

BLOOD

Washable items: Soak immediately in strongly salted cold water. Keep changing the salt water solution until it runs clear, rub any remaining marks with a salt paste. If the stain is obstinate, try saliva for small spots (spit on to some cotton wool) or meat tenderizer. Then soak in biological detergent and wash in the normal way. Be sure all the stain has gone before you do this as the slightest heat will seal in the mark. If the stain is old, try loosening it overnight with a cool solution of biological detergent. In the case of wool fabrics, if possible, leave under a cold running tap so the water runs through the material. This will prevent it felting which is a danger if you rub the stain. Try this solution for obstinate blood stains: soak in a solution of 10 ml (2 teaspoons) of household ammonia to half a litre (1 pint) of water and a few drops of hydrogen peroxide. Follow by a wash in biological detergent.

Non-washable items: Sponge the spot using cold water with a few drops of ammonia in it. Rinse with cold water and blot dry. Take to a dry cleaner if necessary. Blood on suede and leather should be wetted immediately with cold water, then rubbed with a clean white cloth. Otherwise take to the dry cleaner.

Furnishings, carpets: Small stains on upholstery can be tackled with a paste of cornflour and salt. Allow it to dry, then brush off. Repeat if necessary. Place the object in the sun to dry if possible as this will help the cornflour to absorb the blood. Blankets should be soaked in cold salt water, then washed in biological detergent. For treatment of bloodstained mattresses, see page 233. Blood on carpets should be soaked out with cold water, blotted with paper tissues or kitchen towels until clear, then the carpet should be shampooed.

BUTTER, MARGARINE, FATS

Washable items: Take off as much of the surface deposit as possible, then treat with a proprietary grease solvent. The article should then be washed at the highest temperature that the material can stand.

Non-washable items: Use a proprietary grease solvent, preferably an aerosol one. If the stain is very big, then it will be necessary to take the articles to the dry cleaner.

Furnishings, carpets: Treat as for non-washable items, in the case of carpets, follow up with a dry carpet cleaner.

CANDLE WAX

Washable items: If possible put the article in the freezer to harden it. The pieces then break off easily. If any wax is left, put the fabric between two clean pieces of blotting paper or towelling and press with a warm iron. Use a low setting to melt the wax, which should be absorbed by the paper underneath. Shift the paper to a clean patch and continue until no more wax appears. Use a dry cleaning solvent to flush out any wax remaining and use methylated spirit to get rid of any residual colour – use this diluted with an equal quantity of water on rayon or nylon fabrics. Finally, give the garment the hottest wash that it can stand.

Non-washable items: Use the freezer method, then the iron, then dry cleaning fluid.

Furniture, furnishings and carpets: Wax on a wooden table top should be chilled first with a bagful of ice cubes, then gently scraped off, finally rubbed away with a hot clean cloth. Or, try washing it down with a solution of water and vinegar. Furnishings should be treated as non-washable fabrics. Carpets should have the wax picked off gently from the pile (chill first with ice cubes) then melted with a warm iron on blotting paper. Rub with methylated spirit, then sponge with diluted carpet shampoo and rinse.

CAR WAX AND POLISH

Blot all items with dry cleaning fluid, then liquid detergent, then rinse.

CARBON PAPER

Washable items: Rub with undiluted liquid detergent, then rinse well. If this doesn't work, then add a few drops of ammonia to the solution and try again.

Non-washable items: Dab with methylated spirit or white spirit (this method can be used for washable fabrics, too). On acetate or rayon, use a proprietary stain remover only, or take to the dry cleaner.

CHEWING GUM

Washable items: Get off as much as possible, then place the garment in a plastic bag in the freezer for an hour or so, when the gum should break off easily. Loosen any traces that are left by soaking in white vinegar or rubbing with egg white before washing.

Non-washable items: Freeze as above, then treat any marks left over with methylated or white spirit except for acetates or rayons. Then take to the dry cleaner if necessary.

Furnishings, carpets: Patient application of ice cubes to the spot may well harden chewing gum enough for it to be picked off. Follow up with methylated spirit to remove any traces left. Do not be tempted to use a vacuum cleaner on chewing gum in carpets, as it may gum up the works. Proprietary chewing gum remover in aerosols is available, which freezes the gum prior to removal.

CHOCOLATE

Washable items: Scrape off as much as possible immediately, then dab with soapy water with a few drops of ammonia in it, treating it from the back. Wash in biological detergent. If the stain is still there, rub dry borax into the stain, and leave for half an hour, then rinse. Or, rub with glycerine, leave for 10 minutes, then rinse.

Non-washable items: Scrape off as much as possible, take to the dry cleaner.

Furnishings, carpets: Scrape off as much as possible, but be careful not to damage the material, then use a dilute solution of upholstery or carpet shampoo, or use a proprietary cleaner.

COCOA

Washable items: Saturate the material with cool water, then soak in warm biological detergent. If this fails, then wash at the highest temperature the fabric will take. If a grease stain remains, remove with dry cleaning solvent.

Non-washable items: Take to the dry cleaner.

Furnishings, carpets: For furnishings, sponge with cool water and detergent or use upholstery shampoo. Use carpet shampoo on carpets or rub with glycerine and warm water in equal parts for really stubborn stains. Leave the mix on for some time then rinse off, taking care not to saturate the carpet.

COD LIVER OIL

Washable items: Scoop up as much as you can, treat with cleaning solvent from the back of the fabric, then wash in strong detergent. Act quickly, as old cod liver oil stains are almost impossible to remove.

Non-washable items: Treat with cleaning solvent from the back.

Furnishings, carpets: Treat with cleaning solvent.

COFFEE

Washable items: Soak in a biological detergent in hand hot water. Then, if the stain persists, treat with methylated spirit or a solution of 20 vol. hydrogen peroxide in a strength of 1 part to 6 parts water but check for colourfastness first. Soak until the stain has disappeared. Alternative useful first aid for colourfast clothing is to stretch the patch over a bowl (hold in place with an elastic band) then pour boiling water over the stain. If it remains, sprinkle some borax on it and pour again. Then use methylated spirit or peroxide as above if necessary. Residual grease can be removed by dry cleaning solvent.

Non-washable items: Sponge, try solvent and, if necessary, take to the dry cleaner.

Furnishings, carpets: Sponge with clear water and blot, then treat with cleaning solvent. Alternatively, most coffee stains on carpet will respond to being sprayed with soda from a syphon. If the stain is old, then glycerine with equal parts of warm water may shift it if you leave it on for a while, then rinse carefully. However, coffee is a natural dye, so swift action is the best remedy.

COLAS

Washable items: Rinse with cold water, work in liquid detergent from the back of the fabric and rinse. If the stain persists, try methylated spirit mixed with a little white vinegar and water, rinse well and wash.

Non-washable items and carpets: Dab with cold water or, in the case of carpets, spray with soda from a syphon but do not overdo it or you may damage the backing. Then treat with methylated spirit and rinse well.

CRAYONS AND CHALKS

Washable items: Brush off any chalk or pieces of crayon, then sponge with detergent until the stain disappears. If the crayon is indelible, then use a cloth dipped in methylated spirit instead. But do not continue this treatment for long or the colour may start to come out of the fabric, use a dry cleaning solvent instead.

Non-washable items: Brush off what you can, then take to the dry cleaner.

Furnishings, carpets: Try methylated spirit on furnishings if the mark does not brush off. Chalks trodden into carpets can be brushed, then vacuumed out; indelible crayons can be treated with methylated spirit or dry cleaning solvent as above – rinse well afterwards.

CREAM

Washable items: Scrape off as much as possible, then rinse in cold water first before soaking in a biological detergent. If necessary, follow up with dry cleaning fluid to remove the last of the grease.

Non-washable items: Scrape, treat with dry cleaning fluid. If this does not work, take to the dry cleaner.

Furnishings, carpets: Tackle with dry cleaning fluid, rinse well afterwards and blot dry. On carpets, use a dry cleaning solvent, followed by carpet shampoo.

CREOSOTE

Washable items: Sponge well with eucalyptus oil (see page 230), then wash.

Non-washable items: Take to the dry cleaner.

Furnishings, carpets: Take to the cleaners if possible. Otherwise rub the area with a pad soaked in eucalyptus oil. Be careful not to spread the stain and rinse well afterwards, then blot dry.

CURRY

Washable items: Dip into lukewarm water until it runs clear, then rub in a solution of half and half glycerine and warm water, leave for a while, then rinse. Soak in biological detergent then wash. If the stain persists, and the fabric is suitable for treatment, soak in 1 part 20 vol. hydrogen peroxide to 6 parts cold water, rinse well afterwards.

Non-washable items: Sponge with solution of borax and warm water, if the stain remains, send to the dry cleaner.

Furnishings, carpets: Treat furnishings as for non-washable items. Treat carpets with the borax solution of 15 ml (1 tablespoon) borax to 500 ml (1 pint) warm water. If the stain persists, use a half and half solution of glycerine and water. The carpet may have to be cleaned professionally if the stain is large.

DEODORANTS (see **Antiperspirants**)

DYE

Washable items: Splashes should be dabbed up immediately they are made. Always use cold water or you will 'set' the colour. If the spill is a major one, try rinsing in *cold* water in the washing machine, then soak in biological detergent. A mix of 1 part 20 vol. hydrogen peroxide to 6 parts water will often take dye out of silk and woollen materials, but use it with care, patterned garments may 'run' with this treatment. If the dye persists, a drastic solution is to strip the garment of its original colour and re-dye.

Non-washable items: Take to the dry cleaner immediately.

Furnishings, carpets: Small splashes can sometimes be removed with methylated spirit, on both furnishings and carpets. If a large area of the carpet is affected, it is best to call in a professional cleaner.

EGG

Washable items: A soak in biological detergent will usually remove egg stains. But if they look as though they have set, soak first in cold water and then follow up with the biological detergent solution. You may need to follow up the treatment with a dry cleaning solvent.

Non-washable items: Try dabbing with washing-up liquid, followed by a grease solvent.

Furnishings, carpets: Scrape off any excess, then treat with grease solvent. A carpet shampoo will usually remove the stain on carpets.

FATS (see **Butter**)

FELT-TIP PENS

Washable items: Treat with methylated spirit unless the fabric is an acetate, then rub soap into the area and wash.

Non-washable items: Small spots can be tackled with methylated spirit, otherwise take to the dry cleaner.

Furnishings, carpets: Treat fabrics as non-washable items. Plastic and leather should be tackled with a non-abrasive household cleaner if methylated spirit is not effective – wrap a finger in a piece of clean rag and apply to the area.

FRUIT STAINS

Washable items: Rinse immediately in cold water until no more colour comes out, then stretch the fabric over a bowl or pudding basin (use an elastic band or piece of string to keep it in place) then pour boiling water over the area from a kettle. The more force you do this with, the better. So, hold the kettle as high as possible. If the stain is shifting easily, then wash the garment at the highest temperature the fabric will stand (check the label first). If the stain is stubborn, then soak in 1 part 20 vol. hydrogen peroxide to 6 parts water – but be sure the material is colourfast first. Or use a proprietary stain remover. Acetate fabrics should be soaked in borax – 15 ml (1 tablespoon) to $\frac{1}{2}$ litre (1 pint) instead. Dried-on fruit stains can be loosened before treatment with a solution of equal parts glycerine and warm water. On woollen fabrics, try white distilled vinegar after the glycerine.

Non-washable items: Sponge immediately with cold water and send straight to the dry cleaner, or use a proprietary stain remover.

Furnishings, carpets: Follow the advice for non-washable fabrics on furnishings. Blot up the stain on carpets with kitchen paper towelling, sponge with cold water, then shampoo the area with carpet shampoo. If any stain remains, try methylated spirit.

Fruit stained fingers: These can be cleaned up with a cotton wool pad soaked in nail varnish remover.

FURNITURE POLISH

Washable items: Treat with a dry cleaning solvent, then wash in the usual way.

Non-washable items: Try dry cleaning solvent, otherwise take to dry cleaner.

Furnishings, carpets: Treat with dry cleaning solvent, then follow up with upholstery or carpet shampoo.

GLUE (see Adhesive)

GRASS

Washable items: Treat the affected area with methylated spirit unless the fabric is acetate, when you should use a proprietary stain remover, rinse, then wash in the usual way.

Non-washable items: Apply a paste made of equal quantities of salt and cream of tartar, plus a little water, to the area. Leave it to dry then brush out. Use a proprietary stain remover if a mark remains or send to the dry cleaner. This method applies to cricketing flannels that are non-washable.

GRAVY

Washable items: The staining ingredient in gravy is often grease-based, so it is necessary to use a grease solvent on the stain. Plunge the area into cold water first, then treat with dry cleaning fluid before washing in hot water.

Non-washable items: These can be cautiously treated with dry cleaning fluid if a test patch shows no ill effects. If the colour begins to run, however, take it to the dry cleaner.

Furnishings, carpets: Try dry cleaning fluid first, then follow up with upholstery or carpet shampoo.

GREASE

Washable items: If the stain is newly made, scrape, then pat talcum powder, Fuller's earth or cornflour into it to absorb as much of the grease as possible, then brush off and remove the rest with dry cleaning solvent. Finally, wash at the hottest temperature the fabric can stand. On white cotton, where a stain may still show, the fabric can be soaked in a solution of washing soda – be careful to follow the instructions on the packet, too much may damage the fabric. If the stain persists, try using the technique for candlewax – iron it between two sheets of clean blotting paper (see page 239). Delicate fabrics sometimes respond to soaking in a solution of borax in warm water. Use 15 ml (1 tablespoon) to $\frac{1}{2}$ litre (1 pint).

Non-washable items: Scrape off the excess, pat in talcum powder as above, then use a spray dry cleaning solvent. Otherwise take to a dry cleaner.

Furnishings, carpets: Treat furnishings as for non-washable items. On carpets, blot up as much grease as possible with absorbent paper towelling, then sprinkle with talcum powder, Fuller's earth or cornflour. Leave to absorb the grease and then vacuum. If the stain is still there, use a dry carpet shampoo. Grease marks on wallpaper can sometimes be removed by pressing a paste of Fuller's earth to the wall. Brush off when dry and repeat if the stain is still there. Aerosol dry cleaner will sometimes remove grease stains on sturdy wallpaper. Spray, wait for it to dry to a powder, then brush off.

HAIR COLOURANTS

Washable items: Tackle immediately, once the stain has dried it is almost impossible to remove. Soak in cold water, rub with liquid detergent, then with white distilled vinegar, then soak in biological detergent if the stain persists. Henna stains respond to treatment with neat household ammonia or if the marks are stubborn tackle them with methylated spirit. Light coloured garments can be left for a while in a mix of 1 part 20 vol. hydrogen peroxide to 6 parts water. Rinse well afterwards.

Non-washable items: Rub with liquid detergent, rinse. Take to the dry cleaner if the mark persists.

Furnishings, carpets: Dab with cold water, then rub with liquid detergent and blot dry. Professional help may be needed if the mark does not come out.

HONEY (see JAMS)

INK

Washable items: Rinse thoroughly in cold water, if possible leave under a running tap. Then treat from the back with liquid detergent and rinse again. Any stain that remains should come out if treated with a mix of lemon juice, ammonia and water in equal quantities.

Non-washable items: Take to a dry cleaner, dabbing with cold water may simply spread the stain.

Furnishings, carpets: Blot, then treat with methylated spirit. Ink stains on a carpet can be sprayed with soda before the methylated spirit treatment is used.

ICE CREAM

Washable items: Scrape off the excess with a blunt-edged knife, soak in a biological detergent, then, if a mark still remains, use a dry cleaning fluid to remove the rest. Dried-on stains can be treated with a solution of 15 ml (1 tablespoon) of borax to 500 ml (1 pint) of warm water, sponged over the affected area.

Non-washable items: Treat the stain with a grease solvent then, if necessary, take to the dry cleaner.

Furnishings, carpets: Furnishings should be treated as non-washable items. Treat carpets first with a grease solvent then follow up with a diluted carpet shampoo.

IODINE

Washable items: Remove brown stain with hypo crystals – used in photography – 15 ml (1 tablespoon) dissolved in 330 ml ($\frac{3}{4}$ pint) water. Soak stain in the solution for about ten minutes, then rinse carefully and wash.

Non-washable items: Try treating with methylated spirit, if this fails, take to the dry cleaner.

Furnishings, carpets: Blot up any excess iodine then sponge with hypo solution, or methylated spirit. Rinse well.

IRON-MOULD

Washable items: Light stains can be removed by rubbing lemon juice and salt into the mark. Leave for about an hour, then rinse well. Repeat if necessary. If the stain does not shift, use a proprietary iron-mould or dye remover or a solution of oxalic acid: 5 ml (1 teaspoon) in a litre (2 pints) of water but be careful as the acid is extremely poisonous. Do not use on silks and woollens.

Non-washable items: Take straight to the dry cleaner.

Furnishings: Try the salt and lemon treatment or try a proprietary remover. If this fails, get professional help.

JAMS, MARMALADE, HONEY, ETC.

Washable items: Scrape, soak in biological detergent and then wash in the usual way. If the stain persists, soak in a solution of 15 ml (1 tablespoon) of borax to 500 ml (1 pint) of warm water, then rinse and wash in the usual way, OR, use a solution of 1 part 20 vol. hydrogen peroxide to 6 parts water, rinse well.

Non-washable items: Scrape, rinse in cold water then rub with washing-up liquid. If a mark remains, rub a little borax into the stain, leave for a minute or two, then sponge. If still stained, take to a dry cleaner.

Furnishings, carpets: Scrape off excess, sponge with warm water, then treat with upholstery or carpet shampoo.

KETCHUP, PICKLES, ETC.

Washable items: Scrape off excess, rinse thoroughly in cold water, then sponge with warm water and liquid detergent and, if the fabric is colourfast, soak in 1 part 20 vol.

hydrogen peroxide to 6 parts water, rinse and dry. If a mark still remains, as may happen with tomato sauce, try using methylated spirit and rinse.

Non-washable items: Scrape, sponge with cold water, blot, then try an aerosol stain remover. Tomato sauce stains may need the attention of a professional dry cleaner.

Furnishings, carpets: Scrape, sponge with cold water, blot. Then try upholstery or carpet shampoo. If the stain persists, try rubbing a little glycerine into it to loosen it, then shampoo again and rinse.

LIPSTICK

Washable items: Scrape off any excess with a knife, then rub some glycerine or petroleum jelly into the stain to loosen it or, on nylon fabrics, methylated spirit. If the mark shows no sign of shifting, try using a proprietary stain remover, or grease solvent, then wash.

Non-washable items: Use a proprietary dry cleaner. If necessary take for professional cleaning.

Furnishings, carpets: Scrape off excess, treat with pro- prietary dry cleaning solvent, then use upholstery or carpet shampoo.

MAKE-UP

Washable items: Remove any excess with a knife. Then pat with talcum powder to mop up any grease. Treat light stains with detergent and warm water, soak heavier ones in a solution of 5 ml (1 teaspoon) of ammonia to 500 ml (1 pint) lukewarm water or treat with a dry cleaning solvent before you wash in the usual way.

Non-washable items: Scrape off any excess, pat in talcum powder to absorb grease, then use an aerosol dry cleaning solvent or methylated spirit.

Furnishings, carpets: Scrape off excess, use techniques described for non-washable items. Follow up with upholstery or carpet shampoo.

MARGARINE (see BUTTER)

MARMALADE (see JAMS)

MASCARA

Washable items: Rub in neat washing-up liquid, then wash as usual. If this does not completely remove the stain, treat with a dry cleaning fluid.

Non-washable items: If colourfast, treat with methylated spirit. Otherwise use aerosol stain remover and if a mark persists, blot with 1 part ammonia diluted in 3 parts cold water, on colourfast fabrics only. Rinse.

Furnishings, carpets: Tackle as for non-washable items.

MAYONNAISE

Washable items: Scrape off excess, then treat with a proprietary grease solvent. Soak in a solution of biological detergent and water according to the packet instructions, then wash in lukewarm water only. If a mark remains, continue to treat with grease solvent.

Non-washable items: Remove as much as possible with a warm damp cloth, treat with grease solvent. If a mark remains, take to the dry cleaner.

Furnishings, carpets: Blot off as much as possible, then spray with aerosol stain remover, finally wash with upholstery or carpet shampoo.

MEDICINE

Washable items: Soak immediately in cold water, then wash in the usual way. If a mark remains, remove it with methylated spirit.

Non-washable items: Take to a dry cleaner.

Furnishings, carpets: Blot with kitchen towelling, then rinse several times with cold water, blotting between each application. If a mark persists finish up with upholstery or carpet shampoo.

METAL POLISH

Washable items: Blot, to remove as much moisture as possible, then treat with white spirit or proprietary dry cleaner. Wash in the usual way.

Non-washable items: Blot with a cloth moistened in proprietary dry cleaning solvent, then use an aerosol dry cleaner. If a stain persists, take to the dry cleaner.

Furnishing, carpets: Blot excess moisture, then treat with white spirit. Allow to dry then vacuum. If a mark remains, treat with upholstery or carpet shampoo.

MILDEW

Washable items: If tackled in time, ordinary laundering may remove the marks: rub well with washing soap beforehand. Otherwise, soak white cottons and linens in a weak solution of 15 ml (1 tablespoon) bleach to just over a litre (2 pints) of water plus 5 ml (1 teaspoon) of white distilled vinegar. Other fabrics can be soaked in 1 part 20 vol. hydrogen peroxide to 6 parts of water, but watch for possible bleeding of colour. Any residual marks should disappear after a wash or so.

Non-washable items: Take to a dry cleaner.

Furnishings, carpets: Sponge with a mild solution of anti-septic. If this does not work, call in professional help. Mildew on books and paper should be wiped off with a soft cloth just moistened with mild antiseptic.

MILK

Washable items: Rinse in cold water, soak in biological detergent, then wash in warm detergent. Follow up with a proprietary dry cleaning solvent if necessary.

Non-washable items: Sponge with warm water. Allow to dry, then treat with proprietary stain remover. If a mark remains, take to the dry cleaner.

Furnishings, carpets: Mop up as much as possible, then sponge with diluted upholstery or carpet shampoo. On carpets, spray with soda from a syphon first to avoid unpleasant sour smells that may linger afterwards. If a stain remains, treat with proprietary dry cleaner.

MUD

Washable items: Allow the mud to dry and then brush off, working the fabric with a rubbing motion between your hands to remove as much as possible. Then wash in the usual way. If any marks remain, treat with proprietary dry cleaner and wash again.

Non-washable items: Leave to dry completely then brush off. Sponge if necessary with detergent solution and follow up with aerosol dry cleaner.

Furnishings, carpets: Allow to dry, brush thoroughly and then vacuum. Use an upholstery or a carpet shampoo to follow up.

MUSTARD

Washable items: Sponge, then soak in liquid detergent

before washing. If a stain remains, treat with a solution of 5 ml (1 teaspoon) of ammonia to 500 ml (1 pint) of water. Rinse well.

Non-washable items: Spot treat, if possible, with mild detergent, then the ammonia solution above. If necessary, take to the dry cleaner.

Furnishings, carpets: Treat as for non-washable items. Dried-on stains on upholstery can be loosened with a solution of half and half glycerine and warm water.

NAIL VARNISH

Washable items: Blot as much as possible, then treat from the back of the fabric with amyl acetate, if you have some, failing that, *non-oily* nail varnish remover, then white spirit. Follow up, if necessary, with methylated spirit to clear the colour, but not on acetate fabrics.

Non-washable items: Take straight to a dry cleaner.

Furnishings, carpets: Blot, clean up with amyl acetate or *non-oily* varnish remover. Follow up with white spirit then upholstery or carpet shampoo.

NEWSPRINT

Washable items: Sponge with methylated spirit, then wash in the usual way.

Non-washable items: Sponge with methylated spirit then cold water. If the stain does not disappear, take to the dry cleaner.

Furnishings, carpets: Treat as for non-washable items.

ORANGE JUICE

Washable items: Soak immediately in cold water, then wash in the normal way. If any colour from the stain remains, lift it by soaking in a solution of 1 part 20 vol. hydrogen peroxide to 10 parts water. If the fabric is synthetic, use a warm solution of 30 ml (2 tablespoons) of borax to a litre (2 pints) of water instead.

Non-washable items: Sponge with cold water, take to a dry cleaner as soon as possible.

Furnishings, carpets: Sponge with cold water, then treat with upholstery or carpet shampoo and rinse.

PAINT, ACRYLIC

Washable items: Blot immediately and wash out as fast as possible with soap and cold water. If the paint has almost dried, scrape off what you can, then try proprietary dry cleaning fluid, methylated spirit or paint removing solvent. Acrylic paint that has dried on a garment is almost impossible to remove.

Non-washable items: Keep the stain damp, scrape off what you can and take to a dry cleaner as fast as possible.

Furnishings, carpets: Almost impossible to remove unless you tackle it while still damp. Scrape or blot, treat with upholstery or carpet shampoo and warm water, then try methylated spirit or paint removing solvent.

PAINT, CELLULOSE

Washable items: Treat immediately with cellulose thinners, then wash in the usual way. Rayon fabrics must be treated as non-washable.

Non-washable items: Take immediately to the dry cleaner.

Furnishings, carpets: Spot treat with cellulose thinners. Then use upholstery or carpet shampoo. If the patch is a large one, call in professional help.

PAINT, EMULSION

Washable items: Scrape or wipe off any excess as soon as it happens, then flood with cold water immediately, rinse until all traces of the paint have gone. Then wash in the usual way, finally use a grease solvent to take out any remaining mark.

Non-washable items: Keep damp, scrape or blot then take to the dry cleaner as fast as possible.

Furnishings, carpets: Tackle immediately with plenty of cold water, then follow up with carpet or upholstery shampoo and, if necessary, grease solvent.

PAINT, ENAMEL

Washable items: Treat with a paint remover and a clean cloth, keep treating until the stain has gone, working from the front and back of the fabric. Then wash in the usual way, but do not immerse in water until you are satisfied the stain has gone.

Non-washable items: Take to a dry cleaner as fast as possible.

Furnishings, carpets: Blot as much as possible then treat with dry cleaning fluid or paint remover.

PAINT, GLOSS

Washable items: Treat immediately with turpentine or white spirit or brush cleaner except on acetate fabrics. Sponge carefully with cold water then wash in the usual way. If necessary, follow up with proprietary stain remover.

Non-washable items: Treat with turpentine, white spirit or brush cleaner, except on acetate and rayon fabrics. If necessary, take to a dry cleaner.

Furnishings, carpets: Treat with white spirit or brush cleaner, then follow up with upholstery or carpet shampoo.

PAINT, OIL

Washable items: Flood immediately with white spirit (hold a pad of clean white cloth under the stain), then use a proprietary stain remover, if necessary. Wash in the normal way.

Non-washable items: Take to the dry cleaner as soon as possible.

Furnishings, carpets: Clean up with white spirit, then use a stain remover if necessary, finish up with upholstery or carpet shampoo.

PAINT, WATER COLOUR

Washable items: Rinse well in cold water, if a stain persists, treat with a little neat ammonia. Rinse carefully.

Non-washable items: Try sponging with cold water, if this fails, take to a dry cleaner.

Furnishings, carpets: Sponge with cold water, then spot treat with neat ammonia if necessary, follow up with upholstery or carpet shampoo.

PARAFFIN

(N.B. This stain is highly inflammable)
Washable items: Scrape off any excess, then pat talcum powder, Fuller's earth or cornflour into the patch to absorb as much of the grease as possible. Finally, use a dry cleaning solvent and wash in the hottest temperature the fabric will take.

Non-washable items: Pat talcum powder, Fuller's earth or cornflour into the patch and try treating with a dry cleaning solvent. Larger areas can be treated by placing between two sheets of blotting paper and pressing with a warm iron (see Candlewax, page 239). Follow up with dry cleaning solvent. If this fails, send to a dry cleaner.

Furnishings, carpets: Blot the patch, apply aerosol stain remover. Treat large areas by placing a piece of blotting paper on top and pressing with a warm iron, then apply stain remover and shampoo.

PERFUME

Washable items: Rinse out immediately in lukewarm water, if a stain persists, treat with neat ammonia, then wash in the usual way. For dried-on perfume, rub a solution of equal parts glycerine and warm water into it, then wash.

Non-washable items: Rub a half-and-half glycerine and warm water solution into the stain, then sponge over carefully with a cloth wrung out in warm water. Precious fabrics should go straight to a dry cleaner.

Furnishings, carpets: Loosen the stain with a half-and-half mix of glycerine and warm water, then sponge carefully with a cloth wrung out in warm water. Blot well, follow up with upholstery or carpet shampoo if necessary.

PERSPIRATION, FRESH

Washable items: Soak in biological detergent (follow packet instructions) and if the stain persists, treat with neat ammonia and rinse quickly. If the colour has been affected, sponge with a solution of 15 ml (1 tablespoon) white distilled vinegar to 250 ml ($\frac{1}{2}$ pint) warm water, then rinse. White fabrics can be lightly bleached in a mix of 1 part 20 vol. hydrogen peroxide to 6 parts cold water. Finally, wash in the normal way.

Non-washable items: Sponge with a solution of 15 ml (1 tablespoon) white distilled vinegar to 250 ml ($\frac{1}{2}$ pint) warm water. If the colour is affected, follow with methylated spirit, but not on acetate or rayon fabrics.

PERSPIRATION, OLD

Washable items: Sponge with vinegar solution as above, then soak in biological detergent. If the stain remains, follow up with 1 part 20 vol. peroxide to 10 parts water. If the smell remains, soak in a solution of 5 ml (1 teaspoon) borax to half a litre (1 pint) of warm water. Then add a few drops of ammonia to washing water and hang out to dry.

Non-washable items: Sponge with the vinegar solution as above, then take to a dry cleaner.

PETROLEUM JELLY

Washable items: Scrape off as much as possible, then wash in the hottest water the fabric will stand, adding plenty of detergent. If a stain remains, use a dry cleaning solvent.

Non-washable items: Scrape, use a dry cleaning solvent and, if a stain remains, take to a dry cleaner.

Furnishings, carpets: Scrape off as much as possible, then treat with a grease solvent, follow up with diluted upholstery or carpet shampoo, rinse and blot.

PICKLES (see KETCHUP)

POLISH (see FURNITURE POLISH or SHOE POLISH)

PLASTICINE

Washable items: Scrape off as much as possible, then tackle with a grease solvent or, failing that, a little lighter fuel on a piece of clean cloth. If the fabric is a man-made fibre, check first, on the inside of a pocket or of a seam, to make sure no damage is caused. Wash in the hottest possible water that the fabric will take.

Non-washable items: Scrape, spot treat with a grease solvent. If this does not work, then take to a dry cleaner for professional attention.

Furnishings, carpets: Furnishings should be treated as non-washable items. Plasticine trodden into the carpet should be scraped off, then the area treated with grease solvent. Follow up with carpet shampoo, rinse well. If a stain remains, allow the carpet to dry, then try methylated spirit.

PUTTY

Washable items: Chill in a fridge or freezer first, then pick off the excess and treat with dry cleaning fluid. Wash in the hottest possible water that the fabric will stand.

Non-washable items: Chill in a fridge or freezer if possible, then pick off surface putty, spot treat the stain with dry cleaning fluid. If necessary take to a dry cleaner.

Furnishings, carpets: Scrape off excess, then treat with dry cleaning solvent and follow up with upholstery or carpet shampoo.

SALAD DRESSING

Washable items: Blot, treat with an aerosol grease solvent, then wash in the hottest water that the fabric will take.

Non-washable items: Blot, spot treat with an aerosol grease solvent. If necessary, take to a dry cleaner.

Furnishings, carpets: Mop up as much of the excess as possible, then treat with an aerosol dry cleaner. Follow up, if necessary, with upholstery or carpet shampoo.

SCORCH MARKS

Washable items: Rub the fabric under a cold running tap, then soak in a solution of 10 ml (2 teaspoons) of borax to 1 litre (2 pints) of warm water. Wash as usual. Any marks that remain on white cottons or linens can usually be bleached out.

Non-washable items: Sponge with the borax solution as above, rinse, blot dry.

Furnishings, carpets: Treat upholstery as for non-washable items. Scorch marks on carpets can sometimes be removed by sponging with 1 part 20 vol. hydrogen peroxide to 10 parts of water. Failing that, snip off the affected tufts if possible, or rub them over with fine wire wool, using a circular movement.

SHOE POLISH

Washable items: Scrape off excess. Tackle with white spirit or, if the stain is bad and the fabric sturdy, with paint brush cleaner. Small marks can often be removed with an aerosol grease solvent. Wash with detergent and hot water with a little ammonia added.

Non-washable items: Scrape, spot treat with aerosol dry cleaner. If this does not work, try white spirit or paint brush cleaner, failing that, get professional help.

Furnishings, carpets: Scrape off excess, tackle with white spirit, or methylated spirit and follow up with upholstery or carpet detergent.

SICK

Washable items: Take off as much as possible with a spoon. Rinse well under a cold tap, then soak in biological detergent – add disinfectant if necessary. Wash in the usual way. If any mark remains, and the fabric can take it (see pages 208–23), soak again in a mixture of 1 part 20 vol. hydrogen peroxide to 6 parts water.

Non-washable items: Scrape, try sponging with a little ammonia in warm water. If this does not work, take to a dry cleaner.

Furnishings, carpets: Scrape, sponge with warm water and detergent with a little disinfectant added. Carpets should be sprayed with a soda syphon first, if you have one to hand, then tackled with carpet shampoo. Mattresses should be sponged well with warm water and detergent, then rinsed in cold water with a little disinfectant added.

SOOT, SMOKE

Washable items: Tackle the marks with an aerosol dry cleaner, then wash.

Non-washable items: Use an aerosol dry cleaner, if this fails, get professional help.

Furnishings, carpets: Vacuum thoroughly, or shake, then use an aerosol stain remover. Alternatively, on light coloured carpets, rub in Fuller's earth, then vacuum again.

SPIRITS

Washable items: Sponge with warm water, then wash in the usual way.

Non-washable items: Spot treat with warm water and a little liquid detergent, then sponge with clear warm water and blot.

Furnishings, carpets: Sponge over with warm water then follow up with carpet or upholstery shampoo if necessary.

STOUTS (see BEERS)

TAR

Washable items: Scrape off as much as you can, soften with a little glycerine, then remove the rest with eucalyptus oil, working from the back of the fabric. Small marks can often be removed with a dry cleaning solvent. Finally wash in the hottest possible temperature that the fabric will stand. Any stain that remains can usually be removed with a paint brush solvent.

Non-washable items: Scrape, soften with a little glycerine then try a dry cleaning solvent. If this does not remove the mark, take to a dry cleaner.

Furnishings, carpets: Scrape, soften with glycerine, then use a grease solvent, or eucalyptus oil. Dark marks will usually come out with a paint brush solvent. Finish up with an upholstery or carpet shampoo.

TEA

Washable items: Soak in warm water with a little borax added, 15 ml (1 tablespoon) to 500 ml (1 pint) of water, then soak again in a biological detergent and wash as usual. Dried-on stains should be softened before treatment with a solution of equal amounts of glycerine and warm water. If a stain remains, after washing, try methylated spirit. It may be necessary to bleach cottons to remove all the stain.

Non-washable items: Treat with a solution of 15 ml (1 tablespoon) of borax to 500 ml (1 pint) of water, follow up with an aerosol stain remover.

Furnishings, carpets: Treat with a solution of 15 ml (1 tablespoon) of borax to 500 ml (1 pint) of water, follow up with an aerosol stain remover.

Cups and mugs: Tea-stained cups and mugs can be cleaned with a damp cloth dipped in bicarbonate of soda or soaked in a weak solution of bleach. Rinse thoroughly.

TOBACCO

Washable items: Treat the stain with methylated spirit, or if the fabric is acetate, benzine. Failing that, a solution of equal parts of hydrogen peroxide 20 vol. and water may remove the mark. Rinse well afterwards.

Non-washable items: Take to the dry cleaner.

Furnishings, carpets: Sponge with methylated spirit, then rinse and finish up with carpet or upholstery shampoo.

Tobacco-stained fingers: These can be cleaned up with the sterilizing fluid that is used for nappies or babies' bottles.

TREACLE

Washable items: Blot off the excess, soak in warm water, then wash. Old stains can be soaked with a mixture of 10 ml (2 teaspoons) of borax in a litre (2 pints) of water.

Non-washable items: Wipe with a damp cloth, and sponge with warm water. If this does not remove the stain, take to a dry cleaner.

Furnishings, carpets: Blot with a damp cloth, then rinse with warm water, follow up with upholstery or carpet shampoo.

TURMERIC

Washable items: Soak in warm water and a little ammonia to loosen the stain then follow up with white spirit and wash. White cottons and linens may need bleaching.

Non-washable items: Try sponging from the back of the fabric with neat ammonia, then white spirit. If this does not remove the yellow colour, take to a dry cleaner.

Furnishings, carpets: Treat with neat ammonia, then white spirit, follow up with upholstery or carpet shampoo.

URINE

Washable items: Rinse well in cold water, then soak in biological detergent and launder in the usual way. Old stains, which can be difficult to remove, may be improved if you soak the garment in a mix of 1 part 20 vol. hydrogen peroxide to 6 parts of water with a few drops of household ammonia added.

Non-washable items: Sponge with cold water, then with a solution of 10 ml (2 teaspoons) of distilled white vinegar to 1 litre (2 pints) of water. If this fails, take to a dry cleaner.

Furnishings, carpets: Mop up, sponge with warm water and blot. In the case of carpets, squirt with a soda syphon first and finish up with warm water to which a few drops of ammonia have been added. For the treatment of mattresses, see page 233.

VARNISH (SHELLAC)

Washable items: Wipe immediately with methylated spirit unless the fabric is acetate, wash in detergent and rinse well.

Non-washable items: Tackle immediately with methylated spirit (not on acetate fabrics). If a stain remains, take to the dry cleaner.

Furnishings, carpets: Treat as for non-washable items.

WAX POLISH

Washable items: Treat with dry cleaning solvent, then wash in hot liquid detergent solution and rinse.

Non-washable items: Treat with dry cleaning solvent, sponge with warm detergent solution and rinse.

Furnishings, carpets: Treat as for non-washable items.

WINE, RED

Washable items: Pour salt on to the stain to blot it, then soak in cold water and rinse. If a mark remains, stretch the area over a basin, sprinkle on borax and pour over boiling water. In an emergency, white wine poured on to red wine stains will often take most of the offending colour out.

Non-washable items: Sprinkle with talcum powder to blot, take to a dry cleaner.

Furnishings, carpets: Sprinkle upholstery with salt or talcum powder, follow up with white wine or lukewarm water. In the case of carpets, squirt soda from a syphon on to the area, or mop with white wine. Sprinkle with talcum powder and vacuum dry. Repeat this process until the stain is unnoticeable.

WINE, WHITE

Washable items: Sprinkle salt on to the stain, then soak in cold water. Wash as usual.

Non-washable items: Blot, then sprinkle talcum powder on to the stain immediately. If a ring remains, take to a dry cleaner.

Furnishings, carpets: Blot with kitchen paper, sponge over using lukewarm water with a little detergent. Old stains can be reduced if you treat them with methylated spirit.

Some handy home-made solutions

Oven cleaner: Ammonia makes an inexpensive oven cleaner but it can burn the skin, so wear rubber gloves and handle it carefully.

Stain remover: Bicarbonate of soda and water paste makes a good emergency treatment for fruit, tea or coffee stains. Rub on, leave for half an hour, then sponge off.

Improved polish: Cider vinegar, 5 ml (1 teaspoonful) added to a cupful of liquid furniture polish, makes it go on more smoothly, improves its performance.

Window cleaner: Cold wash detergent, diluted 1 capful to 1 litre (2 pints) of cold water, makes a good window cleaner.

Glass polisher: Crumpled newspaper gives windows and glass items a polish after they have been washed.

Bottom of the oven cleaner: Dishwasher powder will clean up burned-on food in the bottom of ovens. Wait until the oven has cooled, sprinkle on the offending spot, cover with a damp paper towel and leave overnight. Wash off with warm water in the morning.

Floor mop rinse: Fabric softener, a capful added to a pail of water, makes a good rinse for a cotton floor mop, leaves it soft and fluffy for the next time.

Marble top polish: A lemon slice wrapped in a strip of clean cloth, dipped in borax will make marble table tops shine.

Furniture polish: Linseed oil, 2 parts to 1 part of turpentine and 1 part of water makes a good furniture polish.

Upholstery cleaner: Liquid detergent and boiling water mixed at a ratio of 1:4, will cool to make a jelly. Whip it up with an egg beater and it makes a good foam for cleaning upholstery.

Flannel rinse: Malt vinegar and water as a rinse will get soap out of face flannels. Use 10 ml (2 teaspoons) of vinegar to 500 ml (1 pint) of water. Combined with a few grains of uncooked rice, it will clean out a narrow necked bottle.

Chrome and paintwork cleaner: 2 parts paraffin, mixed with 1 part methylated spirit makes a good polish for chrome and paintwork.

Drain cleaner: Salt in a solution of hot water, will help to clear drains and gets rid of an unpleasant smell. Use 15 ml of salt to 500 ml of water (a tablespoon to a pint).

Emergency upholstery cleaner: Shaving cream in an aerosol can is another good emergency upholstery cleaner. Use it in exactly the same way as upholstery foam.

First class furniture polish: Turpentine, vinegar and boiling water mixed in equal parts, make a first class furniture polish.

Wall cleaner: $\frac{1}{4}$ cup of washing soda, combined with $\frac{1}{2}$ cup of ammonia and $\frac{1}{4}$ cup white distilled vinegar, added to a bucket of warm water, make a good solution for sponging down grimy walls.

Tiled floor cleaner: One cup of distilled white vinegar in a pail of water makes a rinse for linoleum or PVC tiled floors, leaves them sparkling.

Metal and china stain remover: Wood ash used as a scourer, will take some stains off metal and china objects.

Stains
on household surfaces

ALUMINIUM COOKWARE

Burnt-on food should be removed by boiling some water in in the pan, then working on the softened deposit with a nylon brush or scourer. **Stains** can be removed by soaking the pan in a solution of 15 ml (1 tablespoonful) of borax to 500 ml (1 pint) of water. **Tide marks** left by hard water when it is boiled can be removed with lemon. Boil up some pieces of lemon peel in the saucepan, making sure the water level comes above the tide mark. The same effect can be achieved by boiling up apples or rhubarb in the pan. **Bad stains** can often be removed by simmering a strong solution of vinegar in the pan for about 15 minutes. Use 3 parts of vinegar to 1 part of water. **Surface pitting** will often occur if food is left in aluminium pans overnight, so transfer it to another container. When removing stains with steel wool, rub in one direction only to avoid scratch marks and make sure that you rinse the pan out well afterwards. Roasting tins can be treated in the same way.

BATHS, ACRYLIC

Surface scratches can be buffed out with a little silver metal polish on a clean rag. **Light stains** can be rubbed with some liquid detergent on a soft cloth. **Bad scratches or stains** should be rubbed cautiously with 'wet and dry' sandpaper, used damp. Use the same piece of sandpaper until it is worn right down, follow up with silver metal polish. You could also try a proprietary gently abrasive liquid cleaner on the stubborn stains. Do not try these techniques on glass fibre baths, ask the manufacturer's advice.

BATHS, CAST IRON, PRESSED STEEL

Yellow marks and discoloration can sometimes be removed with a wedge of lemon dipped in coarse salt. Rinse well, or the acid in the lemon may take the shine off the surface. For tougher cases, try a salt and turpentine paste rubbed well in. For other marks there are good proprietary cleaners that will do a good cleaning job, but follow the manufacturer's instructions carefully: left on too long, they can eat into the enamel or porcelain surface. **Tide marks** that won't respond to normal cleaning techniques can be rubbed off with white spirit, then rinsed with a solution of washing-up liquid and warm water. (See also page 172 for tips on everyday care of the bath.)

BRASS

Lacquered brass that has become discoloured and stained can be treated by removing the finish with nail varnish remover or, if the area is large, cellulose thinners. Rinse, clean with a mixture of equal quantities of vinegar, salt and flour, used as a paste.

BRONZE

Green spots on bronze should be rubbed over with turpentine. Allow to dry, brush with a dry nailbrush, then apply a little oil to the surface and polish. Lacquered bronze sometimes cracks and peels but in this case it will have to be treated professionally.

CAST-IRON COOKWARE

Burnt-on food should come off if you boil up a solution of water with a few crystals of washing soda added. The pan must be dried immediately or it will tend to rust. If this happens, clean off with fine steel wool and rinse well. Dry thoroughly, then rub a little cooking oil into the surface before storing, to prevent further rusting.

CERAMIC TILES

Rust stains left by metal objects can be cleaned off with abrasive cleaning powder. **Lime stains** should be rubbed with neat white distilled vinegar. Leave on for ten minutes then rinse off. **Soap marks** can be rubbed off with paraffin. **Mild stains** can be removed with a solution of 1 cup ammonia, 1 cup white distilled vinegar to a bucket of warm water with a few washing soda crystals added. **Other stains** that cannot be removed by general cleaning should be treated with a paste of bicarbonate of soda and bleach. Wear rubber gloves to protect your skin, rub in well with a piece of damp cloth, then scrub with a nail brush. Rinse well afterwards.

COOKERS, ELECTRIC

First turn off the electricity supply at the cooker point. **Burnt-on marks** on vitreous enamel surfaces should be tackled with a mild abrasive cleaning powder (make sure the mark is thoroughly moist first). Follow up, if necessary, with a special vitreous enamel cleaner. See **Ovens** for instructions on cleaning inside the cooker.

COOKERS, GAS

First turn off the pilot lights. Any removable parts should be soaked in hot detergent solution. Add a few crystals of washing soda in really bad cases, then clean up with steel wool. Rinse and dry thoroughly before replacing. See electric cookers, above, for other surfaces. Be sure to relight the pilot flames after cleaning. See **Ovens** for instructions on cleaning inside the cooker.

COPPER

Stains on the outside of copper saucepans can often be removed by a cloth dipped in vinegar, sprinkled with coarse salt. Follow up with a proprietary cleaner and polish. They will work better if you do not clean the base.

ENAMEL COOKWARE

Burnt-on food stains should be shifted by boiling up a solution of 10 ml (2 teaspoons) of bicarbonate of soda in a panful of water. Otherwise, soak the pan in washing-up liquid in hot water, then rub with a paste of bicarbonate of soda. **Residual stains** should go if you fill the pan with cold water and add 5 ml (1 teaspoonful) of bleach. Leave overnight and rinse well afterwards.

GLASS

Scratches on tabletops and glass-fronted cabinets can be improved if you rub a paste of olive oil and toothpaste into them. Stubborn **grease stains** can be wiped off with methylated spirit. Finish up with window-cleaning liquid and polish. **Bad marks** can be improved with proprietary oven cleaner. Allow to dry, wipe off. **Stains on cut glass** should be rubbed off with a solution of 1 part vinegar to 3 parts warm water. **Interior stains** should be soaked in the vinegar solution for some hours, failing that, try using 1 part lemon juice to 3 parts distilled water. If the stain persists, pour in some coarse table salt, cover with vinegar and swill. If the glass has **discoloration** after long storage, soak, then wash in warm detergent with 15 ml (1 tablespoon) of ammonia added. Rinse well afterwards.

IRONS, ELECTRIC

Melted synthetic or starch stains should be tackled while the iron is still warm, but unplugged. Scrape off any excess, taking care not to scratch the soleplate, then rub the iron over a piece of coarse damp cloth, e.g. sacking or coarse linen. An aluminium soleplate can be rubbed with fine steel wool if the mark persists, but chromium or non-stick surfaces would be scratched by this technique. Sometimes stubborn deposits can be removed by turning the iron up to its highest setting so that the deposit burns off. **Burn marks** will usually come off if you rub them with a hot salt and vinegar paste.

IRONS, STEAM

Proceed as for electric irons, but hold the iron at an angle while cleaning the soleplate so that any debris falls on to the working top and not back into the steam vents, clogging them. **Furring** inside steam irons can be removed with a proprietary kettle descaler.

KETTLES

Furring and scale deposits will affect the performance of the kettle. Try boiling up a solution of half water, half vinegar in the kettle. Leave for about six hours, then rinse thoroughly. If this does not work, use a proprietary kettle descaler, following the manufacturer's instructions. Rinse well afterwards.

LAMINATED PLASTIC SURFACES

Treat **difficult stains** with neat washing-up liquid or, if that fails, with mild cream bath cleanser. Never use abrasive powders. Tea stains and other stubborn stains on white laminated plastic can be sponged off with a mild bleach solution, 5 ml (1 teaspoon) of bleach to 500 ml (1 pint) of water, but rinse well immediately afterwards and do not use on coloured or patterned surfaces, as it will damage them. One-step car cleaner will often lift stains on laminated plastic surfaces.

LAVATORY

Avoid staining as much as possible by installing a proprietary flush deodorizer/cleaner in the cistern, which contains detergent. Otherwise tackle stains with a proprietary lavatory cleaner but never mix two different brands of powder or they may set up an unpleasant chemical reaction. **Bad stains** can be tackled with a paste of borax and lemon juice. Rub it on to the surface and leave for several hours. Stains under the rim can be treated this way, or use a proprietary lavatory cleaner.

LEATHER COVERED SURFACES

Desk tops are usually made from washable leather. **Ballpoint pen marks** will often come off if they are treated immediately with milk, otherwise rub very gently with white spirit. **Fountain pen ink** should sponge off if treated immediately with water. Try the same methods on leather upholstery. Call in expert help immediately for stains on non-washable leather. Do not use detergent or dry cleaning fluid or ammonia on leather articles or it will harm them. Use only soap. Moisten the soap and then rub over the affected area. Wipe off with a damp flannel.

MIRRORS

Remove **hair lacquer** stains with methylated spirit. **General stains** can be rubbed off with a mild solution of white distilled vinegar and warm water or ammonia and water. Use 5 ml (1 teaspoon) to 500 ml (1 pint) of water. Cold tea will also often remove marks on mirrors. If the stain persists, then treat it with a solution of 15 ml (1 tablespoon) of borax to half a litre (1 pint) of water. Be careful not to wet the mirror backing. Otherwise it may cause spotting or make the 'silver' flake off.

NON-STICK COOKWARE

Always keep a note of the manufacturer's cleaning instructions as non-stick surfaces scratch very easily. **Bad stains** can sometimes be removed by soaking in a solution of 60 ml (4 tablespoons) of bicarbonate of soda, 90 ml (6 tablespoons) of bleach. In the case of saucepans, boil up this mixture inside the pan for 5 minutes. Ovenware should be left to soak in this solution. Rinse thoroughly.

OVENS

Self-cleaning models should keep themselves clean. Otherwise follow the manufacturer's instructions. Unplug an electric cooker at the cooker point, turn off the pilot lights on a gas cooker, then wipe up **general stains** with a soft cloth and washing-up liquid solution while the oven is still warm after a cooking session. Take out oven shelves if necessary and soak in hot detergent, scrubbing with a nylon pot scourer if necessary. For **stubborn stains** use a proprietary aerosol or pad oven cleaner, following the manufacturer's instructions. **Stains on glass oven doors** should be removed by rubbing over with bicarbonate of soda or liquid bath cleaner while the door is still warm. Do not use aerosol cleaners on glass oven doors as they could lead to the glass shattering. If using ammonia (see page 176), tackle the oven when it is still warm after a cooking session, or put it on a low setting for 20 minutes to warm through. Turn off, put a small dish of neat ammonia on the top shelf and a large dish of boiling water on the bottom shelf. Leave overnight. In the morning, open the oven door and allow the fumes to die down, then wash off the inside of the oven with detergent and water. Repeat if necessary the next night. Ammonia will also clean the chrome rings on cookers. Put the rings in a plastic bag, add a large cup of ammonia, seal and leave for several hours. Rinse out of doors with a garden hose or throw a bucket of water over them.

SILVER

Heavily tarnished silver can be treated with aluminium foil and washing soda. Lay a strip of aluminium foil in a non-metal basin. Put the silver object on top of it, add a few crystals of washing soda, then cover with hot water. Leave for a few minutes then rinse. Otherwise use a proprietary silver cleaner, following the manufacturer's instructions.

SINK, ENAMEL

Light stains can usually be removed by rubbing with fresh lemon or a paste of lemon juice and borax. For **stubborn stains,** use a proprietary vitreous enamel cleaner. Do not use bleach unless you have to, for this will tend to make the sink look yellow. Do not use abrasive scouring pads.

SINKS, STAINLESS STEEL

General stains should come off if you rub them with neat detergent. **Rust stains** can be removed with mild cream bath cleaner or, failing that, rub with lighter fuel. **Water marks** can be removed by polishing off with methylated spirit on a soft cloth. Do not use steel wool or it may scratch the surface.

STAINLESS STEEL COOKWARE

Burnt-on food should be tackled with a very mild abrasive cleaner or very fine steel wool, using a paste of soft soap. **Mild stains** should come out with mild detergent in hot water, follow up if necessary with a proprietary polish for stainless steel.

STAINLESS STEEL CUTLERY

General stains should come off with a hot solution of detergent. Otherwise, try using a proprietary stainless steel polish. Use very fine steel wool and soap to take off marks left by burnt food, or if the metal has become pitted.

WALLPAPER

General stains can often be removed if you rub over the surface with a soft India rubber, or a ball of moistened white bread. **Candlewax and wax stains** should be softened carefully first with a hair dryer – do not allow them to get too hot, cover with blotting paper, then press with a warm iron. Finally, blot the remainder carefully with methylated spirit. **Crayon scribbles** on washable wallpapers can often be removed with dry cleaning fluid or by rubbing gently with a moist cloth sprinkled with bicarbonate of soda. **Grease stains** should be treated in the same way as wax, or tackled with dry cleaning fluid. All these treatments should be tested out first on a spare piece of wallpaper. If the stain will not come out and you have some paper to spare, tear out the wallpaper for the affected area in a jagged shape and patch. It will be less noticeable repaired that way than if you cut out a neat square. As a last resort, hang an ornament or picture over the spot.

WINDOWS

Treat **general stains** with a mild solution of vinegar or ammonia, or try cold tea. **Paint marks** should be tackled immediately: scrape off the excess, then treat with white spirit or nail varnish remover. If the paint has hardened, soften it first with white spirit. **Putty stains** can be softened with white spirit, then scraped off. **Bad stains** can be removed by spraying the area with proprietary oven cleaner. Allow to dry, wipe off.

WOOD FURNITURE

Furniture with a veneered or French polished finish needs very special care when treating stains. In the case of antique furniture, always get a professional's opinion first.

Spirit stains (including alcohol, perfume and some medicines) should be treated immediately as they can dissolve surface finishes, especially French polish. Blot, then wipe up immediately what you have spilled with cold water rubbing the wood with the palm of your hand as it dries. French-polished furniture will almost certainly need professional treatment to restore its shine. If the stain persists on other surfaces and is still fresh, try rubbing with a paste of oil and cigarette ash worked in with a circular motion. Waxed surfaces will need re-doing after this treatment.

Blood stains should be mopped up, sprinkled with salt and then wiped over. If the wood has been affected, rub gently with fine sandpaper and rub down with a hydrogen peroxide solution. Use 1 part of peroxide to 6 parts of water. Do not use this treatment on French-polished furniture.

Dents in solid wood can sometimes be treated by filling the hollow with very hot water, so that the fibres swell.

Heat marks which usually appear as white rings, can be tackled by rubbing turpentine into them, going in the direction of the grain, not round in circles.

Water marks should be treated in the same way as heat marks. If this fails, then try rubbing metal polish into the marks, going in the direction of the grain. Water marks in solid wood can be treated by rubbing with very fine steel wool dipped in liquid wax floor or furniture polish.

Ink stains need quick treatment: blot, dab with bleach and blot again. Do not rub or you may be left with a bleached spot. Rinse well afterwards. Old stains can be tackled with a proprietary wood bleach.

Scratches can sometimes be saved in solid wood furniture if you pour hot water over the affected area to make the wood swell. If this fails, disguise by rubbing with a wax crayon of a similar shade to the wood or shoe polish, eyeliner or a proprietary scratch dressing.

Cigarette burns and scorch marks: if the mark is a light one, rub with metal polish, going with the grain of the wood. If the wood has a wax finish, rub with turpentine instead. If the surface is roughened and blackened, scrape with a sharp craft knife, and then rub with very fine sand paper. If necessary fill with wood stopping, then tint to match the table with shoe or professional wood polish.

Finger marks: rub with a soft cloth dampened with a solution of 1 part vinegar to 8 parts water. Rinse, dry well afterwards.

WOOD, PAINTED

General stains should come off in a hot, mild solution of washing soda or strong solution of washing-up liquid. Do not use abrasives on gloss painted surfaces or they will rub off the shine. To clean off stains before repainting, use a strong solution of sugar soap.

"Don't Spoil the Ship For a Ha'p'orth of Tar"

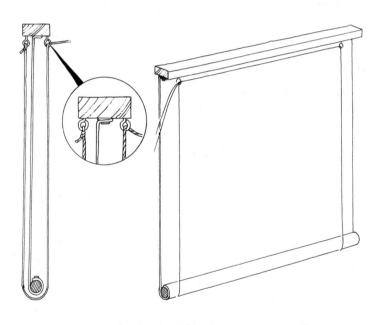

Tips on machine care, furniture care and improvizing

Machine
and furniture care

MACHINE FAULTS

Who to telephone: If your machine develops a fault, it pays to telephone the manufacturer, rather than the shop you bought it from, unless the latter has a Service Department. When you obtain the machine, write out the address and telephone number you need on a sticky label and glue in place somewhere handy on the machine.

Appliance documents: If for any reason you have to return an electrical appliance to the manufacturer for repair under guarantee, you will need the receipt or guarantee registration card that came with it. The best thing is to keep all documents relating to electrical appliances, including instruction books and serial numbers, in a safe place.

Plugs: Always pull the plug out of the wall socket before examining any electrical machine for faults.

Sockets: Before you unscrew the plug on an appliance that has stopped working, plug it into another socket which houses something you know is working. It could be that a power cut, or a faulty socket, is an explanation for the failure, not the machine.

MACHINE MAINTENANCE

Flexes: Keep flexes of portable household items like irons, hairdryers, kettles, as short as possible, whilst still allowing room for manoeuvre. You are then less likely to trip over them or hook them up in something.

Short flexes: If the flex on a household appliance is too short to reach the socket, always plug into an extension lead rather than join an extra length of flex on to the existing one. For a more permanent arrangement, the entire flex should be replaced by a professional.

Filter cleaning: Save on unnecessary visits from the repair man. Clean the filters of washing machines, tumbler driers and dishwashers, whether they seem to need it or not. This will help to keep the machines running smoothly.

Surgical tape: Use wide surgical tape to make temporary repairs on household hoses until you are able to replace them.

Frayed flexes: Generally speaking, it is dangerous to repair frayed flexes, even with insulating tape, although this will work as an emergency measure. It is much safer to replace them instead.

Hoses: Make sure that the hoses on your washing machine or dishwasher are free from kinks, are not pinched against another appliance or against the wall. Otherwise the machine may not fill or empty properly.

Blocked hoses: Check the outlet hose on washers and dishwashers from time to time, it can become blocked, with the result that the contents of the machine will stay sodden. Most outlet hoses are attached to the machine by means of a clip and can be easily removed. You can then check for blockages by looking through them or running a wire up them.

Door seals: Clean regularly round the door seals of dishwashers, washing machines to make sure that they stay watertight.

Dishwashers: Never put real silverware in contact with other metal items in a dishwasher. Otherwise it may become marked and pitted.

Spin drier: Always make sure that the load in your spin drier is evenly distributed, otherwise it could cause bumping, excessive vibration and possibly damage the machine. Also, the clothes will not be dried efficiently.

Tumbler drier: Never fill a tumbler drier more than two-thirds full of clothes. Make sure that they have been well wrung out or spin-dried first to save money.

REFRIGERATORS AND FREEZERS

Position: To save money when running a refrigerator or a freezer, site it in the coolest possible place, leave it at least an inch from the wall to allow the air to circulate and hot air to escape.

Door seal check: Check for a faulty door seal on refrigerators and freezers by putting a sheet of writing paper over the door edge, then shutting the door. If it is difficult to pull out, the seal is intact. If it comes away easily, the seal needs replacing.

Noisy refrigerator: If your refrigerator or freezer is making a great deal of noise, it is probably not standing on a level surface. Adjust the leg screws accordingly or level it up by placing a sliver of wood under one leg.

Dusting: Dust the unit at the back of your refrigerator regularly. A build-up of dust and dirt can cause the motor to run excessively.

When not in use: If you are not going to use the refrigerator for any length of time, always defrost and clean it first. Always leave the door propped open – otherwise mildew will form and an unpleasant smell will develop inside.

Ice-cube trays: Put a sheet of waxed paper under your ice-cube trays before you put them in the freezing compartment of the refrigerator. It stops the tray from sticking to the bottom.

Shelf use: When filling the refrigerator, store raw meat and fish in the coldest zone, cooked food and fats in the centre and salad items in the base. Dairy products and eggs should be stored in the door.

Wrapping: All food should be wrapped in the refrigerator to stop it from drying out. Strong smelling foods should be wrapped with cling-film to stop odours escaping and contaminating other food.

Warm food: Never put warm food in the refrigerator, it will cause it to ice up more quickly.

Broken racks: Broken pieces of plastic rack or accidental holes in the plastic in a refrigerator can sometimes be repaired with a resin repair kit sold in car accessory shops. Always allow it to dry thoroughly before re-using the refrigerator.

VACUUM CLEANERS

Blocked hose: If a vacuum cleaner hose becomes blocked, try reversing it by putting the nozzle on to the suction end, in the hope that will shift the blockage.

Spares: Always keep a spare rubber ring or fan belt to hand for your vacuum cleaner. They have a habit of breaking at times when the shop is shut.

ELECTRICAL GOODS

Steam iron: Always use distilled water when filling a steam iron or it will fur up in time and become faulty.

Kettle: Never fill your electric kettle when it is still plugged into the socket, and always make sure that the element is covered.

Toaster: Save on chores by standing your electric toaster on a tray to catch the crumbs. Remember to clean out the toaster's own crumb compartment regularly. Always switch off and unplug the appliance first.

Electric blankets: Remember to get your electric blanket serviced during the summer months.

GAS APPLIANCES

Ventilation: If you are using gas appliances in a room, remember that there must be adequate ventilation or they will not work properly. In particular, never block up air bricks or built-in ventilators.

Water heaters: Do not run small 'instantaneous' gas water heaters for more than five minutes at a time. Otherwise you may burn out the appliance.

COOKERS AND HEATING

Ovens: Always take a look inside the oven before you turn it on. You may have inadvertently left a dish or a baking tin with food in it, inside.

Radiant fires: Always keep the reflectors of radiant fires shining and clean to get the maximum benefit from them. Use metal polish and a soft duster to bring up the shine.

Radiators: Patchy heat on radiators is almost certainly caused by an air block. Keep a special venting key to hand to turn the valve and let the air out. Always place a bowl underneath the valve when you are doing so as a little dirty water may escape, too.

Wood-burning stoves: If you are using a wood-burning stove, or burning wood in a fireplace, remember that the chimney will need sweeping more frequently than if you are burning coal. Usual chimney sweeping intervals are: wood, 3 times a year; coal, twice a year. If you are burning smokeless fuel, then the chimney will only need attention once a year.

FURNITURE

Leg marks: To stop the legs of furniture marking the floor, glue small pieces of foam plastic to their bases.

Wall marks: To avoid the backs of sofas and armchairs from hitting and marking the wall, fix thick strips of draught excluder to them.

Upholstery studs: If you are putting decorative upholstery studs or tacks into a piece of furniture, fix a tape measure alongside the seam with masking tape. It will then give you regular marked intervals to guide you.

Protective covers: To protect the arms and backs of newly upholstered furniture, ask the store to supply you with an extra length of material. Use this to make protecting covers. The fabric can also be sprayed with silicone water and dirt repellant before use.

Screws: When screwing small items like knobs on drawers or doors in place, dip the screws into a little nail varnish before you use them. They go in more easily, set hard and won't rust.

Plastic foam: If you are stuffing a cushion with pieces of plastic foam, rub some fabric softener over the palms of your hands first. This will stop the foam from sticking to them.

CHAIRS

Cane seats: If the cane seat of a chair has become stretched and is sagging, try this method of tightening it up: sponge it carefully on both upper and lower sides with hot soapy water. Then leave it to dry, away from heat, preferably in the open air. It should shrink back to its original shape.

Wobbles: A table or chair that wobbles may have loose joints. If these are screwed in place, replace the existing screw with a larger one, or put a plastic plug into the hole and re-screw.

TABLE TOPS

Working tables: To avoid unnecessary scratches when using a dining table as a work table – i.e. for anything from sewing machines to typewriters – have a special heavy duty cloth to hand cut from thick plastic. Don't be tempted to use sheets of newspaper, etc., because they may shift during working without your noticing it.

Scratches: To avoid items like book-ends, candlesticks, lamp bases from scratching the polished top of a table, cut out pieces of felt or wool from a discarded jacket to fit them and glue to the base. Or, use foam plastic held in place with a suitable adhesive.

Large tablemats: Patchwork squares made from crocheted odds and ends of string make good tablemats to take large dishes.

FURNISHINGS AND ACCESSORIES

Newspaper: Use thick layers of newspaper as underfelt for a carpet. It not only saves wear but keeps in heat and cuts down noise.

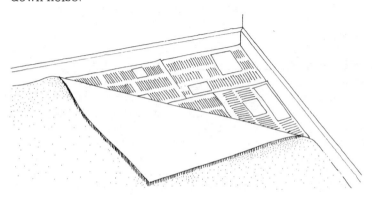

Curtain lining: When lining curtains, leave the bottom hem of the lining unstitched. Hang the curtains for a week to allow the fabric to stretch and any creases to drop out, then hand-hem the lining in situ.

Net curtains: Hang unpatterned net curtains upside down from time to time, they will last much longer.

Waste paper baskets: Large party beer tins, covered with the type of adhesive plastic sheeting used for shelving, make good waste paper baskets.

Sheets: Give plain sheets a luxury look by sewing a band of broderie anglaise, gingham or lace, along the top turn down. Add a matching edge of frill to pillows.

Bathmats: Several same-sized bath towels that have become worn, can be quilted together to make a useful bath or beach mat. Sew decorative patches over the worn places.

Oil cloths: Old-fashioned oil cloths can be given a new lease of life if you rub the surface over with beaten white of egg, using a soft cloth. When it has dried it can be polished with a duster to make it shine.

Odd pieces of soap: Another way with odd pieces of soap: Put them into a basin with a few drops of glycerine, steam in a pan of boiling water until the mixture is soft. Allow to almost cool, press it into shape of a tablet (see also page 86).

Decorative cord: Use nail varnish or sticky tape to stop decorative cord unravelling until you have time to tackle it.

Fuzzy fabric: 'Shave' the surface of a fabric with a razor blade to remove small balls of fuzz, or, rub with very fine sandpaper.

Gift tags: Save last year's Christmas cards to make gift tags for the following year: cut out colourful decorations, thread with a cotton tie, write a message on the back.

NYLON TIGHTS AND STOCKINGS

Vacuuming: Fasten a piece of nylon tights over the nozzle of a vacuum cleaner. You can then use it to vacuum out the insides of drawers and other difficult places, without blowing the contents around. It's also a useful way to pick up contact lenses out of carpets.

Storage: Use discarded nylon stockings to store onions and other items. Hang them up in a corner or a cupboard. They'll store better that way.

Fastenings: Old nylon stockings make good ties to fasten the tops of large plastic garbage bags.

Odd stockings: If you have a lot of odd stockings, boil them up quickly together in a large saucepan, leave them to cool and they should all come out the same colour. Add a teabag or two if you want to intensify the shade.

Starching: If you apply a little starch to tights when you wash them, they are much less likely to snag and are easier to put on.

NEW LEASE OF LIFE

Bras: Turn a white bra into a flesh-coloured one on a temporary basis – to wear under see-through clothes for instance. Soak it in a solution of 60 ml (4 tablespoons) of instant coffee to 1 litre (2 pints) of water. Check the colour after a while, rinse in cold water and dry. After a few washes, the colour will come out.

Fabric shoes: Linen and canvas running shoes and sandals will resist dirt much longer if you spray them with fabric protector before you wear them. Spray white tennis shoes with starch for the same reason.

Make-up bags: A thick polythene bag makes a good plastic liner for a decorative fabric make-up bag.

REPAIRING AND MENDING

Torn pages: The torn page of a book can be glued back together again with the white of an egg. Place the pieces in position on a smear of egg white, cover lightly on top with egg white and allow to dry thoroughly before you move.

Broken china: When mending china, clean the breaks first with cottonwool dipped in neat hydrogen peroxide, to remove any discoloration.

Broken crockery: A cup, plate or saucer that has just one break in it can be mended with an epoxy resin glue – colour it to match the china with powdered artists colours.

Waxing a leak: Paraffin wax can be used to mend a leaking vase, just coat the inside with a thick layer and allow to dry.

Filling a crack: A hairline crack in crockery that is causing a leak can be sealed by simmering the offending article in milk for about an hour. The milk should fill the crack and coagulate inside it making a seal.

Black dye: When dyeing a piece of fabric black, it's a good idea to use an equal quantity of blue dye. This avoids that green tell tale tinge that many home-coloured black garments have.

Cracked ivory: Restore the look of cracked ivory or bone pieces by dipping them in white melted candle wax. Wipe off any excess and leave them to set. Provided you keep them away from direct heat, the cracks should not show.

Holed umbrella: Use iron-on mending tape to repair a hole in an umbrella. Place the tape on the underside of the cover then press on top with a warm iron.

Clothes' patches: If you are patching clothes, use pinking shears to cut out the pieces of material to save having to turn under the edges.

Improvization

INSIDE AND OUTSIDE THE HOUSE

Carpet off-cuts: You can carpet a room very cheaply – or even for free. Carpet shops sell off cheaply, or sometimes give away, sample pieces of carpet (sometimes quite large) when they change lines. Ring up carpet shops in your area and ask. the pieces can be glued or stitched together to make a large patchwork carpet.

Patterned flooring: If you can't afford carpets for a room, you can improve the look of the floor by stencilling it. Buy ready-made stencils or cut your own from stencil paper. Hold them in place with masking tape and use either spray paint or use ordinary gloss paint with a stencil brush. A final coat of polyurethane varnish will also give a longer lasting finish.

From door to work surface: An old door makes a handy work surface. If you use the hinges to attach it to the wall and fit hinged legs, you can fold it away when not in use.

Build your own barbecue: Use a few bricks and two wire grills for a cheap home barbecue set. Make it half a metre (two feet) square and two bricks high. Remove one brick to allow air to circulate. Put one of the wire grills on top of the bricks – this is for the charcoal. Build up the square to waist height, then put the other grill on top for the food.

Free-standing shelves: Make your own bookcase quickly and easily. Simply stack planks or floorboards on top of bricks, which act as spacers. Don't build more than four planks high, or the structure will become unsteady.

Home-made blind: An old broomstick can be made into the basis of a cheap rolled blind. First cut it to the width of the window. Choose a piece of material and cut this to the width and length of the window allowing for, then making, narrow hems. Tack one end to a batten (25 × 50 mm/2 × 1 inches) the width of the window and the other to the broomstick. Fix two long pieces of string to the batten a short way in from the edges of, and behind, the material. Fix two screw eyes opposite the string in front of the material. Roll the material up around the broomstick to the top of the window. Pass the two pieces of string through the two screw eyes. Use the string to raise and lower the blind.

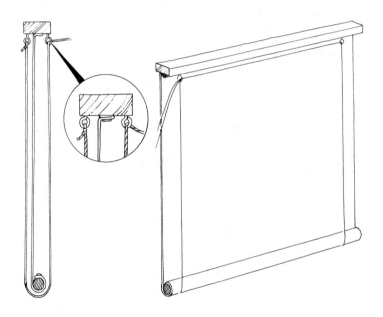

Hang it all: Paint a length of old garden trellis a bright colour, attach it to the kitchen wall, hang a few butcher's hooks from it and you will have instant extra storage for untidy kitchen utensils.

Medicine containers: Four litre (two pint) icecream containers are ideal for keeping first aid and medical supplies in. Remember to keep medicine out of reach of children.

Screw-top jars: Save screw top jars to make under-shelf storage for odds and ends. Simply screw the jar lid to the bottom of a wooden shelf – use at least two screws. Now the jar will hang under the shelf and can be removed with just a twist, leaving the lid still in place.

Improvized wardrobe: Use narrow alcoves for hanging clothes. Attach two or three lengths of strong chain to the wall at different heights near the top. Use fairly large linked chain, so that the coat hangers will slot into them. Attach one end to the wall and let it hang vertically. Use this to hang clothes from, so that they overlap. Hang a piece of curtain over the front of the alcove if you wish.

Kitchen knife holder: Save empty cotton reels to make into a useful kitchen knife holder. Nail a row of them shoulder-to-shoulder on to a piece of board. Add another row 75–100 mm (3 to 4 in) below the first row, taking care to line the two rows up. Attach the board to the kitchen wall and slip the knives in between the reels, so that they hang by their handles.

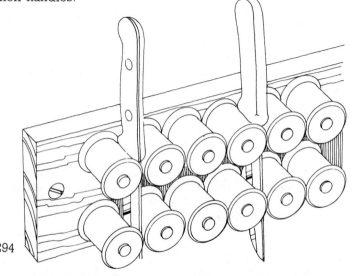

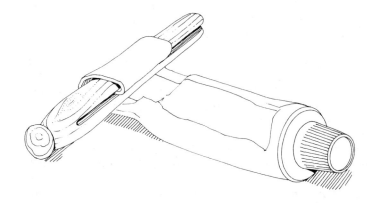

A tight squeeze: Use an old-fashioned clothes peg as a 'key' to get the most out of toothpaste tubes. Slip the peg over the end of the tube when about half of the paste has been used. Twist the tube around the peg to get all the paste out.

Plunger to the rescue: If you accidentally pull one of the handles off a chest of drawers, you may find the drawer impossible to pull out. Wet the end of a rubber plunger and use this as a giant sucker to pull the drawer out.

Handy tool holder: Cut the finger ends off an old leather glove, cut two slots in the palm and thread on a belt for a useful tool holster.

Cork cushions: An old cork will help to save your fingers, when you are rummaging in your odds and ends drawer. Use the cork as a pin cushion for nails, drawing pins and other sharp objects.

There's life in an old paintbrush: A matted old paintbrush can still be of use – cut off the matted bristles to leave a handy dusting down brush to use before decorating.

Plant markers: Save the children's iced lolly sticks to use as plant markers – just write on them with a permanent marker. You can cut one end to a point with a sharp knife to make it easier to stick in the soil.

Bottle top bird scarer: If you grow your own fruit or vegetables, make a useful bird-scarer this way. Save foil milk bottle tops, when you have about thirty, thread them loosely on to a piece of strong cotton or string, with a knot between to make sure they are separated. Hang up between two pieces of bamboo a little way above the ground. The noise and the flashing produced as they move in the wind is enough to keep most birds away.

Non-rust cans: Aluminium drink cans make good paint-brush holders – they won't rust and discolour the paint. Use a knife to cut off the top of the can, then trim any rough edges with scissors. If there are still jagged pieces, either file them with coarse sandpaper or fold over the edges to the inside of the can. Wash carefully before using.

Screen it: Screens are convenient to add privacy to bedsits. To make your own, hinge together four louvred doors or shutters with attractive brass hinges.

Measuring pinta: If you need to measure a pint of liquid but do not have a measuring jug, use a clean milk bottle instead. You could make similar use of a litre wine bottle, if measuring in metric.

RECYCLING IDEAS

Bright plant pots: Cans that have contained tinned food make good containers for small plants – clean them thoroughly, then paint them in bright colours and they will look completely different. Empty paint tins also make cheap and cheerful holders for outdoor plant pots, once they have been cleaned and painted.

Freezer fillers: Fill empty plastic lemonade or squash

bottles with water and use them to fill space in your freezer, if it is low on food. A full freezer functions more efficiently.

Egg-box starter kits: Egg-boxes can be used as starter kits for seeds – fill the hollows with soil or vermiculite, sow the seed in them. They're useful for starting off seed potatoes too, as they hold them in the correct position.

"Strike While the Iron Is Hot"

All about
washing, drying and ironing

Washing techniques

PRE-WASH TIPS

LAUNDRY BASKETS

Wet towels: Don't put wet towels into the laundry basket. Try to dry them first. If you don't, they could start to mildew in the basket.

Plastic bags: Give each person in the household a large plastic bag to hang on the back of the door to put all dirty clothes in. This will help keep rooms tidy as well as helping you. Use the same principle after ironing, allocate everyone a basket into which ironed clothes are put to be collected for putting away.

Two baskets: Get the family to help with the initial sorting of the clothes by having two laundry baskets, one that takes white material and the other that takes coloured items.

SORTING

Table cloths: Do not put table cloths and place mats away with stains on them. Apart from being unhygienic, it will also make any stains doubly difficult to remove when you do come to wash them.

Stains: Look carefully while you are sorting the washing for badly stained items. If you catch the stain before it is sealed in by the hot water, then it will be easier to get out. (See Stains sections, pages 234–67.)

Tears and loose fittings: Inspect all clothes for tears and loose buttons before the clothes are put into their respective piles.

Care labels: Sort all the clothes thoroughly before they are put into the wash. Sort them according to their care label.

Sorting piles: Clothes can usually be sorted into the following piles:
White cotton and linen – which can be washed in very hot water.
Colourfast coloured cottons – hot water, according to care label.
Nylon and synthetic materials – hand hot water.
Rayon and silk – hand hot water.
Delicate articles – warm water.
Woollens – warm water.
Hand wash all articles found to bleed when tested.

COLOURFASTNESS
Testing for colourfastness: To test clothes for colourfastness before immersing the whole garment, wet an inconspicuous area. Then proceed as described on page 227. If the material stays white then wash normally. If there is a faint trace of the colour on the material, then it is safest to wash this garment on its own for the moment. It should stop bleeding after a few washes. If the material is well coloured then the garment is not colourfast and may need to be dry cleaned to prevent all the colour from being bled out of it.

Making colours fast: To make black or red materials colourfast, soak them in a bowl of salty water. For brown, pink and grey items, add salt and alum (obtainable from chemist's), for green just soak in a solution of alum. For blue items soak in a solution of white vinegar.

SOAKING
Overnight soaking: Anything that is exceptionally dirty should be soaked overnight, material permitting, as this is the best way of ensuring that it gets clean. Soak clothes in a bucket big enough for them not to be squashed together.

Soaking and colour change: If you are going to soak an item before you wash it, make sure that the detergent is completely dissolved and that you soak the whole of the article – soaking causes a slight colour change and this will show up if the material is not completely soaked.

Over-soaking: When soaking make sure that you do not over-soak the material. As the water cools the dirt settles back into the material, 20 minutes should be sufficient.

White clothes: Add laundry borax (see page 181) to the water when soaking white clothes, this will help to loosen the dirt.

Milk: Try soaking white clothes with stubborn stains overnight in milk. This will often shift the stain.

BEFORE THE WASHING MACHINE
Loose dirt: Make sure that you brush off any loose mud or dirt before an item goes into the wash.

Trouser cuffs: Make sure that you unroll trouser cuffs before they are put into the wash. They not only harbour dirt but also cause marks if washed rolled up.

Shirt cuffs: Button shirt cuffs to the front of the shirt. This will prevent tangling of the arms.

Folded items: Open out any items that are folded as there may be hidden corners of dirt in the folds.

Wooden buttons: Remove any wooden buttons from items as they may swell and crack after washing.

Fasteners: Close all fasteners before they enter the washer, they can snag other materials and damage delicate fabrics.

Pockets: Make sure that all pockets are completely empty, especially look out for stray bits of tissue which will cover the whole wash in little pieces of fluff. Beware of children's pockets, they will invariably contain some little treasure which could harm your washing machine, or stain clothes.

WASHING TIPS

DETERGENT

Light amounts: Always use the suggested amount of detergent when washing. Too little will mean items will not be clean, too much will cause greyness.

Too much lather: If a detergent produces too much lather in your washing machine, add some fabric conditioner.

Neat detergent: Make sure that the detergent is completely dissolved before any clothes come into contact with it. Neat detergent will cause patchiness in coloured fabrics.

Low lather: In a front loading washing machine be sure to use a low lather detergent.

Twin-tubs: Dissolve the detergent in a twin-tub before putting in the clothes, by setting the machine to wash for a few minutes.

Automatics: Automatics are designed for a particular powder so always use one recommended for your machine.

Cool wash: To dissolve detergent for a cool wash, mix it first with some fairly hot water and then add it to the cooler water.

Warm wash: You will need more detergent for warm water than for hot.

TEMPERATURE

Launderettes: The maximum temperature used in a launderette is usually 60°C (140°F). This will wash cottons or linens as long as they are colourfast, also coloured polyester cotton mix. Whites will probably not come out very white because the bleaching action of the powder will not have started properly at this temperature, so add your own extra bleach.

Cold water: Do not wash items in cold water as this will not get rid of the dirt – the water must be warm enough to start to melt any grease. Detergent, apart from biological ones, will not function at low temperatures.

Towels: Towels are often scratchy when they haven't been rinsed properly. Remember they are absorbent and so will hold detergent longer than other materials.

SPINNING

Synthetics: Synthetic fabric doesn't need much spinning, after a certain point you will be spinning creases into the fabric. If the fabric is still fairly damp when it comes out of the spinner don't worry.

Temperature guide: If you do not have a modern washer with dials that correspond to the temperature shown on the care label, then here is a rough guide. (See also pages 206–7 for information on wash programmes.)
100°C–212°F Boiling Point.
 95°C–203°F Extremely hot – there will be clouds of steam.
 60°C–140°F Probably the highest you will ever get from a hot tap.
 50°C–122°F Highest hand temperature that you will be able to bear.
 40°C–104°F Warm to the hand.
 30°C– 86°F Cool to the hand.

WASHLOAD

Fragile articles: Wash tights, lace and other fragile articles in a pillow case to prevent them from being damaged by or being tangled with other articles.

Mixed load: Try to mix a load of washing so that it contains large and small items.

Washing programme: Set the washing programme correctly acccording to the care label on the garment, this will make sure that the material is washed properly and will reduce the risk of fading of colours, shrinking etc.

FABRIC CARE
White clothes: When boiling white clothes in a pan add a piece of lemon skin, it acts as a natural bleach. If you have a twin-tub be sure to fish out the skin as soon as the clothes are washed. Do not use in an automatic or you will clog up the machine.

Damask cloths: Damask table linen will benefit from a spoonful of methylated spirits in the final rinse.

White socks: A small amount of bicarbonate of soda, added to the washing water, will take the shoe stains out of white socks.

White nylon: Wash white nylon on its own as it often picks up seemingly invisible dyes from the water and will readily turn grey.

White silk: White silk and nylon should be washed in white soap powder; many coloured powders have dyes added to them. When rinsing add a *few* drops of washable blue ink, it will help emphasize the white.

Corduroy: Wash corduroy items inside out as this will stop them picking up any fluff in the water.

Nylon jumpers: Wash nylon jumpers inside out as this will prevent snags and damage to the surface in the wash.

White lace: White lace can get very grubby. Put it into skimmed milk with a little laundry blue. Rinse in warm water and pull back into shape.

RINSING
Bleach: Bleach must always be rinsed thoroughly out of any material. If not, it may continue to act and harm the fabric.

Softener: In the final rinse add a cup of white vinegar, this will neutralize the action of the soap powder and will soften the fabric.

Epsom Salts: Add 5 ml (1 teaspoon) of Epsom Salts to $4\frac{1}{2}$ litres (1 gallon) of water in the final rinse. This will help to prevent colour bleeding from the material. (See also page 301 for information on making colours fast.)

Proper rinsing: Rinsing is a very important part of the wash process, look how much time it takes up on a washing machine cycle. If the article is not rinsed properly then you will often damage fibres of the fabric as well as rendering the fabric a grey colour.

Reducing static: Fabric conditioner, used in the final rinse, helps to reduce the amount of static electricity picked up by man-made fibres. (See also page 62 for hint on reducing static in an ironed garment.)

AFTER WASH TIPS

Sorting: As the clothes come out of the machine, sort them into those that will need to be ironed and those which will get by with just folding. Peg them out separately. When you come to unpeg them, start with those which do not need to be ironed so that they are on the bottom of the pile and do not crush the others.

End of programme: As soon as the clothes have finished washing, take them out of the machine to keep creasing to a minimum.

Sheets and table cloths: Sheets and table cloths should not need ironing if you treat them carefully at the drying stage. Smooth them by hand when still slightly damp.

Damp articles: There is a limited amount of time that articles can be left in a damp state before they start to develop mildew which is difficult to remove.

Washing machine care: Between washes, remember to clean the filter tray of your washing machine. After the last wash, give it a quick wipe over with a damp cloth.

DRYING TIPS

SPECIAL FABRICS

Coloureds: Dry coloured fabrics separately from white materials as until they are completely dry they are still capable of affecting each other.

Starched materials: Starched materials should be dried separately to prevent the starch from spreading to other clothes.

White articles: To store white silk, nylon and other articles, wrap in dark coloured tissue paper. This will prevent light getting to the material and so will stop it from yellowing.

Linen: Linen will be damaged if it is kept too long in a warm airing cupboard.

Tights: If wet tights are needed in a hurry, blow dry with a hair dryer – don't hold the dryer too close.

DRYING CARE

Fabric protection: Protect cleaned garments by using a proprietary fabric protector.

Ironing: Do not wait until the clothes are bone dry as this will lead to extra creasing and added expense in time and energy needed to iron them out. The iron will complete the drying process in most cases.

Sorting: Dry small articles and large articles separately.

Extra space: Spread a net or nylon mesh over the bath, fixed in four corners by suction cups, this will give you extra drying room.

Clothes rack: A length of ladder that is too old to be trusted to support your weight can make a useful clothes rack. Hang it from the bathroom or kitchen ceiling from four hooks fastened into the joists.

Woollens: To speed up the drying of woollens, put a folded towel inside the body of the sweater and two cardboard tubes inside the sleeves.

TUMBLE DRYING

Drier load: Tumble-drying should be used as economically as possible. Do not over fill as this will mean that everything will take longer to dry.

Temperature: Check that anything you put into a tumbler drier can take the heat. Some items may have plastic fastenings and belts that could melt. Rubber and plastic items should not be dried in a tumbler drier, nor should permanent pleated items.

After the drying: Dried articles should be removed from the drier as soon as they are finished to prevent them becoming unnecessarily crumpled. If clothes are not to be ironed immediately, then they should be hung up.

Clothes too dry: If clothes have got too dry to iron, then put them into a tumbler drier with a wet towel and set the drier to cool.

WASHING LINE

Water droplets: Wipe the line clean and free of any water droplets before you hang clothes out.

White clothes: Peg very white clothes out on the line inside out so if they do catch any bits of dirt, these will be on the inside.

Stockings: When hanging out stockings on the line, stop them wrapping around other items by pegging the feet together at the bottom.

Pegging: Clothes should be pegged by their strongest part.

Clothes pegs: Clip your clothes pegs on to a metal hoop made from a wire coat hanger. Slip this over your arm when pegging the clothes out, it will leave both hands free for the clothes.

Wind: When hanging the washing out on the line, stand with your back to the wind, then the wind will help put the clothes on the line and they will not flap back at you.

Skirts: Skirts should be pegged by the waistband as this is really the only feasible place.

Delicate blouses: On delicate blouses which you are afraid will mark from the pegs or on jumpers that may be pulled out of shape, thread a pair of tights through the sleeves, like a child's elastic glove securer. Then peg the ends of the tights, rather than the blouse or jumper, to the line.

Sheets: The quickest way of drying sheets is to let the wind get to them. On a really blustery day they will dry quickly if laid length ways along the line. They take up more space this way but dry more quickly. Otherwise, fold them in four so that they are ready for ironing, but remember to keep turning them to aid drying.

Salt for anti-stick: When washing clothes on icy cold days, save them from sticking together when they're put out on the line by adding a handful of salt in the final rinse.

IRONING

Well-ironed sheets: When ironing sheets, put the board near to a table and as you iron slide the sheet on to the table in gentle folds to prevent it creasing.

Outside in: If you want a perfectly ironed table cloth, iron it from the outside inwards in concentric circles.

The right heat: When the temperature of the iron is critical for a garment don't use the iron the moment it heats up, give it about five minutes to settle down first – most irons overshoot the correct temperature before settling down.

Avoid buttons: Don't iron over buttons, most irons have a special groove at the tip to allow you to press around them.

Base cleaner: To remove a sticky patch from the base of an iron, rub it back and forwards gently on a piece of paper sprinkled with salt.

Avoiding fur: A steam iron will fur up less quickly if it is thoroughly emptied before being put away.

Getting rid of fur: Remove fur from steam irons by partially filling the iron with vinegar. Steam this away, then wash the inside with distilled water (see also page 274).

Dots for temperature: Those mysterious dots on the temperature control of your iron have a purpose. If you examine a modern garment you will find an iron symbol with a number of dots. Just match up the number of dots on the garment to the number on the iron and you'll know you're ironing at the right temperature. (See also page 205 for an explanation of the dots.)

Speedy ironing: You can iron faster if you put a strip of aluminium foil under an ironing board cover – the foil reflects heat back into the underside of the material.

Let garments settle: Try to avoid wearing newly ironed garments – unless they are left for a few hours they pick up creases very easily.

Dry spots: Ice cubes are ideal for damping isolated dry spots when ironing.

Stay sharp: Creases in trousers will stay sharper longer if you rub a little soap on the inside of the crease before ironing.

Crease prevention: When ironing over a zip, slip a strip of foam rubber inside the garment to prevent the iron from making creases.

Iron-savers: Most shirts will need very little ironing if they're taken straight from a tumbler drier and hung up while they cool.

Bleach it out: A light scorch mark in white cotton caused by an iron can often be removed by putting detergent on the spot and leaving it to bleach in the sun. (See also page 262.)

Button up: When ironing a shirt, button the sleeves together to prevent them from dragging on the floor while you work.

Ironing sleeves: When ironing the sleeves on a delicate garment, use a rolled up magazine inside the sleeve to keep the shape. Don't do this with a damp garment, the ink may run and cause staining.

Spray on water: If the clothes are too dry, but you wish to iron them straightaway, use a water-spray (such as is sold for spraying garden plants) and spray on water just before ironing.

Hold it steady: It is useful to have a proper holder for your iron. This serves two purposes, it means the iron doesn't have to be left standing while it cools and it prevents it being knocked over accidentally.

Caring for embroidery: Before ironing a heavily-embroidered article, place a good layer of soft material (such as a blanket) over the ironing-board. Then iron the embroidery on the wrong side. By this method the raised surface of the embroidery should not be crushed.

Too dry: Sprinkle articles that are too dry with water, then roll them up and leave them for half an hour or so before ironing.

"There's Many a Slip Twixt Cup and Lip"

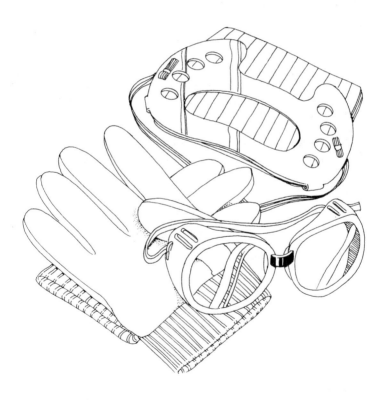

Safety hints about the house

Safety tips about the house

IN THE KITCHEN

Sharp knives: Blunt knives are even more dangerous than sharp ones because of the extra force needed to cut with them – keep yours sharp.

Loose handles: Loose saucepan handles are a danger as the handle may come off while you are carrying something hot. If the handle is screwed on, this just needs to be tightened up. If the handle is held by rivets, these can be tightened by putting one end of the rivet in contact with something hard (a brick, for example) and hitting the other end with a hammer.

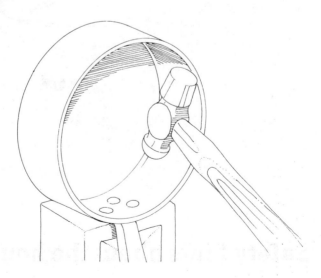

Handy surface: When planning a kitchen, try to arrange to have a surface next to the cooker on to which you can place pans from the cooker. It is dangerous to carry a heavy pan full of hot food across the kitchen.

Sensible storage: Another point to remember when planning a kitchen is that heavy items should not be stored above shoulder height. Reaching up to get a heavy pan from a top shelf is an ideal recipe for a domestic disaster. Even if the item is light, it is better to step up rather than reach up, to it. Invest in a sturdy set of steps; never balance on an old chair.

Cork it: Embed points of skewers and other sharp objects in old corks before putting them away in a drawer – that way you won't hurt your hands when you hunt for them.

Mince meat: When putting meat through a mincer use a wooden spoon, not your fingers, to push it down.

KITCHEN FIRE HAZARDS

Deep frying: When deep frying make sure the fat (without food in) doesn't come more than a third of the way up the side of the pan.

Fat on fire: If fat catches fire while you are cooking meat, sprinkle the meat and fat with bicarbonate of soda to put out the flames. When the soda is rinsed off, the meat will still be edible.

Steam: When pouring hot water out of a pan into the sink, partially fill the sink with cold water first to prevent steam from rising up and scalding your hands. Don't be put off if there seems to be more steam than usual – really hot steam is invisible, it shows up only as it cools.

Smoking oil: Remember that oil doesn't need a naked flame to light it. Once oil is sufficiently hot it will ignite on its own. Never let it get hot enough to start smoking – at this temperature, as well as being a fire hazard, it starts to break down and will make food taste bitter.

Damp heat: Never use a damp or wet teacloth for handling anything hot. The water will transmit the heat through the cloth and burn your hands.

The right clothes: When cooking, don't wear extravagant clothes that may trail and catch alight on the cooker.

Flame stopper: If a fire breaks out in the oven, don't open the oven door. Keep the door shut and turn off the heat – the fire will go out through lack of air. As an extra precaution with a gas oven, turn the mains supply off as well.

Teacloths: Never hang teacloths to dry over the cooker – this is a common cause of kitchen fires.

Safety blanket: Keep a fire blanket near the cooker to put out flames involving fat and/or electricity, then you won't be tempted to put water on the flames, which will only make matters worse.

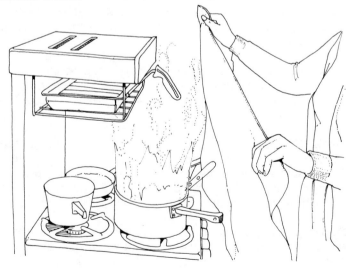

Dry fry: Make it a rule: never put wet food into hot fat – to do so causes the fat to spit violently. Dry the food (chips, for example) with a cloth before sliding carefully into the pan.

Hot surface: Never use the surface of an electric hob as a place to leave empty pans, etc. The hob may be turned on inadvertently.

GENERAL FIRE HAZARDS

Deep ashtrays: If you smoke, use stable, deep ashtrays where there is no risk of the tray being knocked over, or the cigarette falling out of it.

Flammable products: Don't store anything flammable near the entrance to the house or under the stairs (this includes many common household products). In the event of a fire they may ignite and make it difficult for you to get out of the house.

Decorations: When buying Christmas decorations, make sure that they are flame resistant.

Low beams: After you have moved into a new house you'll find that it takes some time for you to get used to any low beams. To avoid constantly banging your head, draw attention to the doorway by hanging something brightly coloured over it. The same applies to a doorway that is frequently used by guests.

Oil heaters 1: Never attempt to fill an oil heater when it is alight, this is often the cause of a fire.

Oil heaters 2: If possible, take the heater to the source of fuel rather than vice versa, to avoid unnecessary spills inside the house.

Oil heaters 3: Never move an oil heater around the room when it is alight and do not position it in a draughty spot. Never dry clothes on it.

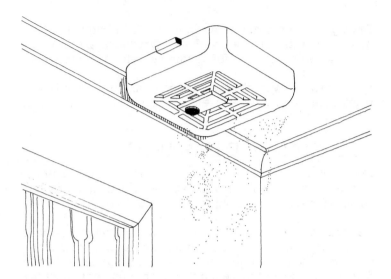

Smoke detectors: Most people die in fires due to asphyxiation from smoke rather than from the flames. Fit smoke detectors to give you an early warning of a fire.

T.V. grill: Make sure that the ventilation grill at the back of your television is not blocked by curtains.

Microcooking: Microwave cookers do not always heat food evenly – stir it before eating or you may be badly burned.

Escape rope: If there is only one way down from upstairs in your house, keep a length of knotted rope upstairs which is long enough to allow you to climb out of the window in case of a fire.

Chimney care: Chimney fires can be a danger – keep your chimney well swept (see page 286). If one does start you can put it out either by placing damp newspaper on the fire (the steam puts out the fire) or by throwing common salt into the flames. If these remedies don't work, starve the flames of air by shutting all the doors and windows and putting a damp blanket across the entrance to the fireplace.

Rubbish fire: Cigarette ash put into a rubbish bin is a common cause of fires. Empty ashtrays into an empty tin can and pour a little water in with the ash before throwing away.

SERVICES

Mains stopcock: Make sure that not just you, but everyone in the family knows where the mains water stopcock is and can turn it.

Cut-off rules: If you have coin-operated gas or electricity and it runs out, remember to turn off any appliances *before* putting more money in. Remember with gas that you will probably have to re-light pilot lights. During a power cut, the same rules apply to electrical and gas appliances.

Electricity in the bathroom: Electricity and water together are a recipe for tragedy. Never touch or operate any electrical appliances with wet hands, and never take any kind of appliance into the bathroom. The availability of electricity in the bathroom is limited deliberately to pull-cord operated light and heating fittings, and isolated shaver points, for your safety.

ELECTRICAL APPLIANCES

Cleaning: Switch off all appliances before cleaning them. The same applies when removing bread that's stuck in the toaster. Even when a toaster is switched off the elements should not be touched as they are easily damaged (see also page 285 for further information on toasters.

The right amp: Putting a 13 amp fuse in a plug on an appliance that draws very little current (a table light, perhaps) is almost as bad as by-passing the fuse altogether. Use a 3 amp or 5 amp fuse instead. As a guide to which to use, remember that a 3 amp fuse is for up to 600 watts and a 5 amp fuse for up to 1000 watts. Most appliances have their wattages marked on them somewhere.

Correct wattage: Most lampshades have a maximum wattage bulb recommended by the manufacturer. Make a note of this and don't be tempted to use larger bulbs, they may cause a fire.

Cable grips: Always use the cable grips when wiring a plug. Many people 'save time' by not using them – however, if they are not used the strain on the wire will mean that the plug soon has to be rewired; it can also cause the wires to short, fusing the plug or causing a bad accident.

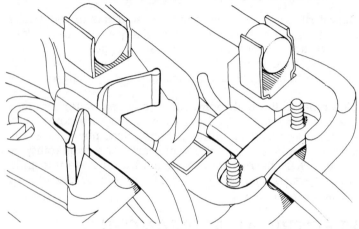

Switch off appliances: To avoid fire, unplug, or switch off at the socket, as many appliances as is possible before retiring to bed. This is particularly important for the television.

Socket adaptors: Never use more than one socket adaptor in any one socket; to do so can cause sparking and be a fire hazard.

Electrical imports: Many other countries have different, or much lower, standards when it comes to electrical safety; be watchful when buying imported items or bringing things back from holiday. If in doubt have them checked by a qualified electrician.

Fuses: Never replace the fuse in a plug with anything but the correct fuse. Never be tempted to use pieces of wire, silver foil, etc. At a pinch you can use a fuse of a lower rating if you do not have exactly the right one, but you may find it blows very easily.

Electrical check-up: If you buy a secondhand electrical appliance, have it checked by a qualified electrician before using it, even if it seems to be in perfect condition.

Extra insulation: Most tools designed for electrical work are insulated. For extra safety, if you find yourself having to use tools that are not, simply wrap insulating tape around the handles.

AND GAS APPLIANCES

Secondhand gas appliance: When considering the purchase of a secondhand gas appliance don't forget that you will need to have it checked by a qualified engineer, not only for your peace of mind, but also in order to satisfy the gas board. You should therefore add the cost of this on to the price of the item.

Gas water heater: If you have a gas water heater in the bathroom, don't get into the bath while it's running.

Back from holiday: Remember to relight any pilots on gas appliances, once you have turned on the mains supply on your return from holiday.

ELECTRIC BLANKETS

Overloaded plug: Never plug electric blankets into an adaptor which is shared with another appliance. This could cause overloading.

Avoid creases: Always make sure that an electric blanket is lying flat and smooth on the bed. Creases in it could cause the element to break.

Blanket storage: Never fold an electric blanket to store it. Instead roll it up or keep it flat on a spare bed when not in use.

Overheating: Do not leave heavy objects, such as suit cases, on a bed when the electric blanket is switched on. It could cause the wires to overheat.

HOME SECURITY

New locks: When moving into a new flat or house, it's worth changing the major locks on outside doors. If you don't do this you have no way of knowing how many keys there are in existence and who has them (anyone who had borrowed the keys from the estate agent, for example, could have had copies cut).

Prevention is best: To prevent a lock being slipped using a thin piece of plastic, knock a few carpet tacks into the frame just in front of the bolt recess. Don't knock them in all the way, just far enough for the door to close without scraping them. In this position they will block any attempt to slip the lock.

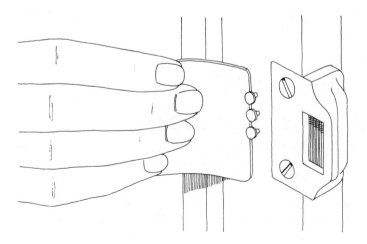

Inner doors: Don't bother to lock inside doors when going away on holiday – once a burglar has got into the house this will not stop him, it will only increase the amount of damage done.

Out of sight: Don't leave valuables on view through windows. These will only tempt people, and may give the impression that yours is a home worth burgling.

No ladders: Don't leave ladders lying around outside if you can help it. If you have to, then padlock them to something, so that they can't be moved.

Keys in the lock: Never leave keys in the lock on the inside of a door. Very often if you do a burglar can either turn it from the outside with a pair of tweezers or make a small hole in the door near the lock and turn it like that.

Mortice bolts: Where possible, fit key-operated mortice bolts rather than ordinary barrel bolts. Mortice bolts are much stronger because they are set into the door itself and from the outside the burglar has no way of knowing where and how many of them there are.

Insurance: Make sure you are fully insured. Also, keep your insurance updated in line with inflation and any new valuable contents added since the last estimate.

Beware strangers: Don't let strangers into the house without making them show you identification. Many burglars carry out thefts by tricking their way into the house.

No notes: Never leave a note on the door saying that you are out, or when you will be back.

Safe for people

WITH CHILDREN IN MIND

Drink bottles: Never use bottles that once contained soft drinks to store anything else in. Small children may well recognize the bottle and help themselves.

Stair gates: Use safety gates across all stairways until you are confident that a small child is old enough to cope with them.

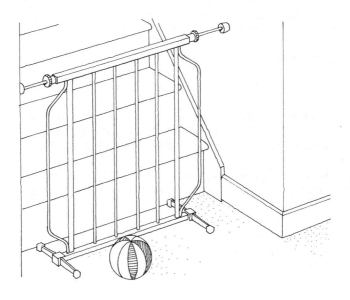

Baby bath: A baby can easily slip in a bath and bang its head. To prevent this, put a small towel or flannel on the bottom of the bath before filling.

Safe saucepans: Small children will reach up to grab at anything. When cooking keep all saucepans and frying pans turned in from the edge of the cooker. Put a guard rail round the edge, and never leave a child alone in the kitchen. If possible, use the kind of pans that have two small handles, one on each side, rather than those with just one large one.

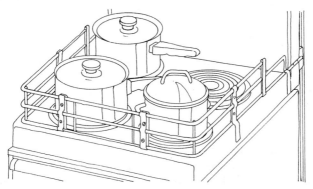

Storage places: If you have a child about your home for the first time, you will have to alter some of the places that you usually keep things – don't keep cleaners and chemicals under the sink, for example.

Eating code: Children are not always good at remembering which growing things are safe to eat and which are not. To be on the safe side tell them not to eat anything that is growing.

Washing machines: If you have small children, make sure that the door of your washing machine and tumbler drier cannot be opened while the machines are running. When buying a new machine, get one where the door can be locked when not in use.

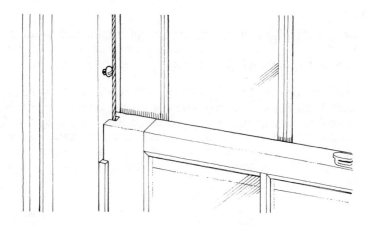

Sash windows: If you have small children around, make sure that they can't fall out of a sash window by putting a screw in the way of the runner 15 centimetres (six inches) above the top of the lower sash. You'll still be able to open the window for fresh air, but not far enough to be a danger to children.

Socket covers: Although modern sockets incorporate a mechanism to prevent children pushing things into them, accidents can happen. Be on the safe side, use plastic socket covers when the socket is not in use.

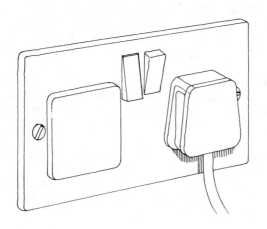

Emergency locks: Discourage children from using the locks on bathroom and toilet doors. If possible replace existing locks with the kind that can be opened from the outside in an emergency.

Bathroom locks: If a child locks him or herself in the bathroom and can't get out, distract his or her attention by passing a favourite comic under the door. Many bathroom locks can be opened with a minimum of damage by levering the frame and the door apart at the point where the bolt enters the frame. If this doesn't work you can try shouldering the door – but remember to tell the child to stand well clear. If this, too, fails call a locksmith or, finally, dial 999. (See Emergency Locks above.)

Plastic bags: Never leave plastic bags within the reach of children.

Electric flex: Don't let animals or children play with flexes, they are easy to bite through.

Pond netting: If you have very small children about, fix netting over all ponds and pools – even ornamental ones. A small child can drown in only a few inches of water.

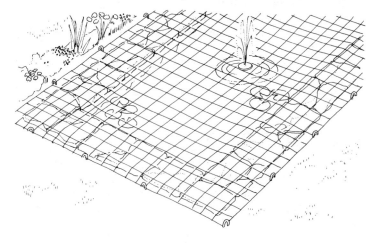

Glass stickers: Children often cannot see whether an all-glass patio door is open or closed until it's too late. To help them, stick something on the glass at their eye level.

Babysitters: When using a babysitter, give her a list of what to do if a fire breaks out, the telephone rings, someone comes to the door, she smells gas, the fuses go, or a child becomes ill. You should also leave her the telephone number of the place you are going to.

It's no bother: If a child is late home inform the police if this is in any way abnormal. Don't be afraid of 'bothering' the police. They never mind being alerted unnecessarily.

Friend not foe: Never give your children any cause to be frightened of the police. They may need a policeman's help at some stage, but they will not go to him if they think he is a bogey-man.

Delayed reactions: If you pick your child up from school consider the consequences if you are delayed for any reason. If you know you are going to be late 'phone the school secretary. If possible make an advance arrangement for another mother to pick your child up, you can do the same for her when needed.

Strange stories: When warning your children about going with strangers don't forget that the stories used may not be obvious. For instance, what would your child do if told that what they were doing was 'very naughty' and they were to get in the car – the person was going to take them home and tell their mummy about it?

PERSONAL SAFETY

Slipping rugs: Never polish the floor under a rug. If you have a small rug that tends to slither about dangerously on a polished floor, hold it in place by brushing strips of latex adhesive around the edges. Leave this to dry before replacing the rug.

Razor blades: Press one edge of a double-sided razor blade into the disused match stub end of a bookmatch. It will protect your fingers when you use it.

Pins and needles: Don't hold pins and needles in your mouth while sewing or put them in your clothes – use a pincushion.

Waxed floors: When waxing floors make sure you apply the wax thinly and evenly. An uneven, or too thick, coating of wax will cause accidents. For similar reasons never wax uncarpeted stairs.

Many a slip: Roughen the soles of slippery footwear with sandpaper to avoid accidents.

Slippery soles: Crêpe soles, from which the tread has worn, can be very slippery in wet or greasy conditions. You can renew the tread by cutting shallow V-shaped grooves across the soles with a razor blade.

Dark stairs: Many bad falls are caused when somebody has to come up or down stairs in the dark. Avoid them by getting two way switches fitted.

Toys: It's not just in cartoons that someone steps on a roller skate and glides through a window to end up in hospital. Train your children to pick up toys straight after playing with them, and don't let them play on the stairs.

... and pets: Pets can be the source of many a nasty fall, too – don't let them get into the habit of lying in doorways or across stairs.

Sharp objects: Remember that what you throw away can be a hazard to dustmen – never throw out anything sharp (razor blades, broken glass, etc.) without first wrapping it in newspaper. If you are throwing away a large amount of broken glass (from a window, say) it is essential to warn the dustmen about it.

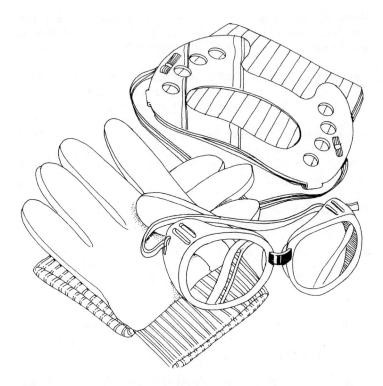

Safe D.I.Y.: Strong gardening gloves are ideal for protecting your hands when working with heavy tools. When drilling or chiselling at brick work or tiling, always wear safety glasses to protect your eyes. Any job that involves a lot of dust can be a danger to your lungs – protect them with a mask obtainable from chemists.

Important labels: D.I.Y. tools and preparations have become very sophisticated and therefore potentially dangerous in recent years. Don't take risks – read through the instructions fully before starting to use them.

Mixed chemicals: Never mix two chemicals together – poisonous fumes often result.

Harmful fumes: Many products, particularly cleaning fluids, emit fumes that are harmful. The effect is often cumulative, that is, the substance enters the body and is not dispersed, so that each small exposure to the chemical adds up to what can in some cases be a lethal dose. Therefore before using any product that gives off fumes or vapours or smells strongly, or has a warning on the packet, open all the windows in a room, then try to avoid breathing the fumes directly.

Hidden poisons: Manufacturers are not always obliged by law to declare that their products are poisonous. For example after-shave, carpet cleaners, detergents, disinfectants, dyes, lavatory cleaners, perfumes, shampoos and white spirit all are, or contain, poisons. They are all safe if used correctly, but should be kept out of the reach of young children.

The right steps: If you are hanging curtains or getting something out of a high cupboard, use a set of steps rather than a chair, which you could tip up. Wear flat shoes, too, otherwise your heels may catch in your hem.

No clocks or mirrors: It is not a good idea to hang a clock or a mirror over the fireplace. People then tend to stand too close to the fire in order to look at them and are in danger of being burnt.

Kitchen curtains: Don't hang curtains at your kitchen window if the cooker is beside it. They may catch fire if they flap when the window is open. A blind is a better idea.

Kitchen sockets: If you are planning to put in new sockets above your work surface in the kitchen, they should be at least 23 cm (10 inches) above the surface and not too near the water source.

Poisonous plants: Some house plants are poisonous – find out whether any of yours are; if so, label them clearly to enable you to identify them in an emergency.

Spray paints: When using aerosol spray paints indoors, be sure to open the windows before you start.

HYGIENE

Natural bristles: Don't use a natural bristle toothbrush. The bristles are hollow and may therefore collect minute food particles which will allow germs to breed.

Tin opening: When opening tin cans remember to wipe over the top with a damp cloth first – this will remove any dust and grease that may have accumulated and stop this getting into the food. Don't try to open a tin when the bottom is resting on a slippery surface – put a damp cloth underneath to keep it steady.

Scrubbable surfaces: When planning a kitchen or bathroom remember that all the surfaces should be scrubbable. Surfaces that are cracked should be repaired since the cracks provide an ideal place for germs to breed in.

Clean grouting: Although wall tiles will be left clean after a quick wipe with a damp cloth, the grouting between tiles will need a good scrub to keep it clean.

Hidden dirt: The dirt and grease that tends to accumulate around, and particularly behind, cookers tends to be missed out in the ordinary process of cleaning. However, this can be highly flammable as well as unhygienic, so make a point of removing it regularly. You may find that there are other places where dust and dirt collect that tend to be missed out; give these a good scrub at the same time.

Dry food storage: Although dry foods will not go off if left in contact with air, they should be stored in sealed containers to keep them safe from insects and vermin.

Meat: Raw meat and cooked meat should always be kept separate. Don't buy either from a butcher who keeps the two together. If you have to keep both in the fridge at the same time, make sure that they are kept well wrapped on the same shelf (if they are kept on different shelves the juices from one may drip on to the other). After cutting raw meat on a board, always scrub it carefully and disinfect with a little bleach before using it for anything else.

Clean seat: It's important to make sure the toilet and the toilet seat are kept clean. Because of their size children have to hoist themselves up on to the seat, and are therefore likely to pick up germs from it.

Personal gear: To restrict the way in which minor (and major) ailments are transmitted to all members of the family, make sure that everybody has his or her own personal flannel, toothbrush and towels. If you have young children, encourage them to stick to using their own things by buying a complete set for each of them in a matching colour.

Cover cuts: When preparing food, keep your hands clean and cover any cuts or sores with sticking plaster. If an existing dressing is dirty, change it before starting to cook.

Dust and germs: Dust from a vacuum cleaner should be wrapped carefully in old newspaper and disposed of in a dustbin, not a wastebin. This dust contains millions of germs which, if allowed to get into the air, can cause infections of the lungs, as well as asthma attacks.

Prompt eating: Foods should be eaten within two days of their 'sell-by' dates.

Pet food: Try not to leave half-eaten bowls of cat or dog food lying around. These will attract flies.

First aid

GENERAL HINTS

Hospital in a hurry: If someone has to be got to hospital in a hurry and he or she can be moved easily, it is often quicker, if you have a car, to take the person yourself rather than call for an ambulance.

Broken bones: If you suspect that someone has broken a bone, don't attempt to move him or make him stand, call a hospital – the same rules apply to suspected internal injuries.

Electrocution: One of the effects that large amounts of electricity have on the body is to operate the muscles. This means that in some cases a person may become stuck to what they are touching – their muscles tighten up and do not allow them to let go. *Do not touch them* or you will receive a shock as well. Instead turn the electricity off at the source. If this is not possible push the person clear with a piece of wood. Be careful when moving someone who has been shocked – the electricity may have operated muscles together that normally only work in opposition (in the upper arm for example). This places great strain on bones and can break them.

No food: If someone has injured him or herself in such a way as to lead you to think an anaesthetic might be needed (a broken leg or arm, for example) don't give him or her anything to eat or drink while waiting for the ambulance. If you do, it will mean that he or she cannot be given an anaesthetic for several hours.

Shock: If a person is suffering from shock after an accident, keep him warm by covering him with a blanket. Stay with him and give plenty of reassurance – send someone else for an ambulance.

Reassured but awake: A person suffering from shock should not be allowed to fall asleep.

Curing cramp: Cramp is caused by a lack of oxygen in the blood supplied to a muscle. Anything that improves the blood supply will cure it – the application of a towel dipped in warm water, rubbing or exercising. A stitch is a cramp of the diaphragm, the cure (and the way to avoid getting a stitch) is to breath in a regular and controlled way.

MEDICINES AND FIRST AID KIT

Old medicine: When you finish a course of treatment of a prescribed medicine, don't put the bottle with any remaining tablets back in the cupboard – flush the tablets or medicine down the lavatory and throw the bottle away.

Medicine safety: Although it may be difficult to get young children to take medicine, never tell them tablets are sweets – they may take you at your word and help themselves to more of them.

Uses for bicarbonate: Keep some bicarbonate of soda in your medicine box: it can be used for treating scalds and mild burns (make up a paste with water), as a treatment for heartburn (drink a pinch in a glass of hot water), and as a gargle for sore throats.

Taking a pill: When swallowing a pill the trick, to avoid tasting it, is not to let it touch your tongue. You can do this by resting it on the back of your lower front teeth, taking a gulp of water and swallowing it down with the water. A child can suck an ice lolly before taking an unpleasant medicine. This will numb the taste buds for a short time and is also a reward for having to take something nasty.

First aid kit: Keep the following in your first aid box:
  1 roll of porous surgical tape
  2 large and 2 medium prepared wound dressings
  1 packet sterilized cotton wool
  2 tubular gauze bandages
  2 large triangular bandages
  1 standard crêpe bandage
  the doctor's telephone number
  tweezers
  an eye bath
  a sharp needle, sterilized
  safety pins
  scissors

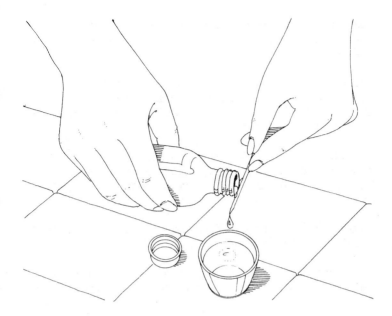

Limited drops: Where medicine requires that you administer a certain number of drops, you can do so accurately by holding a toothpick across the top of the bottle and running the medicine down the length of this.

Timely reminder: When a medicine needs to be taken at rigidly fixed times, use a kitchen timer or an alarm clock to remind you.

No swapping: Never give a medicine prescribed for one person to another, no matter how similar their symptoms seem. Also, never save the remnants of a medicine to treat yourself if the illness recurs.

BURNS AND SCALDS

Clothing on fire: A person whose clothes are on fire should be rolled in a rug, blanket, or piece of carpet. This will stop air getting to the flames and so put out the fire.

Blisters: When treating burns beware of bursting blisters. These become infected very easily and can lead to major complications.

Scalding: Remove any tight fitting clothes from a person who has been scalded (do not do this for someone who has been burnt). Scalding causes swelling and clothing will cause painful constrictions.

No butter: Don't put butter on burns – if they are serious leave well alone and call a doctor. Mild burns should be treated by holding them under cold running water for 5–10 minutes.

Mild burns: The freshly cut surface of an onion can bring relief from mild burns and stings.

Small burns: Painful, but small, burns on hands can be relieved by soaking in water containing a few dissolved aspirins.

FITS, FEVER AND FAINTING

Fits: Don't restrict the movements of a person suffering a fit. Loosen his clothing if it is tight, but do not attempt to put anything in his mouth. Put something soft under his neck. When the fit is over do not move him, let him lie still until he has time to work out where he is.

Fever: Treat a person suffering from a fever with aspirin (the dose recommended for someone of her age). If her temperature is particularly high, sponge her with tepid water (the cooling effect comes from allowing the water to evaporate).

Fainting: Fainting is caused by a lack of oxygen in the blood supplied to the brain. Loosen tight clothing, give the patient plenty of space and, if the room is hot, or smoky, open the windows. To rouse him you must increase the amount of blood going to the head. Do this by putting his head

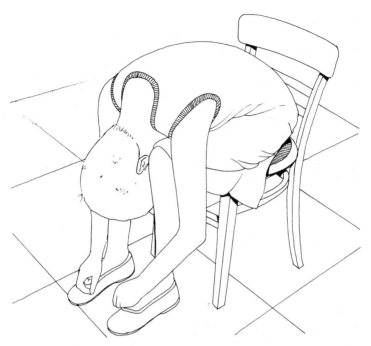

between his knees if he is sitting. If he falls to the ground, raise his legs up above the level of his head. Don't try to pick him up – fainting is to some extent a protective measure, since if a person is lying down more blood is going to his head anyway.

FEET

Cutting toenails: Toenails should be cut straight across, not following the shape of the toe, to prevent them ingrowing. Cure an ingrowing nail by cutting a V-shaped notch out of the middle of the nail, then allowing it to grow out.

Foam lining: Wellington boots transfer the shock of walking to the foot and, as well as tiring the walker, are very cold in winter. A solution is to slip a piece of foam rubber cut to the shape of the foot into each boot.

FOREIGN BODIES

Something in the eye: Most of the time when someone complains of something in his or her eye it will not be on the surface of the eye but on the inside of the lid. It can be removed by pulling the eyelid back, twisting the corner of a clean handkerchief to a point and using this to dab the object off the lid. If there is something stuck to the eye itself, do not attempt to remove it – get medical help.

Splinters: Do not attempt to remove glass splinters or any splinters lodged under a nail – see a doctor and get him to take them out.

Removing splinters: To get a splinter out without trouble, place the effected area of skin over the top of a bottle or jar filled with very hot water. Keep the skin in firm contact with the bottle top. The heat and pressure will push the splinter out.

Choking: Don't panic when dealing with someone who is choking – your panic will be transmitted and cause him or her to constrict his or her throat around the blockage. With serious cases, get medical help straightaway or go directly to the nearest hospital casualty department.

Choking and small children: Small children or babies who are choking can be treated by hanging them upside down and firmly patting their backs to dislodge the object. However, if they seem to be choking very badly, just get them to hospital straightaway.

DAY TO DAY PROBLEMS

Bruises: The pain and the look of bruises can be relieved by applying a little dry starch moistened with water to the area as soon as possible after the injury takes place.

Boils: To draw the core out of a boil, make a poultice as follows: mix together one spoon each of honey, oil and flour, beat a yoke of egg into this and spread on a piece of gauze. Apply to the boil overnight.

Nose bleeds: Nose bleeds only need medical treatment if they last longer than twenty minutes, or if the sufferer is an old person.

Large cuts: Do not apply any material directly to any large cut when you are not sure whether it contains any foreign material (glass, etc.). Instead use clean material around, but not touching, the wound while you wait for the ambulance.

Stings: A bee's sting contains muscles that continue to work after the sting has been detached from the bee. These allow the sting to actually dig its way into the skin, and then to inject the poison into the wound. The trick therefore in removing a sting is to get it out as quickly as you can. Use the edge of a fingernail in a scraping motion to remove it. A wasp's sting is different. The damage is done once it has stung you – no sting is left to be removed.

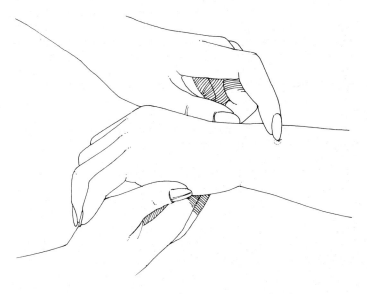

Hangover cure: Most of the effects of a hangover are the result of the dehydration that alcohol causes. It can be prevented by drinking two or three glasses of water before going to bed.

Headache cure: Headaches triggered by foods and drinks which are the products of fermentation can be cured, if they are not severe, with a hot drink of milk and honey.

Expanding the chest: Any kind of activity which involves blowing will expand the chest cavity and therefore be good for a child who suffers from asthma – try bubble blowing, blow football, etc.

Toothache: A clove dipped in a little whisky or brandy and applied to the affected area will provide temporary relief from a toothache.

Poisoning: A person suffering from any kind of poisoning should be taken to hospital as quickly as possible – take a sample of the poison with you if you have it. Don't try to make them sick, don't give them anything to eat or drink, except if they complain of burning of the throat or mouth, in which case give them plenty of water, but nothing else. Never give anything to a person who is unconscious. If someone is poisoned make a note of the time you discover them – this will help the hospital decide on treatment.

Earache: Some relief can be given to a person suffering from earache by keeping the ear warm – use a hot water bottle or warm oil dripped into the ear and retained with a plug of cotton wool.

HEALTH AND SAFETY RECORD

Keep a list of emergency phone numbers as a handy record in case of accidents.

Doctor ....

Dentist ....

School ....

Local police station ....

Gas emergency ....

Electricity emergency ....

It is also useful to keep a record of details of the family's health. Whoever takes the children to the doctor will need to have information on infectious diseases, especially if the G.P. is new to you.

Name ....

Injections ....

Infectious diseases ....

Hospital treatment ....

Blood group ....

Any allergies? ....

Name ....

Injections ....

Infectious diseases ....

Hospital treatment ....

Blood group ....

Any allergies? ....

"Nothing Ventured, Nothing Gained"

Tips on amusing children and keeping pets

Children

This section presents a selection of ideas for keeping children amused as well as some hints for common problems.

RAINY DAY FUN

Fun-printing: Cut the bottom off a cardboard milk or fruit juice carton, leaving 6 mm ($\frac{1}{4}$ inch) of the sides, and use it to make a stamp pad. Cut a piece of sponge to fit inside the bottom of the carton and soak with water-based paints. Make several for different colours. Prints can be made with leaves, fingers, fruit, potatoes or rubbers.

New life for old cards: An old pack of cards can be used to make a flip book. Glue a piece of white paper on to each card so that half the card is covered. Draw a simple figure doing something (throwing a ball for example) on each card. The position should change very slightly in each picture. Watch him come to life when the cards are flicked.

Natty necklaces: Tear glossy coloured paper out of magazines to make into beads. Roll a triangle of paper tightly around and around a toothpick, until it makes a bead shape. Glue the end down and when the glue has dried, slide the toothpick out. This leaves a hole for threading. Repeat until there are enough for a necklace, then thread with cotton or fine ribbon.

Plastic skittles: Save plastic washing-up bottles to make a set of skittles. There are nine in a set. Either paint the outside or stick on brightly coloured paper. Remove the plastic cap and feed a handful of dried pies or beans or even gravel through the neck, to help them stand up. Then put back the cap and close, so that the filling doesn't spill.

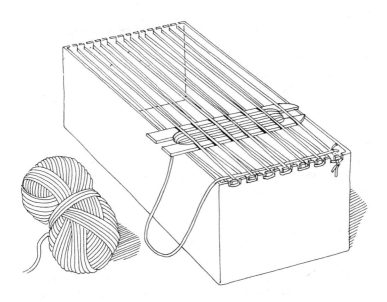

Shoebox loom: An old shoebox can be used to make a simple loom. Take the lid off and cut notches every 12 mm ($\frac{1}{2}$ in) along either end, trying to make the notches fall opposite each other. Wind a piece of string or wool back and forth through the notches so that the top of the box is covered. To weave wool should be threaded under and over the string, back and forth.

Mask a bag: Large brown paper bags can be made into all sorts of masks with a little ingenuity. Cut holes for eyes and mouth in them, then give each child a bag along with a supply of paint, crayons and sticky coloured paper. You could give a prize for the best mask, or get them to write a play using the masks – the lines can be stuck to the inside of the bag to save having to learn them.

Tuneful bottles: Milk bottles can be 'tuned' by filling them with different amounts of water and played by tapping them with a stick. Nails of different sizes can be hung from a coathanger using rubber bands, to produce different notes as well. The shorter the nail is, the higher the note will be. They will ring clearest if struck with something metal.

Rhythm section: Make a pair of maracas from empty washing-up liquid bottles. Take the tops off and put a handful of dried peas, beans or rice inside. Glue or tape a piece of stick to the top of the bottle to make a handle. The maracas can now be decorated, either by painting them or by sticking coloured paper on to them.

Make your own lampshade: Inflate a balloon and smear it with petroleum jelly. Tear brightly-coloured tissue paper into small pieces and soak them in wallpaper paste. Mould this mixture on to the balloon like papier mâché. Leave to dry thoroughly, then pop the balloon. Cut a hole in the bottom of the shade and attach a light fitting.

Make pin pictures: Give each child a piece of corrugated cardboard and about twenty pins, along with a reel of brightly coloured cotton. Each child should push the pins into the cardboard wherever he or she likes, then wind the cotton back and forth between the pins to make different patterns and pictures.

Missing dice: You can replace a dice missing from a board game with a sugar cube – just draw dots on the sides with a felt tip pen. Remember that the opposite sides should always add up to seven, so six is opposite one, five is opposite two and four opposite three.

Replacing lost counters: Save bottle tops, buttons and washers to use as replacements for lost game counters, or let children make up their own games with them.

Home-made jigsaws: Cut coloured pictures out of magazines and use them to make jigsaw puzzles. Glue each picture to a piece of cardboard (use cardboard that is *just* thin enough to be cut with a pair of scissors). Cut the card into pieces with the scissors and jumble up.

Toy telephones: Two empty plastic yogurt pots can be made into a toy telephone or walky-talky. Make a hole in the bottom of each pot with a skewer, then thread a piece of thin string through the bottom of both pots and tie a knot in each end. One person puts one pot to his ear, the other speaks into the other pot. If the string is kept tight between the two pots the sound will travel down the string over quite long distances.

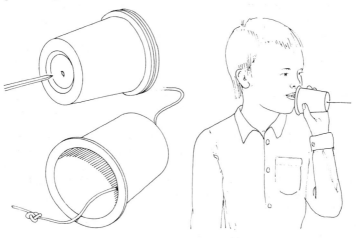

PARTY FUN

Out of order: Give each child a newspaper that has all the pages in the wrong order. They have to try to put the paper back together in the right order – the winner is the first one to do so.

Whispered stories: Write down a very short story or a joke. Seat all the children in a line and whisper the story to the first child in the line. Each child whispers the story to the next, until it gets to the end of the row. The child at the end tells the story out loud, then you read out the original story to see how different they are.

Pea-picking: Give each child two cups and a straw. Put twenty dried peas in one of the cups. Each player has to suck through the straw to pick up one pea at a time and drop it in the empty cup. The first player to get all the peas in the empty cup is the winner.

Pass the matchbox: Divide the children into two teams and make them stand in two lines. Each team is given a matchbox cover, which the first person in the line puts on his nose. Each team has to pass the cover down the line from one child to the next, using only their noses. The team that gets the cover to the end of the line first wins. If the cover is dropped it has to go back to the child behind the one who dropped it.

Hide and see: Show all the children a small object, then make them go out of the room. Hide the object in the room, so that part of it can be seen quite easily. Bring the children back into the room and tell them to start looking for it. When one of them sees it, he or she must sit on the floor and not say anything. The game is over when only one person is left standing. Give the first to find it and the one left standing a prize – but don't tell them at the beginning of the game that you're going to do this.

GAMES TO PLAY WHILE TRAVELLING

Name a pub: Each child chooses a pub name, then has to try to spot as many pubs with that name as possible. Score one point each when a pub has the right name, score half a point when part of the name is right. Or, with one child looking out on the left and the other on the right, count the number of legs in pub signs (e.g. "The Swan" counts two).

Miles away: Get the children to close their eyes. They have to keep them closed and try to guess when a mile has gone by. When each thinks a mile is up, he or she raises his or her hand but doesn't say anything. The winner is the one who is nearest to being right.

Car scores: Each child chooses a car colour and scores a point whenever a car of that colour is seen – the winner is the one with the highest score. Older children may like to play the same game, but looking for makes of car instead.

Strange creatures: Give each child a piece of paper and tell them to draw the head of some kind of creature on it. Now they fold the paper over so that only the very bottom of the neck is showing, then exchange pieces of paper. Next they draw a body, folding the paper again afterwards and swapping again. Finally they draw the legs, swap, then unfold the picture to reveal a funny jumbled-up figure. This game is best played by three people or more. You can make it longer by also adding a funny name on the bottom before unfolding the paper.

Station bingo: When travelling by train, make a list of all the stations that the train passes through on the way. Give each child a jumbled-up list of the station names – missing out two or three different names in each case. These lists are then used to play station bingo. They must cross out the name of a station as the train goes through it, if it is on their list. The first person to get all the stations on his list is the winner.

GENERAL TIPS

Hot seat: When giving babies and very small children a bath, use a hot water bottle to provide a slip-proof seat. Simply fill it with lukewarm water and place it on the bottom of the bath for the baby to sit on.

Fun dusters: Encourage children to help with the housework. Make fun dusters from old white socks – draw a face on each with a felt tip pen. When it's dry get the children to help with the dusting.

Getting a grasp of things: To give a baby practice in grasping objects, thread up some of the following on a piece of string and hang them over the cot: measuring cups and spoons, empty cotton reels, a wooden spoon with a hole drilled in the handle and a plastic beaker.

Cold comfort: If your baby's teeth are coming through and hurting him, you can provide temporary relief by breaking up some ice cubes and tying them into the corner of a clean cotton handkerchief. If you give the handkerchief to him, he will automatically chew on it and the cold ice will relieve the pain from his gums.

Save on calls: Small children often like to play with the phone. To stop them accidentally calling somebody, put a wide rubber band around the phone so that the contact points (where the handset rests) are held down. With them held down, the children can play to their heart's content.

Reflections: Remember that small children often can't see into the bathroom mirror. To encourage them to wash and brush their teeth thoroughly, either give them something to stand on, or, better still, put a second mirror up at their height.

Bath time fun: In an old washing-up liquid container, mix a small amount of washing-up liquid, some brightly-coloured cake dye and some water. Squirt a little of this mixture into the water when running the bath, for a cheap coloured bubble bath.

Sock over shoes: To prevent scratch marks on the floor when your baby is crawling, cover his shoes with discarded socks.

Crayon sharpening: You can sharpen a child's wax crayon by warming the end gently then reshaping into a point.

Hidden stores: Children get more fun out of toys if you keep some of them hidden away in reserve. When a child gets bored, bring out some of the stored toys. At the same time, store away a few of the toys that are out. Keep rotating toys in this way and your child won't get bored with them.

Sugar in the salt container: To prevent breakfast-time sugar trails all over the kitchen, put some sugar in a large salt shaker. Tell the children to use this to shake sugar over their cereal.

Hands up, it's a trick: When taking a lot of children in the car, shout 'Hands up' before shutting the doors. This saves any accidents with fingers and the children enjoy it.

Lighter blocks: Wooden blocks can be too heavy for very small children. Cut blocks out of foam rubber (using scissors) instead.

See-through storage: String bags are useful for storing children's toys. Hang them up on a nail in the wall and they'll be able to see just what's stored away.

Pets

DOGS

Allow for growth: When buying a mongrel dog for a pet, remember that it may be difficult to tell how big a puppy will grow.

Training in the garden: Don't try to lead train puppies in the street – start them off in the familiar surroundings of the garden where there are not too many new and therefore distracting smells. That way they'll be able to pay attention properly and also no harm will be done if they manage to slip the lead.

When to buy: Always make sure that a puppy is fully weaned before buying.

Keeping on the collar: A dog's collar should only ever be removed when he is indoors – to do this outdoors is to invite disaster.

Keep it short: When training a dog, remember that short regular periods of training given frequently are much better than long, irregular periods.

Keep cool: You should never lose your temper while training a dog, if you shout at him or strike him you will only confuse him. Most dogs are eager to please and willing to learn.

Familiar ways: The dog will learn most quickly is he is always taught by the same member of the family.

Food and drink: Don't exercise your dog straight after he has had a heavy meal and don't give him anything substantial to eat late at night. Make sure that there is always a bowl of clean water available to him.

After a bath: Keep a dog inside for a few hours after giving him a bath – if you don't he'll go and roll in earth straightaway.

Preparing for travel: Sooner or later you will almost certainly need to take your dog somewhere in a car. You can prepare for this by training the dog, while he is still a puppy. Take him for very short rides at first and give him plenty of attention. When he is used to being in the car, you can take him for longer rides.

Cars are too hot: Never leave a dog in a car in hot weather – even if the car is in shade. In cooler weather he may safely be left, but make sure that he has water to drink and leave the window open a fraction.

CATS

Cats in cars: When transporting a cat in a car, always keep it in a box or basket – it can be dangerous to drive alone with a cat loose in the car.

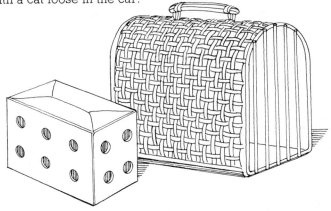

Medicinal grass: Remember that although cats eat mostly meat, they need to be able to eat a certain amount of grass. They eat it to ease upset stomachs – without it fur balls may cause vomiting. A small amount of grass can be grown in a window box if necessary.

Keep off the flowers: If you lay holly leaves round the base of a flower you wish to protect, this will deter cats from walking on it.

Cat-scratching post: Kittens should always be provided with a scratching post. Wrap a piece of old carpet around the leg of a sturdy piece of furniture or a small log. Make scratching motions with the kitten's paws on the post in order to train it.

RABBITS, TORTOISES AND OTHER PETS

Two's company: Rabbits like company – when buying them get two females, but never two males as they fight.

Keeping tortoises: It is best to buy tortoises in pairs of male and female – this discourages wandering. Try to buy them in spring, never buy later than July.

Leave the shell: Do not use oil paint to write on the shell of a living tortoise. A small amount of acrylic paint is alright.

Bark to bite on: Guinea pigs need to be given something to gnaw on – cut a small piece of log with a healthy bark and place this in the cage.

Handle with care: When handling guinea pigs, take care that they cannot jump out of your hands and injure themselves – use both your hands. Don't handle them for too long or let them get overexcited or they may become exhausted.

Mice food: Don't give cheese to pet mice, although they

like it, it will make them smell and may make them fat. The same applies to bacon and green vegetables.

Keep out the rain: If your rabbit's cage stands outside, it must be waterproof. Rabbits like to have room to move as well, so provide them with a secure, wire-netting enclosed run.

"Waste Not, Want Not"

Metric conversion charts of useful measures

SEWING AND KNITTING MATERIALS

Knitting needles and crochet hooks have both gone over to metric sizing. The old and new sizes are compared below.

Knitting needles		Crochet hooks (wool)	
Old size	Metric size	Old size	Metric size
000	10	2	7 mm
00	9	4	6 mm
0	8	5	5.50 mm
1	7½ (7.5)	6	5 mm
2	7	7	4.50 mm
3	6½ (6.5)	8	4 mm
4	6	9	3.50 mm
5	5½ (5.5)	10	3 mm
6	5	12	2.50 mm
7	4½ (4.5)	14	2 mm
8	4	Crochet hooks (cotton)	
9	3¾ (3.75)	1½	2 mm
10	3¼ (3.25)	2½	1.75 mm
11	3	3½	1.50 mm
12	2¾ (2.75)	4½	1.25 mm
13	2¼ (2.25)	5½	1.00 mm
14	2	6½	0.75 mm
		7	0.60 mm

SCREWS AND SCREW SIZES

Below are some suggested guide-hole diameters for standard wood screws. They are only a guide: the holes may need to be slightly larger in hardwood or smaller in softwood.

Screw	Point hole	Shank hole
No. 4	2.0 mm	2.5 mm
No. 6	2.5 mm	3.5 mm
No. 8	3.0 mm	4.5 mm
No. 10	3.5 mm	5.0 mm
No. 12	4.0 mm	5.5 mm
No. 14	4.5 mm	6.5 mm

The following is a list of typical jobs for standard-gauge screws:

No.4 Very small cabinet hinges, keyhole-cover plates.

No.6 Window hinges, curtain rail brackets, door handles, lock-sets.

No.8 Door hinges, light-duty shelf brackets, general box-construction.

No.10 Heavier shelf brackets, wall-cupboard mountings, hinges for heavy doors.

No.12 Adjustable, slotted-steel, heavy-duty shelf systems, small-to-medium central-heating radiators, wall-mounted boilers, outdoor trellis supports.

No.14 Heavy and double-size central-heating radiators, shelf brackets for heavy loads, sturdy frame construction (benches, tables, and so on).

Metric equivalents of screw sizes are as follows:

millimetres	9	12	15	19	25	32	38	44	50	57	63	76	89	101
inches	$3/8$	$1/2$	$5/8$	$3/4$	1	$1\,1/4$	$1\,1/2$	$1\,3/4$	2	$2\,1/4$	$2\,1/2$	3	$3\,1/2$	4

CHILDREN'S CLOTHING

Below is a general guide to metric and imperial
measurements and sizing.

	Age	Weight	Chest	Height
*	3 months	5.5 kg/12 lb		62 cm/24^{1}/$_{2}$''
*	6 months	8 kg/18 lb		69 cm/27''
*	9 months	9.5 kg/21 lb		74 cm/29''
*	12 months	11 kg/24 lb		79 cm/31''
†	18 months	12.5 kg/28 lb		83 cm/33''
†	2 years		51 cm/20^{1}/$_{4}$''	92 cm/36''
†	3 years		53 cm/20^{7}/$_{8}$''	98 cm/38''
†	4 years		55 cm/21^{1}/$_{2}$''	104 cm/40''

* clothes marked by weight/age
† clothes marked by height/age

MEN'S CLOTHING

Collar sizes

inches	14^{1}/$_{2}$	15	15^{1}/$_{2}$	16	16^{1}/$_{2}$	17	17^{1}/$_{2}$
cm	37	38	39/40	41	42	43	44

Waist measurements

inches	26	28	30	32	34	36	38	40	42
cm	66	71	76	81	86	91	97	102	107

SHOE SIZES

The three series of measurements do not exactly correspond, so you may need to try one or two sizes before getting the right fit. American sizes apply only to women's shoes.

British	American	Continental
3	$4^1/_2$ (45)	36
4	$5^1/_2$ (55)	37
5	$6^1/_2$ (65)	38
		39
6	$7^1/_2$ (75)	40
7	$8^1/_2$ (85)	41
8	$9^1/_2$ (95)	42
		43
9		44
10		45
11		46

WOMEN'S CLOTHING

Size	inches bust/hip	cm bust/hip
8	30/32	76/81
10	32/34	81/86
12	34/36	86/91
14	36/38	91/97
16	38/40	97/102
18	40/42	102/107
20	42/44	107/112
22	44/46	112/117
24	46/48	117/122

WEIGHTS AND MEASURES

The exact conversion of 1 oz to 28.349 grams makes exact calculation too complicated for practical weighing, so the Metrication Board suggests that 1 oz is taken as 25 grams for amounts under 1 lb, and 30 grams for amounts over 1 lb.

This is a rough guide, showing approximate equivalents.

1 oz	2 oz	3 oz	4 oz	8 oz
25 g	50 g	75 g	100 g	200 g

When weighing amounts in excess of 1 lb:

1 lb	2 lb	3 lb	4 lb	5 lb
450 g	900 g	1^1/$_2$ kg	1^3/$_4$ kg	2^1/$_4$ kg

LIQUIDS

The litre is the basic unit for measurement in metric. It is approximately equivalent to 1^3/$_4$ pints. 4^1/$_2$ litres are about equal to 1 gallon.

Below are rough equivalents in pints of buying ^{1}/$_8$, ^{1}/$_4$, ^{1}/$_2$ and whole litres.

^{1}/$_4$ pint	^{1}/$_2$ pint	1 pint	2 pints
150 ml	300 ml	600 ml	1200 ml

SPOONS

^{1}/$_4$ teaspoon	1.25 millilitres
^{1}/$_2$ teaspoon	2.5 millilitres
1 teaspoon	5 millilitres
1 tablespoon	15 millilitres

MEASURING LENGTH

The metre is the basic unit for measurement in metric. It is just over 3¼ feet. The following are exact equivalents:

1 inch = 25.4 millimetres

1 foot = 0.3048 metres

1 yard = 0.9144 metres

1 mile = 1.6093 kilometres

1 millimetre = 0.394 inches

1 centimetre = 0.3937 inches

1 metre = 39.37 inches

1 kilometre = 0.6214 miles

On the right, however, is a handy guide to show you at a glance how the two systems compare:

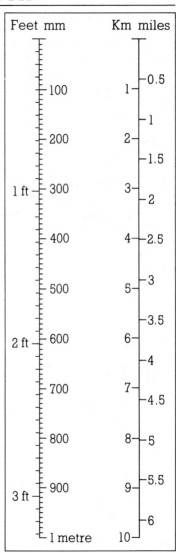

TEMPERATURES

Most temperatures are now measured in Celsius, formerly Centigrade. To convert Fahrenheit to Celsius, subtract 32, multiply by 5, divide by 9. This gives an approximate figure. To convert Celsius into Fahrenheit, multiply by 9, divide by 5, add 32. Normal body temperature (formerly 98.6°F) is now measured as 37°C. Normal room temperature for central heating is 18°C for the bedroom and 22°C for the living room. The tables opposite show conversions for the range of temperatures used for the oven/freezer (left) and for outdoors (right). Below is a guide to electric and gas oven temperatures.

OVEN TEMPERATURES

Centigrade		Fahrenheit	Gas mark
100	very cool	200	Low
110		225	1/4
120		250	1/2
140	cool	275	1
150		300	2
160	moderate	325	3
180		350	4
190	mod. hot	375	5
200		400	6
220	hot	425	7
230		450	8
240	very hot	475	9
260		500	10

FAHRENHEIT/CELSIUS CONVERSIONS

Oven/Freezer

Fahrenheit	Celsius
0	−17.7 deep freeze
water freezes 32	0
50	10
	20
	30
100	40
	50
	60
150	70
	80
200	90
212	100
	110
250	120
	130
	140
300	150
	160
	170
350	180
	190
	200
400	210
	220
450	230
	240
	250
500	260

Outdoors

Fahrenheit	Celsius	
0		
	−15	
10	−10	
20	−5	
32 30	0	freezing
40	5	
50	10	cool
60	15	mild
70	20	warm
80	25	very warm
	30	hot
90	35	
98.6 100	37	body temp.
	40	
110	45	
120	50	

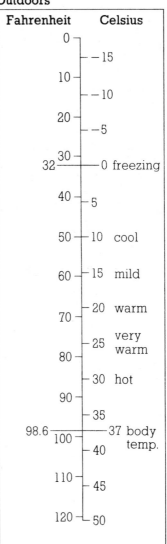

BEDS AND BED LINEN

Sizes of bedding can be confusing now that they are all
metricated. Below is a chart showing what sizes will fit
what size of bed. Variations allow for different mattress
thicknesses and tuck-in allowances.

Bed type	Bed size	
Single	90 cm×190 cm	3′×6′3″
Large single	100 cm×200 cm	3′3″×6′6″
Double	135 cm×190 cm	4′6″×6′3″
Large double	150 cm×200 cm	5′×6′6″

Bed type	Blanket size	
Single	180 cm×240 cm	5′11″×7′11″
Large single	200 cm×250 cm	6′6″×8′
Double	230 cm×250 cm	7′6″×8′
Large double	260 cm×250 cm	8′6″×8′
Extra large	300 cm×250 cm	10′×8′

Bed type	Blended sheets	Cotton & flannelette sheets
Single	175 cm×260 cm 5′9″×8′6″	175 cm×255 cm to 275 cm 5′9″×8′5″ to 9′ 200 cm×255 cm to 275 cm 6′6″×8′5″ to 9′
Large single	175 cm×260 cm 5′9″×8′6″	175 cm×275 cm 5′9″×9′ 200 cm×275 cm 6′6″×9′
Double	230 cm×260 cm 7′6″×8′6″	230 cm×255 cm to 275 cm 7′6″×8′5″ to 9′
Large double	230 cm×260 cm 7′6″×8′6″	230 cm×275 cm 7′6″×9′
Extra large	275 cm×275 cm 9′×9′	270 cm×295 cm 8′11″×9′8″

MOTORING

Tyre pressures, as well as petrol pumps, have also come in for metrication. The following two tables show rough equivalents.

Petrol measures		Tyre pressures	
litres	gallons	lb/sq in	kg/cm^2
5	1.1	10	0.7
10	2.2	12	0.8
15	3.3	15	1.1
20	4.4	18	1.3
25	5.5	20	1.4
30	6.6	21	1.5
35	7.7	23	1.6
40	8.8	24	1.7
45	9.9	26	1.8
50	11.0	27	1.9
		28	2.0
		30	2.1
		33	2.3
		36	2.5
		38	2.7
		40	2.8

Index

C

N

O

P

S

T

U

V

W

Z

We are grateful to Rentokil Limited for
supplying the illustration reference for
the plaster beetle on p. 198.